FAST LANE
ON A
DIRT ROAD

FAST LANE

ON A

DIRT ROAD

Vermont Transformed: 1945–1990

Joe Sherman

The Countryman Press, Inc.
Woodstock, Vermont

© 1991 by Joe Sherman

Permission to quote from "A Tinkerer," "Valley Road," and "Vote Fraud" by Walter Hard, has been graciously granted by the copyright holder, Walter Hard, Jr.

Library of Congress Cataloging-in-Publication Data

Sherman, Joe, 1945–
    Fast lane on a dirt road: Vermont transformed, 1945-1990 / by Joe Sherman.
      p. cm.
    Includes index.
    ISBN 0-88150-213-8
    1. Vermont—Politics and government— 2. Vermont—Economic conditions. 3. Vermont—Social conditions. I. Title.
F55.S48 1991
974.3'04—dc20   91-28005
                                            CIP

Cover design by Catherine Hopkins
Text design by Ann Aspell

Published by The Countryman Press, Inc., Woodstock, Vermont, 05091

10 9 8 7 6 5 4 3 2 1

In memory of George and Lou

CONTENTS

PART FOUR

Beneath our boisterous self-confidence is fear—a growing fear of the future we are in the process of creating.

—Loren Eiseley, *The Immense Journey*

PROLOGUE

One afternoon in June 1979 I squeezed between an old, loose door and its jam and into a colossal brick carcass of Vermont history, the Champlain Woolen Mill in Winooski. Puddles glistened on the floor, wires dangled from massive wooden beams, and a couple of pigeons, startled, cooed and glided out through broken window panes. I went up the long wood-treaded staircase. When I reached the third floor, the air came alive with panicked wings. Glass fell from more ragged panes as dozens of frightened pigeons, like too many schoolchildren shoving through too few exits during a fire drill, sought the safety of outdoors.

I stood there then, the big mill quiet, empty, still. It smelled faintly of lanolin, or wool grease, polished into the hardwood floors by the comings and goings of thousands of people who had worked there for decades. The smell reminded me of the glory days of Vermont textiles, a time not that long ago when I had tagged along behind my dad through just such a colossus as this.

For a child the experience was like moving through the innards of some gigantic beast. Dewey's Mills in Quechee, where my dad worked, smelled, pulsated, and was slippery underfoot. To me, age four, my father huge and smelling like the mill itself, the place seemed like a living thing inhabited by dozens of laughing adults, a few who waved at me. Being near my dad in the belly of this beast was wonderful, scary, a bit intoxicating.

In the basement of the tall, yellow mill sat the picker house. The picker house was where the raw wool, which arrived in big shaggy bales, got blended by men wielding huge forks. The dye house was next door. In there, wooden dye kettles reeking of chemicals whirled the raw wool and gave it colors. Two floors up was the card room. There my dad worked among "alleymen," fellows in green and black T-shirts who took care of the alleys between the loud mechanical monsters, and "feed men," who kept the wool coming from the picker room to the cards, and "strippers," who cleaned the cards. The wool "comes out of the cards about as big around as a shoestring," my Dad always said, "and doesn't have any twist in it." At this stage, it was called "roping." Roping got wound around big wooden spools and then traveled by elevator to the frames on the top floor. The frames gave the wool its twist before the looms, several floors below, their shuttles and spools slamming away in a wild song, wove it into cloth.

Today, of course, Vermont's woolen mill culture is as extinct as the dodo bird. Renovated and upscaled, the surviving mills make different noises than they did forty years ago. Mostly shopping and eating noises, not manufacturing ones. The pigeons who inhabited the mills in the 1970s are out and the boutiques and the eateries of the 1990s are in. No teenager holding a skateboard on his hip and pumping up the stairs of the Champlain Mill Mall, for instance, intent on buying a new rap tape by Public Enemy, has probably ever heard of "carrying roping" or "doffing ends." Yet, only a few decades ago, these were commonly understood terms in Vermont. More than two dozen woolen mills hugged riverbanks in Bennington, Cavendish, Ludlow, Quechee, Hartford, Bridgewater, Johnson, Winooski, and other towns. They employed nearly six thousand people, around fifteen percent of the state's manufacturing force. Other mainstays of Vermont industry were the machine tool factories in Springfield, the Fairbanks Scale Company in St. Johnsbury, the granite sheds and quarries in Barre.

In 1990, the scattered woolen-mill buildings still standing, regardless of their use or their modern rhythms, linked Vermont's recent past to its near future. As long as buying stuff remained popular, the mills would probably continue to connect yesterday with tomorrow. Built in an industrial Vermont in the late nineteenth century, abandoned in a floundering Vermont in the mid-twentieth, they now housed the hip and the commercial, eager to get a jump on the twenty-first, whatever it might bring. The architectural remnants were compelling metaphors for the pervasive transformation that had been taking place in Vermont since the late 1940s, when the woolen mills and their communities and their language made up a large and distinct part of the population. I personally loved them. Not the least because if I took a moment to get down on my knees in a corner of one, I could still catch a whiff of lanolin. It reminded me of what my dad used to smell like when he came home from work.

PART ONE

SLAMMING LOOMS
& ROCKY FARMS

She just kept her hopes up that someday it'd be better.
—Raymond Young, 1987, Tunbridge hill farmer

*I*n those days we lived in Quechee. Dewey's Mills, where my dad fixed cards with wrenches as long as your arm, towered alongside the narrow entrance to the Quechee Gorge a mile from the village. My mom and my two sisters worked in a second mill, the Harris and Emery Woolen Mill, about one hundred yards from our house on High Street. The Harris and Emery Mill was brick, stood four stories at the river's edge, and was so antiquated that the river still powered many of the oily pullies and clapping belts that ran the machines that made the cloth. Their syncopated beat, in tune with the loud, rhythmic slamming of the looms, soothed my boyhood sleep.

A covered bridge crossed the Ottauquechee River downstream from the mill dam. The bridge had played a bit part in the drama of my family. My sister Barbara had been crossing it once, riding her unruly stallion backwards because he refused to enter the shady bridge any other way, when her husband-to-be made a wisecrack from the street. "That girl don't know the front from the ass end," he said. Not long after that they were seen together admiring mill horses stabled in barns alongside the river below our house. Then they got married.

In the years immediately following World War II, Quechee was a typical Vermont mill town. A sampler of nineteenth-century houses was strung out for a mile or so along Main Street, which paralleled the Ottauquechee River. A church steeple jutted above hip, mansard, and gable-shaped roofs. Where the houses petered out, farms took over, along with woods, creating a quilted pattern that spread up the hillsides.

Quechee sat in a natural bowl. It had once been a glacial lake and the lake's outlet had, over a millenium, carved our village's claim to fame, the 162-foot Quechee Gorge.

The village population was around three hundred. We had two stores, Capron's Nation-Wide General Store, which stood next to the covered bridge by the Harris and Emery Mill, and Waterford's Store on the other side of the river. The Catholics used the second-story room above Waterford's for Sunday services. Quechee also had a post office, above which a dim-witted fellow named Elmer Eastman lived with his mother. We had an elementary school, a library, mill barns and sheds, and a tall, green water tower which, if it had ever toppled, might have crashed right through the roof of my house.

At the time Vermont also had a new governor. His name was Ernest Gibson, Jr. He was a war hero, a liberal Republican, and an upsetter of the status quo.

Once in office Gibson proved a little too visionary for most of Vermont's legislators. As a body the lawmakers were an overpoweringly humdrum lot, their eyes on the last century and their fingers guarding the state's cash drawer. Gibson's conspicuous heroism, magnetic personality, and liberal notions steeped in FDR's New Deal populism, didn't impress the legislature enough so that it cooperated with him.

During his inaugural address in 1947, the forty-six-year-old Gibson, who was world-traveled and movie-star handsome, said, "We live in an extraordinary age. Events so various and important that they might crowd and distinguish centuries are compressed in our times, within the compass of a single life."

Despite his assurances, few events in Quechee could be called distinguished in those days. We never saw any of the fast planes, televisions, or rocket-propelled missiles the governor mentioned in his speech. Nor did my parents, as far as I know, lie awake at night, worrying over the fact that "civilization has invented a destructive force so great that man may now destroy himself," another concern Gibson brought up. As for Aristotle, whom Gibson also referred to in his eloquent speech, quoting that "the fate of empires depends on the education of its youth," the Greek philosopher wasn't exactly well-known among the alleymen and the strippers in Quechee either. The reason Gibson quoted Aristotle was because he wanted to improve education, attracting better teachers to Vermont with better pay and benefits, something his predecessors as governor had not done. The governor was also worried about the health of his constituents. The descendants of the Green Mountain boys had not exactly impressed the physicians who had examined them for entrance into military service during World War II. Fifty percent of those called had failed their physicals. Gibson, whose own health broke temporarily while he was commanding troops in the South Pacific, said the statistic was "truly distressing."

No doubt decades of inbreeding had made Vermont "a special world" in a different kind of way than the one tourism would successfully promote in the 1960s. Like most villages in the state, Quechee had, in some ways, changed very little since the second half of the nineteenth century. It was still "a town of the hinterland," as essayist Van Wyck Brooks had called rural villages in *The Flowering of New England,* a place "one seemed to encounter simpletons, and worse, idiots and homeless lunatics, freely walking about."

For a kid, this was great. It meant a number of adults in town acted a lot like us kids. Elmer Eastman, for instance, not only collected tinfoil from us; he also had a deformed arm and such a strong one on his other shoulder that Elmer could thrust it out and two boys could swing from it. Another fellow, Johnny Tucker, was a hermit. He lived in a tarpaper shack in the woods by the side of the gorge. We also had a resident millionaire, or at least we were told he was a millionaire. He lived in the white mansion above the Quechee Fells farm on the back road to Taftsville. An albino buck made rare appearances in the millionaire's apple orchards.

Up above town, along Route 4, there lived a Mrs. Gilson, a devout Catholic widow who was both well-off (my parents didn't, to my recollection, call people "rich" or "poor," but rather "well-off" and "not so well-off") and a little eccentric. Before I was born, both my sisters, Barbara and Gerry, had taken turns boarding with Mrs. Gilson, helping her clean her big farmhouse and keeping her company. One of Barbara's duties was to check under the beds every night and to look in the closets because Mrs. Gilson insisted the Ku Klux Klan intended to kill her.

"She was afraid to be alone," Barb told me many years later. "She was afraid of her ex-husband coming back and killing her, or the Ku Klux Klan doing it. So one night—she had a porch roof that come up to one of the stories of the house—we looked out there, and there was a whole mess of people dancing around in white sheets. I got the gun, and I shot in the air and sca'rt 'em away."

The fact that both the Ku Klux Klan and less bigoted eccentrics found Vermont hospitable in the forties was due to a long tradition of tolerance, at least if you were white or able to pay someone like my sisters to look after you. The rich who were odd seemed to command a special respect, as though they possessed unique powers. The message seemed to be: be weird, if you could afford it.

Adulation of the eccentric well-to-do, I realized when I got older, was not uncommon in primitive places. And much of Vermont in the 1940s, vis-a-vis the rest of America, was quite primitive in its sociology and economics. It was close in some ways—its isolation, its patriarchal mill towns with a couple of rich families and with practically everyone else working for them or for businesses that depended on their mill's vitality, its local mores and educational control and social network centered by churches and the poorhouse, its lackluster economy and absence of raw resources to stimulate that economy—to what people later came to associate with Third World countries, places conspicuously underdeveloped. And as in those countries in Vermont you could be strange, particularly if you had money, and people would mostly just smile at you tolerantly, if not with a little envy.

In Barbara's case, her relationship with the worried Mrs. Gilson didn't lack for some counterbalancing humor. One time, for instance, the widow bought some lobsters for a special treat.

"I looked in the sink and she had two live lobsters," Barb told me. "She said she was gonna put them in boiling water. Well, I guess I told her! 'You put those lobsters in boiling water, that's the last you're ever gonna see of me!' Then I did a fool thing myself. I took them down the river and let them go."

In 1946 Josephine Dupuis moved to Quechee from Hanover, New Hampshire, an intellectual oasis in the North Country because of Dartmouth College. Dupuis, twenty-six, was startled by how backward the people in Vermont were.

"It was like going back in the Dark Ages," she remembered vividly even thirty-four years later, when I talked with her in her kitchen overlooking the one-time mill town that had been transformed into a second-home mecca. "You couldn't believe how behind they were," Dupuis said, shaking her head. "It was awful. The people worked so hard for those mill owners. They were afraid to open their mouths." Yet, as Dupuis added moments later, sounding a bit flabbergasted by the other side of her recollection, "they said they were one big happy family."

One reason the mill workers said they were happy when more worldly types saw them as exploited was that they had a rather narrow view of their options. Families lived for generations in the same town. Husbands and wives often first met in a mill. Cousins fell for each other as they skinny-dipped at night in mill ponds. If you didn't like mill work, or wanted a union, or thought the mill owner ought to give bigger Christmas bonuses, your avenues for expressing grievances were limited. Some owners could be approached, as could some mill superintendents, like Mr. "My My" Talcot who ran the Harris and Emery Mill. Mr. Talcot was called "My My," my sister Barbara said, because whenever somebody swore or asked him something thought-provoking, the first words out of his mouth were always, "My, my." Other superintendents, often mean and penny-pinching, were best left alone. My father told me that one super he worked for only seemed pleased when he found him sitting down, because that meant nothing needed fixing, the machinery was going full blast.

The forties were a time when the word "union" brought frowns to the foreheads of many Vermonters. Most family-owned woolen mills and other industries across the state would not have allowed a union in without a real fight, preferring to act as though the Vermont Marble Company strike of the previous decade hadn't even happened. Yet in late 1935, hundreds of mostly Italian workers at Vermont Marble Company in Proctor—a typical paternalistic operation, with company stores and housing—walked out of the marble sheds and quarries. Guns and guards promptly appeared. What Vermont state government thought about the strikers was evident when state funds were used to hire deputies to protect those who continued working from those who didn't. Dynamite explosions, rallying socialists, and the fact that "labor strife contrasted starkly with Vermont's pastoral image," as Peter Jennison noted in *Roadside History of Vermont,* brought reporters and national attention on the Rutland area. In the spring of 1936, with the Proctor family shaken up but still firmly in power, the strike ended in arbitration.

Most mill owners, including the well-known Proctors (three of them had been governor, including Mortimer Proctor, who was upset during his bid for reelection by the upstart Gibson in 1946) saw themselves as humane capitalists upon whose success the future of their respective towns depended. Unions, a threat to their control and security, scared them.

Dewey's Mills, located at the mouth of the Quechee Gorge, epitomized the paternalistic mill community rooted in one family's wealth and power. Albert Galatin Dewey had founded the A. G. Dewey Company in 1836 when he built America's first "shoddy" mill on the Ottauquechee. Shoddy was reworked wool, mostly rags and remnants collected by rag merchants, or rag men, in the cities. One hundred and ten years later the company operated under the leadership of the fourth generation of the Dewey family. Their little principality contained sixty-three buildings scattered over fourteen hundred acres, and included the five-storied, wood-framed mill that seemed so alive to me, a three-storied office building with a French mansard roof, a machine shop, an ice house, a dormitory for single workers (with a dining room and a cook), eighteen family houses with apartments, a company ball field, a gun club free to employees, and various barns and sheds for wagons, horses, and machinery. William Dewey, the company president, lived in a large house on a plateau above his mill.

"We were more spoiled than the average kids," one of his three daughters, Carol Dewey Davidson, told me when we talked about her childhood. "We lived on the hill top overlooking everybody else in town," she said. "Our grandfather had built the school we went to, so we felt that we owned that as well." There weren't many kids in the Dewey's Mills community, Davidson recalled, but she confirmed my memories about how strange many of the adults were. "Towards the end of the mills' functioning," she said, "my father brought in more normal people."

Alongside Route 4 by the gorge was Dewey's Mills Outlet. The outlet caught a lot of passersby off guard. It was a flat-roofed, modern-looking building in a land of gable ends. It had won an award from *Progressive Architecture*. A sidewalk led out onto the high arching steel bridge off which a number of depressed Vermonters, as well as some out-of-staters, had leaped.

In 1990 a sign on the fence bordering the sheer drop read:

WARNING
Climbing gorge wall is
prohibited. $500 fine
if rescue is necessary.

No such sign had existed the afternoon my sister Barbara and her friend, Kay Bagley, back in the 1940s, had bloodied their hands and ripped their clothes during an ascent. They considered going back down, Barb told me, but that proved harder than continuing upward. Folks spotted the two teenage girls on the sheer granite ledges, and soon a crowd gathered, pointing and speculating on the outcome of the risky climb. Somehow my dad got wind of the fact his older daughter was pulling "a damn fool stunt," as he would call it later. With some other fellows from the mill he was soon peering over the edge of the cliff, smoking cigarette after cigarette until Barbara and Kay, smiling, exhausted, hands cut, pulled themselves up to end their wanton gesture of youthful optimism.

Although Dewey's Mills was rather progressive for the forties, providing employees health insurance, a week's paid vacation after a year, and a small pension, it did have a problem. A veteran who returned from World War II and went to work there best summed it up: "It'd go like hell for a while, then shut right down."

Business fluctuated because the woolen mills in New England were dying out. Historically, New England had been *the* textile center. In the late 1800s it had produced fifty percent of the woolens and eighty percent of the cotton goods in the United States. Sprawling complexes lined rivers in New Bedford and Fall River, Massachusetts. The Amoskeag Mill in Manchester, New Hampshire, employed seventeen thousand, boasted its thousand slamming looms could weave a mile of fabric each minute, and by 1915 stretched for a mile along the Merrimack River. Such mills, with their durable, versatile buildings made of heavy timbers, double-thick wooden floors (they were called "slow burning," because their heft retarded the spread of fire), and thousands upon thousands of bricks, were a symbol of Industrial Age power. Architecturally, they spoke a common visual language. Stair towers often decorated fronts. Clocks and cupolas towered over tenement roofs. The ubiquitous smokestack helped loft pollutants high into the air. They descended on neighboring villages and their farmers' crops. Vermont's mills, small compared to those in southern New Hampshire and Massachusetts, often copied their styles. The Vermont mills relied heavily on overflow work from the larger mills to keep busy. After World War II, however, everything changed. Textile manufacturers headed South and overseas where wages were lower, unions non-existent, and officials more cooperative. Huge, old, inefficient behemoths like those strung along the Merrimack River and clustered in the Lowell, Lawrence, Haverill area of Massachusetts, closed. The work coming to Vermont dried up.

Nevertheless, many Vermont mills hung on. Being small helped, as did the fact the mills had a reserve of skilled workers in the White River and Black River valleys, where waterpower had dictated locations during the wool industry's heyday. Some desperate towns even voted to give mill owners tax breaks, so they didn't go under. Workers tolerated insecurity and seldom complained. The scattered locations of the mills made temporary layoffs and rehirings less conspicuous (and easier to use as an economic throttle by mill owners who had little fear of unruly labor reactions) than they would have been in a single city. Because of these factors, and because the Vermont work force, isolated by mountains and the weather and poor roads, had little choice but to tighten its already cinched belt, many woolen mills kept running well into the 1950s. The Hartford Woolen Mill kept making a special grade of wool for baseball uniforms that outfitted Little Leaguers everywhere. The Champlain Woolen Mill in Winooski, which belonged to the American Woolen Company, kept twenty-two hundred people working, more than any other single private employer in the state.

The Harris and Emery Mill in Quechee, however, closed in 1952. Four years later, Dewey's Mills closed its doors when the Hartland dam, a flood control project, put the picker house and other basement functions below high water level. Bought for $288,000 by the federal government, the one-time principality became a ghost town awaiting the wrecking ball. Bridgewater Woolen Mill, where my dad worked for years beyond retirement age, managed to keep going well into the 1970s. He often grumbled about working conditions. "They can chuck the whole darn place into the river far as I care," he'd say when he was exasperated about the shortage of help or the age of the machinery, which required him to spend a lot of hours on his back wrestling with oily nuts the size of donuts. My sister Barbara also worked in Bridgewater right up until it closed. But her story had another side to it, that of the hill farmer.

*I*n 1946 Barbara and Raymond Young, the fellow who had accosted her while she rode her stallion backwards through the covered bridge in Quechee, bought the 126-acre Roy Russ farm in the egg carton-like hills of Tunbridge. They paid nine hundred dollars for it.

Raymond Young was the kind of Vermonter that Ernest Gibson, Jr., then campaigning for governor in the Republican primary against incumbent Mortimer Proctor, was worried about. One of eleven kids raised on a farm in East Randolph, Raymond had left school during the Depression (he was sixteen) and had gone to work for the Civilian Conservation Corps, cutting the Nose Dive Trail on Mount Mansfield. He'd worked with a crew of about thirty other farm boys and townies for two years, 1934 and 1935, dropping trees, wrestling rocks, and digging stumps. Then he came down with rheumatic fever.

After that, Barbara said, Raymond had "a leaky valve of the heart. The doctors said he'd never live to see thirty. He had these bad spells where they had to give him shots in the neck to bring him to."

Raymond's health was so marginal that following his physical for the Army at the outset of World War II, a doctor pulled him aside and advised the young man "to find a quiet stall and plenty of good food." Raymond appreciated the advice, but who was going to pay for the food and the stall? In order to make a living once the Army had rejected him Raymond decided to have a go at the one thing he knew something about. Farming. He rented the old Roy Russ farm, about a mile from the one-room Ward Hill School where he'd learned the three R's—reading, 'riting, and 'rithmetic—bought eight heifers, and started hauling milk cans to the Tunbridge Creamery, a two-hour round trip by horse and buggy down and up a windy dirt road.

The work soon wore him out. Raymond sold the cows, moved to Quechee and got a job carrying filling (bobbins on which yarn was spun) in the Harris and Emery Mill. There, he spotted Barbara on horseback in the covered bridge. She was, he recalled with a grin decades later, "madder than hell" about his method of introducing himself.

In April 1946, when the Youngs saw their future farm together for the first time from the seat of his horse and buggy, Raymond was thirty and Barbara twenty-one. They had two kids, Lizzy, age two, and Francis, one.

"You couldn't drive a car up there then—no way!" Barb recalled. "It was mud. The house was a worn-out situation that we jacked up seventeen inches on one side. In fact, if you started mopping the floor up there, and if the pail tipped, it went right outdoors down in the other corner. The toilet was a backhouse, about fifty feet from the house. You used it winter and summer. There was no electricity. You used lamps. There was no running water. You went to the spring and got water and carried it to the house. The road was so that during the middle of the summer you could get up here with a car. But the rest of the time, if you didn't have a horse, you'd be pretty bad off."

At the time the family farm was a Vermont institution. There were upwards of 24,000 of them, scattered across the state: in the river valleys, down the length of the Green Mountains, in the Champlain Valley, on the rolling plateaus. The typical farm had a fifteen to twenty cow herd, 150 acres, a sugarbush, a woodlot, and the Vermont look: the two-story farmhouse, the gambrel or gable-ended barn, the muddy barnyard, rocky pastures, smooth meadows, and dark woods. Thousands of farms were as primitive as Roy Russ's old place, some even more so. Dirt floors, chickens in the kitchen, wet milking (you squirted your hands with a little milk from the cow's tit and rubbed them together for lubrication), and corn. The farms were everywhere: in villages, on hillsides, on high shoulders of mountains, their fields often white with snow in early October as leaves still turned in the valleys. There were also a few spectacular farms originally built as nineteeth-century country estates: Shelburne Farms, the Billings Farm in Woodstock, the Theodore Vail Farm in Lyndonville.

Yet, by the late 1940s, the state had far fewer farms than there once had been. A walk into the woods along any abandoned road invariably brought you to stone walls, foundation holes, possibly even a wobbly stone chimney standing like a sentinel over lilacs. And the number of farms was declining fast. The 24,000 farms of 1946 became 9,200 farms by 1964. Over eighteen years, that's an average loss of 822 farms a year, two or three, every day, for more than six thousand days in a row. By 1970 there were 6,800 farms. By 1990, 2,400. As the number of farms had declined, their nostalgic value had risen, however. By the seventies, many Vermonters had never been on a farm, never mind milked a cow, and there was a tendency among them to gloss over the post-World War II years, before the interstates and the growth of tourism and skiing, with a romantic haze. They mistakenly saw that time as the twilight of a Vermont filled with snug farmhouses, canned vegetables in the cellar, dry cordwood stacked in the shed, and a diversified animal kingdom in the barn. The truth was another matter. The tractor, the bulk tank, price regulation, and breeding programs were redefining dairy farming. Most Vermont farmers, but especially those in the hills, where growing seasons were short, the soils stonier, and the creameries further away, simply could not make enough money. Big gardens, canning, and a "patch it up and make do" ethic helped many make ends meet. But there were always property taxes to pay, poll taxes, too, if you wanted to vote, feed for the animals to buy, shoes to put on children's growing feet, and, most expensive of all, new machinery to acquire. So many farmers "worked out to boot," holding second jobs in woolen mills, tanneries, quarries, sawmills, and in local garages and stores.

Milk was the cash crop on the farm, supplemented usually by maple syrup. Farms tended to be diversified, although that was changing. "Christ, they had everything," Raymond Young said about the farms in the vicinity of the old Roy Russ place. "Ducks, geese, a few sheep, chickens, hogs someone would come and dress out in November. You'd cure and smoke the hams, fry out the lard, and use it for frying donuts." There were lots of horses: Percherons, Belgians, Clydesdales, and Morgans, veritable mountains of warm flesh that required bridles, bits, and hobbles to work, as well as good horse sense to get along with.

But a new era had dawned. It was called the car culture, although in Vermont its presence was symbolized as much by the noisy tractor, which scared the animals in the barn at dawn when it coughed awake, as by the fat-tired, sleek roadster with suitcases strapped to the trunk, or the family sedan. The new culture was reshaping much of America—its landscape, its mindset, its habits. The car, with its promise of freedom and mobility, altered the American Way of Life in fundamental, far-reaching ways. The Vermont Way of Life, with its horses, dirt roads, and skepticism about change, proved stubbornly resistant to the car culture—but it gradually gave way.

On the farm new advances in technology and science were encouraging less diversity and more specialization. That meant tractors, machinery, chemicals. It meant selling the horses and the bull, converting acreage used for oats and corn, which fed them, to sileage and hay, which fed more cows, and going to the bank to get loans, not only for the tractor, which was the lynchpin of the new, but for such things as bulk tanks and milking machines. After that there were other things for a farmer to think about, like improving his herd's bloodline, what nutrients to add to depleted soils, how to control pests with sprays.

A lot of soul searching went on inside the hearts of Vermont farmers during this time. Agriculture had been steadily changing since the turn-of-the-century, with such things as pasteurization, cement floors in barns, and newer implements. But not at the rate it was changing now. And the lure of the new was strong and regional market pressures unrelenting. Extension agents were go-betweens, linking the farmer to the milk companies via the University of Vermont, which had an unshakeable faith in the latest science and technology and wanted farmers to know how to apply them. The extension agents didn't let farmers forget for too long what was out there either and that they were always available to help.

"What they were saying to our farmers," recalled a former manager of the St. Albans Cooperative, a fellow who worked a lot with extension agents during the fifties, was " 'Get more milk, that's your cash crop.' And how do you get more milk? 'Eliminate something's a non-producer. The bull don't produce nothing—get rid of him! You can use artificial insemination! And you need more grass feed!' "

One tradition Vermont farmers had to be weaned from was something called "the spring flush." The spring flush was a consequence of the natural birthing cycle of cows. They calved in the spring, so milk production peaked to feed the newborn. From a marketing standpoint, though, this was bad business. The human thirst for milk and milk by-products was steady; it didn't fluctuate with the seasons. So extension agents recommended to farmers that they get their stock to freshen at different times throughout the year, rather than primarily in the spring. There was a lot of resistance to this. Farmers with young stock were used to letting a bull run with them and only reluctantly tied the bull up.

The price every farmer got for his milk was set by the federal government. The loss of control over the price farmers received for milk had begun during the Depression. In 1933 President Franklin Delano Roosevelt had signed the first farm pricing law, assuring politicians and the public alike that it was only temporary, the government had no intention of propping up agriculture. By the fifties the temporary crutch had become a national milk-pricing complex in which Vermont occupied a niche in Federal Milk Marketing Region Number One. Region Number One's headquarters were in Boston. There the Big Four—they included Hood Milk Company and Whiting Milk Company, both well established in Vermont—had processing plants in Milk Alley in Charlestown.

The system was a political concoction that created a pipeline with government's hand on the control valve. Need more milk? Open the valve with incentives. Need less milk? Close the valve and put some farmers out of work. The pipeline, which led indirectly from tens of thousands of udders in Vermont to the stomachs of children and adults in populous southern New England, needed more milk in the fifties. The baby boom generation had a giant thirst. Three glasses a day, minimum, in an era when breast feeding had become a a victim of cultural stereotyping; breast feeding was something only poor and backward people still did.

Across Vermont the installation of the bulk tank became the litmus test of keeping up with changing agricultural times. Installing one meant you were a modern dairy farmer. Lifting milk cans, like those Raymond Young had hauled to Tunbridge, meant you weren't.

The bulk tank is a large, stainless steel, temperature-controlled tank that stores milk for pick-up, usually by a stainless steel truck, which pumps the fluid out of the milk house. The truck looks like a bulk tank on wheels, but is significantly larger. A bulk tank, which maintains a constant cool temperature, reduces the odds of the bacteria in the raw milk multiplying rapidly. A tank also eliminates costly and time-consuming handling. In the fifties the bulk tank, clean and shiny and with its own well-lighted, concrete-floored addition to the barn, could look rather alien in a manure-rich, hay-littered, and animal-inhabited environment. And *having* to put a bulk tank in lifted the hair on the necks of many old-timers. The gleaming tank, separated as it was from the less sanitary stanchion area with its flies and gutters, stood for changes they felt were being shoved down their throats. In truth, it was only one piece of a package, one stainless steel element of an attitude change—not the end-all or be-all of the transformation. To induce farmers to convert milk cans to bulk tanks, the system began paying them a premium for bulk-tank milk. Extension agents urged farmers to phase out cans. In the early 1970s all of Vermont's processing plants shut off can lines completely, and the last holdouts finally installed bulk tanks.

Production volume became a critical factor if a farmer was to handle his debt load. The Holstein, a bigger, more docile cow than the traditional Jersey, became the dairy cow of choice because it produced more milk. Farmers debated the worth of one kind of cow over the other. They made jokes. For instance, Jersey farmers often said, "You can always tell it's Holstein milk because if you throw a silver dollar in it, you can still see the dollar." Holstein farmers shot back, "Well, that's right. But if it's Jersey milk, you wouldn't cover the coin." One thing was for sure. If you switched from Jerseys to Holsteins, you had to either enlarge your barn or build a new, bigger one, or else the tails of your Holsteins would be just about touching, with their necks in tight stanchions and their hooves in the gutter. A clumsier cow, the Holstein also was more at home on the flatter terrain of Addison, Grand Isle, Franklin, and Orleans counties, where soils tended to be better and farms survived iɪ greater numbers.

Though some farmers held onto their old ways in the post-World War II era, the power of the new won most of them over. Many farmers practically fell in love with the first skinny red Farmall or squat green John Deere they laid eyes on. Just to be riding, they thought, instead of walking. All that horsepower and you didn't have to grow its feed! Some farmers paid their new tractors more compliments in six months than they had paid their wives in twenty years. But then the withholding of compliments, at least towards those you loved, was another time-honored Vermont tradition.

There was a chronicler of the older, disappearing Vermont. His name was Walter Hard. Hard, a druggist in Manchester, wrote weekly columns for the *Manchester Journal* and the *Rutland Herald*. He explored the mythical complexity of the Vermont character, both on and off the farm.

Myths, of course, personify a culture's self-image. They dress up its vision of its own goodness and of its evils. The good Vermont myths deal with independence, frugality, and common sense. The bad ones, less frequently heard, though just as true, admit of physical abuse, intolerance, and ignorance in a rancorous mountain people. Many myths hung over the small farms. Like misty mornings and snowy blizzards, they added character and mystery and sometimes obscured hardship and poverty.Hard, a traditionalist, concerned himself more with the good myths, though in some of his characters there lurked a dark side.

Robert Frost, a contemporary of Hard's and already on his way into the pantheon of poetry's immortals, was a modernist. Using Vermont imagery to stir the mysterious and often darker side of life, Frost plumbed Frost. It was Hard, however, writing on Sundays after church for his newspaper columns, who painstakingly brought to focus the times the two poets both knew well, Vermont in the last decades of the nineteenth and first decades of the twentieth centuries.

Walter Hard "absorbed all the folklore, traditions, stories, anecdotes, and tall tales that his Yankee forebears and their neighbors had passed down over the years," J. Kevin Graffagnino, curator of the University of Vermont's Wilbur Collection, wrote in his introduction to Hard's *Vermont People*.

Already forty-six when his first book, *Some Vermonters,* appeared in

1928, the druggist/poet published ten more. During that time he watched his home town of Manchester, "a sleepy village in a peaceful valley," as he put it, become a haven for second-home owners, tourists, and, after World War II, for skiers schussing the slopes of Fred Pabst's Mount Bromley in nearby Peru. Hard's byline appeared in the first issue of *Vermont Life* Magazine in 1946. He wrote about characters, incidents, and landscape that he knew or had heard of from others who knew what they were talking about. In the process, he wrote about all of Vermont, because in those pre-interstate days, unassuming, laconic, indomitable Vermonters who spoke of a part of America still out-of-step with modern times pretty much inhabited the whole state.

Dry humor, whether in a judge or a drunk, a housewife or a carpenter, runs through Hard's work like a stream. It waters the personalities of characters like Gard who, in "Hard Cider," likes his drink so much he lets his farm go to hell, all except one tree. Its apples make Gard's winter's supply. Then there's Egbert Buckley in "A Tinkerer." Egbert can fix just about anything. Uses junk parts that have been thrown away. Fills the yard of his blacksmith shop with wrecks. Once the summer people get lawnmowers, it's Egbert who keeps them working. Over the years, though, the nature of his toil changes how Egbert looks. Hard writes:

> In general Egbert looked as though he himself
> Might have been made of cast off parts.
> Even his eyes weren't mates—
> One was blue and the other brown.

Walter Hard's characters are almost always unpretentious. "Big enough not to amount to much," he calls them. And born philosophers. Some have a knack for puncturing phoniness with barbed one-liners. And his characters are not quaint. They don't sit around smoking corncobs by pot-bellied stoves, mouthing "yup" and "nope," although there are loafers who do plenty of sitting around. The characters who inhabit Hard's tales are distillations of rural people whose lives are understated in a way that harps back to a simpler, more direct America.

When Walter Hard walked the streets of Manchester, the car culture was already honking its horns at slow buggies. Youngsters smiled through the passenger windows as drivers went by slowly in respect to the horses, whose hooves clattered on the hard-surfaced streets. Vermont was becoming "surrounded by a nation growing sadly out of touch with the small-town traditions on which it was built," Graffagnino wrote.

In Hard's stories the characters believe unshakeably in the continuity of established tradition. Changing just to change seems foolish. They question the new from every angle, then . . . maybe, cautiously embrace it. Or parts of it anyway. The good parts. They are even tolerant of the local petty thief. In "Jed Gets in His Wood" Hard reminds readers that even such a minor scoundrel fits in the nature of things:

> . . . with Jed out of the way who'd there be
> To blame when something turned up missing.

By the early 1950s, the Vermont that Hard wrote about was coming apart under economic and social pressures, although the state legislature did its best to ignore them. In the hills, the kerosene culture of wicks and lamplight gave way at an accelerating rate to fuses and sixty-watt light bulbs, thanks to the efforts of rural electric cooperatives, which had been stringing power lines along back roads, through gores, and into tight valleys since the 1930s. With electricity came indoor plumbing. No more trips to the spring with a bucket. No more midnight shuffles to the backhouse or gropes in the dark for the cornhusks.

In the fields, the tractor, along with new implements, displaced the workhorse. Not that farming still wasn't tough, and didn't form character and respect diligence, doling out harsh consequences for the weak. But it wasn't as backbreaking or as primitive as it had been.

Still, thousands clung to farm life not because they loved it, but because they were afraid to change. Others felt the obligations of inheritance. They farmed out of necessity, not desire. Farm women remained the driving force behind many better operations. They managed the money, the children, the food. They were the hub of the family wheel, the pillars of the church, the soul of the Grange.

The successful family farm became more of a hybrid, both a bastion of the past and a showcase for the future. It also was, in most instances, financed by a local bank. A tractor, for instance, frequently the first step a farmer took towards modernizing, meant big debt. The small farmer had traditionally hoarded his cash, of which he seldom had much anyway. But to get a tractor, the farmer had to go to the bank. The bottom line was that tractors, bulk tanks, hay balers, seed planters, and all the other implements it only made sense to buy once you had the tractor, cost a farmer more than money. To become modern, he also had to mortgage his old-fashioned independence.

Farmers back in the hills in particular tended to do some pondering before borrowing. For a great many of them going to a bank for a loan was about as foreign as going to the town hall to vote Democrat.

"The hill farmers died when they bought their first tractors," claimed Esther Swift, librarian at the Billings Farm and Museum in Woodstock. Before the tractor, "with the village idiot and his brother you could get along," she insisted. But not afterwards.

Vermont farmers got inexorably drawn into the maw of a rapidly changing agricultural world. Physically isolated yet more and more part of a large web of markets and government price regulation, they had to produce more milk to survive, and to produce milk they needed to invest in machinery. To invest they needed credit. To make debt payments to the bank they needed to produce more milk. That meant more cows. And to feed more cows they needed the other new labor-saving equipment.

It was a spiral. At the center of the spiral was an uncontestable axiom: you could only have as many cows as you could feed, and growing and handling feed was a lot of work and expensive.

In agriculture whirl was becoming king.

On the Roy Russ farm, going against the current, another Vermont tradition, Barbara and Raymond Young didn't buy a tractor for years, until 1952. Before then Raymond farmed with Ned and Dick, a team of workhorses. He did the chores, fed the babies. Barbara helped in the mornings, then commuted to the second shift at the Harris and Emery Mill, riding her horse five miles down to Eaton's Sawmill on the North Branch in South Royalton each afternoon, stabling him there and traveling to Quechee with a boss who lived in Tunbridge.

In those days the infamous "drunkard's reunion," otherwise known as the Tunbridge World's Fair, offered the Youngs a break. The final fair on the annual state circuit, which included similar extravaganzas in Barton, Addison County, Essex Junction, and Rutland, where the Vermont State Fair was held, the Tunbridge World's Fair was Vermont's oldest.

I remember going to it as a boy. From South Royalton we rode up to the farm and once there my dad began working on getting drunk, a fair tradition. I wandered into the barn where the air was thick with the pungent smells of urine and cowshit. I talked to my niece Frances, who was a week older than me, and hoped my dad would take me for a ride on the tractor. After dark we drove down a twisting dirt road, rumbled through a covered bridge, and parked inside the oval racing track, in sight of the noisy, brightly lighted, and wonderful midway. At either the 1952 or 1953 fair, I remember sitting in the wooden grandstand, the barn smell of farmers and the buttery smell of popcorn mingling in the chilly air, and being so excited I could hardly stand it. There was an auto thrill show on the oval dirt track. The drivers revved their engines, the spinning wheels threw arcs of dirt, and the cars zoomed up wooden ramps and flew off over the bashed and dented roofs of a dozen wrecks. At a tent pitched on the edge of the midway my dad and Raymond joined staggering farmers who, smelling like whiskey and manure, paid to see the strippers at a girly show. Years later I would see my share of these shows. They were debauches really. Farmers and hooting locals cavorted on stage with the girls. Their antics and sexual gymnastics fired the imaginations of wide-eyed boys who had lied about their ages to get in and mesmerized grizzled old-timers who hung back so they didn't get shoved up on stage by some smartass.

Just before the 1952 fair, having decided they had to do something to make their farm work and to get out of debt, Barbara and Raymond bought a thirty-five horsepower Farmall Super A with a set of harrows, a set of plows, and a mowing machine.

"I think I bought the whole business for five thousand dollars," Raymond recalled. "That's when we sold the horses."

But success continued to elude the Youngs, as it did roughly seven thousand other small farmers who stopped milking cows for a living during the fifties. To modernize effectively it took a different kind of character than a lot of farmers had. Many farmers remained anachronisms, throwbacks to an era confined more and more to the pages of Walter Hard's books, and no amount of talk about improvements was going to change that. Vermont had been just fine like it was, they grumbled.

Those farmers who had the knack, or larger dairies, often thrived. But for every success story there were six, seven, or ten tales of woe. The Youngs weren't successful.

In 1952, the same year they bought the tractor, their barn burned. Twelve hundred chicks went up in smoke. Determined to make it in a business in which thousands of folks very much like them were giving up from exhaustion, burdensome debt, and prolonged despair over a deteriorating situation that the state seemed reluctant to ease, the Youngs kept at it, buying more cows, Barbara working at Dewey's Mills after the Harris and Emery Mill closed, then at the Bridgewater Mill after Dewey's closed in 1956. A truck from the creamery came up the narrow dirt road every other day to collect the milk, but sometimes the truck couldn't make it through the mud or snow. The day after Christmas in 1959 the house burned.

"It started, I guess, up in the old attic part," Raymond said. "Those airplanes going through here had something to do with it—those sonic booms. Breaking the sound barrier. Shook the whole house." The booms had been going on for two or three years. "I think it must have cracked the chimney up there. It didn't have a lining.

"The mailman came along. He was late that day, but I'd been cutting wood down on the bank, and I'd run out of oil and gone into town. He got out quite a lot of stuff. I guess the last thing he got out was the TV, and the goddamn ceiling fell in right behind it. He just barely made it."

Frances Clark, the Young's oldest daughter (they had four children, but one, Lizzy, died of leukemia in 1951), was a teenager before she realized her folks were not really getting ahead. In fact, by the early sixties, she understood "they were going backwards. I remember putting all this money into grain and haying and all this work. When you add that together, with your kids working, too—really, you didn't get much out of it."

Raymond agreed. "Couldn't seem to get a foothold," he said, echoing the lament of thousands of small farmers. "Always something seemed to be happening. Barb and I threw our lives away fooling around with it."

When I drove Maggie, my wife, to the farm in the early seventies, one of her first questions was "which is the house and which is the barn?"

The lean-to that housed a few cows and some pigs was the barn. You could tell, I explained, by the hay sticking out the gaps between boards. The replacement house, begun when twenty or so neighbors had chipped in free labor one weekend after the old place burned, had never been finished. It sat beside a foundation, out of which good-sized saplings grew. By that time Raymond's health had deteriorated even further. My sister was still "working out to boot." Every woolen mill except the one in Bridgewater had closed. The number of farms in Vermont was down to around sixty-five hundred. But the indomitable spirit of my sister, despite all the hardships and disappointment she had seen, still seemed alive. Raymond said she stayed cheerful on the surface, but not underneath. In the fashion of the Vermonter of old we so love to imagine, "She just kept her hopes up that some day it'd be better."

*T*he Joseph Bortugno farm is three miles from the Raymond Young farm. On a wet November day in 1989 I visited Bortugno. Rain pounded on the silver roof of his empty barn and danced in wind-driven sheets across a large pond. Retired from farming since 1967, when "farmer's lung," a reaction to silage-born dust, locked him out of the barn, Bortugno was a trim, youthful-eyed, rugged man with unruly grey hair and ruddy cheeks. Despite his lung ailment, he stood erect and walked a lot differently than Raymond, who darted around his kitchen hunched over in a bow-legged shuffle.

Bortugno acted surprised I wanted to interview him. A bit warily he told me he had moved to Tunbridge in 1945 from Litchfield, Connecticut, because land prices down there were rising. Farms were going out in

Connecticut just as they would go out in Vermont a decade later, agricultural dominoes falling northward through New England. For this farm, which was more fertile and closer to the Tunbridge Creamery than the old Roy Russ farm, Bortugno paid $3,500. He tore down everything in sight, he said, and built new. He ran a much different, and much more successful, farm than Raymond and Barbara Young ever did.

Beginning with fifteen Holsteins, Bortugno worked up to sixty. He steadily bought more land—forty-two acres adjacent to his original ninety-six, then seventy-six, then a large parcel of just over two hundred. He bought tractors, worked hard, and stayed out of entanglements that might have kept him from increasing his milk production. He didn't raise hogs or chickens like the other farmers, he said, nor did he sugar or belong to the Grange. He didn't go to Town Meetings much. He just worked, harvesting crops, building his herd, increasing his milk check. Mrs. Bortugno kept a big garden and canned a lot. Bortugno had a hired man.

The details of his farm life consumed about fifteen minutes. They contrasted sharply with Raymond's tale. Strangely enough, before I left Bortugno's house, he started lamenting the loss of the old Vermonters, the kind who did attend Town Meetings, who joined the Grange, who drank whiskey in the sugarhouse until they fell over into the boiling pan and got scalded, laughing afterwards even as skin blistered.

"Now they're all different," this old man with the wild hair said, raising his voice. "They're either writers or painters or something else that move up here!" Shifting his attention from the rain on the windows he fixed me with a stare. "And you're another one, huh?"

I admitted I was.

"My neighbor up here is a writer," Bortugno went on, gesturing, visibly riled. "Two or three painters up here. What else we got?" He glanced at Mrs. Bortugno in the kitchen. "A masseuse?"

Was there a masseuse in Vermont in the 1940s? I pondered this as I drove away from Bortugno's farm in the pounding rain.

BEFORE HIS TIME

I stress that it is my firm conviction that the two
foundation stones upon which Democracy must stand if
it is to survive in this world are education and health.
—Governor Ernest Gibson, Jr.
Speech to Vermont legislature, 1949

In the summer of 1943, on the island of Rendova in
the South Pacific, Colonel Ernest Gibson, Jr., of Brattleboro became a bona
fide war hero. Shrapnel from a bomb, combined with a powerful
photograph—face twisted in a grimace, shocked eyes angled skyward
towards hands tying a white bandage around his forehead—landed
Gibson's picture on millions of Americans' laps. The photograph made it
into the national papers, including the *Washington Post,* and was reprinted
in dailies from one end of Vermont to the other. In those pre-television days,
such a dramatic shot left a vivid and lasting impression. Colonel Gibson later
received a Purple Heart for his wound and a Silver Star Medal for valor.
Vermonters were proud of him. After the wound, Gibson also seemed to
become a little more attuned to his mortality. After all, he was forty-three,
with a wife and four kids. Besides, the tropical jungle fighting had wasted
him. He got word to his close friend, U.S. Senator George Aiken, that he
would appreciate some help getting stateside. Late in 1943 Gibson was
furloughed back to Vermont. His voice filled with emotion, his body frail,
his hair gray, the decorated colonel spoke at bond rallies around the state,
considerably enhancing his reputation.

Two years later, after the war's end, thirty-three thousand veterans, out
of forty thousand who had enlisted, returned to Vermont. They found a
place not much different from the one they had left. There were those
countless farms, the villages, the small mills. And little promise for the future.
One veteran, General "Red" Wing of Rutland, who had commanded the
Forty-third Division in which Gibson served, was promptly courted by the

Republicans to run for governor. But protracted jungle combat had ravaged Wing's health and he died suddenly in late 1945, leaving Gibson his heir-apparent.

Most of Gibson and Wing's fellow veterans were not generals, of course, nor colonels or officers of any stripe, for that matter. They were simply ex-GIs, young, restless, energetic guys glad to be home and still alive. But now they'd seen Paris, marched along German autobahns, and peered up at droning squadrons of B-17s from the decks of aircraft carriers, a job carrying roping in a woolen mill, if it was hiring, or the prospect of taking over the family farm, didn't entice them to forget about the big, exciting world they had experienced. Once they realized that the Old Guard had little desire to make Vermont any different than the state had been in 1940, the great expectations with which many of them had been filled when they first got home gradually drained out like water through an unattended hole in a tub.

Thousands decided to leave Vermont. They wanted possibilities and newness, not the same old jobs and dirt roads and low standard of living most Vermonters had accepted—it seemed like forever—as their inheritance and destiny. By the hundreds, month after month, they packed their bags, hugged loved ones good-bye, wiped away the tears, and headed out into the mid-twentieth century. Of those who stayed, hundreds, deferring the necessity of facing dismal prospects, enrolled at Norwich University and at the University of Vermont on the GI Bill. But even with an education, a spanking new life wasn't available for them here. When Ernest Gibson appeared on the political horizon, it looked as if he might change that. But for those in a hurry, his years as governor would prove a disappointment.

The veterans who left Vermont, on the other hand, accompanied by high school graduates and others who were disenchanted, went looking for their fates elsewhere in New England, in New York, down south where the woolen mills were hiring, out west in California where the weather was good twelve months a year. Those with some knowledge of Vermont history knew they weren't doing anything new. The list of Vermonters who had preceded them during the last century was impressive. The heavyweights had included Frederick Billings of Woodstock, who had built the Northern Pacific Railroad through Montana, Henry Wells of Thetford, who had become the Wells of Wells, Fargo Company, Elisha Otis of Halifax, who invented the Otis elevator, Harvey Hood of Chelsea, who started his own milk business in Boston, and Francis Asbury Pratt of Woodstock, who had been a partner in Pratt Whitney Aircraft in Connecticut. "Eight of the first eighteen governors [of Wisconsin, which became a state in 1848] were native Vermonters," wrote Charles Morrissey in *Vermont: A History,* "as were seven of its early senators." Temperance societies everywhere had Vermont to thank. William Wilson of East Dorset, who became a heavy-drinking Wall Street lawyer, and Robert H. Smith, a doctor from St. Johnsbury who also imbibed to excess once he moved his practice to Akron, Ohio, joined hands and founded Alcoholics Anonymous in 1935. Out in the Utah territory, three Vermont women had tied the knot with Brigham Young in the previous century. Possibly the Mormon patriarch, who had sixty-seven other wives, leaned favorably towards the Green Mountain girls because Joseph Smith had been born in the hills of Sharon.

Smith, granted, was an unusual case. Once he left Vermont he became a prophet. In Sharon, the young Smith was, according to the *Encyclopedia Britannica* (11th edition), "a good-natured, lazy boy suffering from a bad heredity physically and psychically." At age eleven he left Vermont with his parents, who, "like his grandparents," the encyclopedia continues, "were superstitious, neurotic, seers of visions, and believers in miraculous cures and in heavenly voices and direct revelation." Smith was seventeen and living in Manchester, New York, when the angel Moroni, he claimed, appeared to him in a vision and directed him to a spot on a hillside where he dug up the Gold Bible, a book six inches thick, made of thin gold plates secured with gold rings. Once translated, the ancient script on the plates became *The Book of Mormon*. Would the former Green Mountain boy have located the Gold Bible, which the angel Moroni subsequently and mysteriously took away, and have founded a religion if he had never left home?

Thousands of lesser known, hard-working Vermonters joined wagon trains, and later boarded real trains to head west. They made more of their lives than they probably would have if they had stayed home. Returning infantrymen, pilots, seamen, as well as their younger brothers and sisters graduating from Vermont high schools in 1947, 1948, and 1949, continued the exodus.

The revelation that dawned on the attentive was usually the same: Vermont was a losing hand in cards, the wrong card in Bingo, it meant decades of peering out the glass window of the drugstore or the hardware store or the bank office if you were a merchant or small businessman. Life lay out there, in Connecticut, Boston, New York, Michigan, Wisconsin, points west. Vermont remained a great place to be from, a scenic backwater of covered bridges, farmers, and mill towns where slamming looms still lulled boys to sleep. But as far as challenging a young adult who wanted to get ahead, it was nowhere.

Once elected governor in the fall of 1946, Ernest Gibson, Jr., at least tried to do something about that.

*V*eterans, along with the poor, the unhealthy, and the young, found an ally in Vermont's "New Dealing Yankee," as the press called Gibson. He was a magnetic guy who might bring about some major changes in areas his pinch-faced predecessors had tended to ignore, such as health care and education. In retrospect Ernest Gibson, Jr., was kind of a John F. Kennedy figure in Republican gray a decade and a half before the sixties. But his efforts on behalf of Vermonters were thwarted by a conservative Old Guard, many of whom despised him. He put himself on their bad side with his victory over the incumbent Mortimer Proctor in the 1946 Republican primary.

The enormous upset broke a century-old Vermont political tradition called "the mountain rule," which was "the strength of the Republican party," according to Gregory Sanford, Vermont's State Archivist, a big, bearded, encyclopedia of a man who rules over the accumulation and chaos of state records in Montpelier. "The mountain rule really dates back to the creation of Vermont, and in various manifestations is a way that political offices were informally apportioned," Sanford told me. "In terms of the governorship, it meant that each governor was allowed two two-year terms, then stepped aside forever." The rule took its name from the Green Mountains that split the state, creating both physical and political divisions. The rule said that "a governor from the east is always followed by a governor from the west is always followed by a governor from the east. The lieutenant governor is a mirror image of the governorship. The rule is used by the party to avoid factionalism."

Until Gibson, that is. When Gibson beat Proctor in the 1946 primary, he also ended a political dynasty. Redfield Proctor had been governor from 1878 to 1880, and Fletcher Proctor had served a single term, from 1906 to 1908. The Proctors had towns named after them; they were rich and powerful. Mortimer Proctor was also an incumbent. Incumbents did not lose in Vermont. So neither the Proctors nor the Old Guard they represented were real happy that an alliance of GIs, the poor, and crossover Democrats, many of whom had recognized a Republican steeped in the populism of FDR, voted the upstart in. Not in, actually, but made him a shoo-in once the general election came around because Vermont was a one-party state. No Democrat had been governor since before the Civil War.

Once Gibson took office, it became an old political story: the progressive newcomer versus the conservatives in power.

To most of the Old Guard's way of thinking Gibson had started out his political career just fine. He came from a respected, well-connected family. His father, Ernest Gibson, Sr., had been one of Vermont's U.S. senators. Gibson, Jr., had graduated from Brattleboro High School, where he was a pole vaulter and played baseball. He went to law school at George Washington University while his father was in office. Moving back to Vermont he became secretary of the state senate in the mid-thirties. He rode back and forth to sessions with George Aiken, whose political ascent was in process: Speaker of the House, lieutenant governor, and in true mountain-rule style, governor, all in a span of six years, 1930 to 1936. Gibson rode with Aiken because they had been friends ever since Aiken, a Putney horticulturist, had become Gibson's first law client in the mid-twenties and they had discovered they thought a lot alike. That is to say, liberally for young Republicans. It was Governor Aiken who appointed Gibson to serve out his father's term when Gibson, Sr., died in office in 1940. Once in Washington, Gibson made friends with Senator Harry Truman from Missouri and embraced FDR's New Deal populism. It was his infatuation with the New Deal that started conservatives in Montpelier grumbling.

Gibson, handsome, wavy-haired, articulate, with an affinity for pin-striped suits, cut a debonair figure in the Capitol for a politician from Vermont. He also kept "the seat warm until Aiken mounted his own candidacy," writes University of Vermont history professor Samuel B. Hand in "Friends, Neighbors, and Political Allies: Reflections on the Gibson-Aiken Connection," a paper about the long-term alliance of the two men. When Gibson's short term expired, he didn't return to Vermont. He remained in Washington as chairman of the Committee to Defend America by Aiding the Allies and appeared at rallies with vivacious, crowd-pleasing movie starlets. He traveled by train and made speeches, urging isolationist Americans to help the allies fight the Nazis in Europe. He received more attention from the press than he ever had as a senator.

In June 1941, six months before Pearl Harbor, Gibson enlisted in the Army. Senator Aiken objected. After all, his friend had turned forty, had kids and a wife. Please "get back on the domestic firing line [where] you would be worth ten thousand well-meaning individuals," Aiken urged. If Gibson would change his mind about active duty and want to back out gracefully, Aiken promised, "I shall do what I can to bring this about."

Gibson said he'd stick it out for the year he'd committed himself to. Letters written to Aiken during this time, Hand notes, reveal an older officer losing patience with military tradition. The War Department, Gibson told Aiken, "has adopted a policy—in writing—that no officer not a regular army man can hold a key position in a new division." That excluded Army Reserve and National Guard officers, like himself and Red Wing. "Once again our brass hats are showing a tremendous inability to understand human nature," Gibson said. The promotion policy changed in the Army, but the parallel between its blindness to caliber and reliance on a narrow, and harmful, tradition and a similar blindness and preference for the party faithful in Republican Vermont didn't escape Gibson.

After Pearl Harbor, Colonel Gibson found himself digging foxholes under the command of General Wing in the South Pacific. Aiken, aware that the twist of fate could make Gibson politically unbeatable in Vermont after the war, kept him informed of politics back home. "The Old Guard is still operating," he wrote, "but I think weaker than ever." In another letter he joked, "There is no one at home to knock them down every morning after breakfast."

Gibson, as a former senator, attracted plenty of wartime press. Not only did journalists seek him out, but, as Professor Hand points out, "Gibson was hardly a shrinking violet." The head wound Gibson received during the bombing raid on Rendova Island made him a hero and set the stage for him to return home and, as Gregory Sanford put it, "mortally wound" the mountain rule.

As governor, Gibson's timing was good and his message clear, but his political muscle proved weak. He lacked experience in the political trenches. It was his first elected position and he couldn't get many of his reforms past the Old Guard. He did push through a minimum wage and a pension plan for teachers, and he established the State Police, much against the wishes of the county sheriffs who lost power. His first head of the police was former Army General Merritt Edson. A short, rugged disciplinarian, Edson later got into a battle with Gibson's successor, Lee Emerson, who tried unsuccessfully to shift law enforcement back to the county sheriffs. Arguably, Gibson's most pervasive contribution to state government was the graduated income tax, which shifted higher payments onto those who could afford them. His efforts to upgrade public health, though, were constantly thwarted by a legislature not yet ready to take seriously the idea that workers had health rights.

At the time workers' rights of almost any kind were given short shrift. On the farm and in the factory workers were perceived by many as little more than beasts of burden. The prevailing attitude was that if you couldn't make more of your life than a mule or a Percheron, well, that was your problem. The attitude had grave consequences, of course, not only for adults, but for children. The fate of empires, as Aristotle had foreseen it, couldn't rely much on education of the mind if the body was a ruin.

In an attempt to rally support for health care legislation, Gibson appointed a committee to study occupational diseases. Statisticians reported there were now forty-one thousand workers in manufacturing jobs across Vermont. Fifty-eight hundred of them worked in twenty-seven textile mills. The largest number of jobs, seventy-three hundred, were found in lumber and timber businesses. The machine tool industry employed sixty-eight hundred. Health experts looked at the most common Vermont ailments, including silicosis in the granite quarries, asbestosis in the Lowell asbestos mine, dermatology problems in the tanneries, and dust, oil, and chemical dangers routinely handled without many precautions in the woolen, machine-tool, and paper mills. Farms, with their finger-eating machinery ("People with missing digits are more interesting," went an old adage), and dust problems, such as the common "black lung," which barred many farmers from their own barns if they wanted to keep breathing, were excluded from the study—the dozens of farmers in the legislature saw to that.

Gibson hoped the committee would come up with some solid amendments to Vermont's Workman's Compensation Law, which offered minimal workplace protection. But the thrust of the committee's evaluation of the "Industrial Disease Problems in Vermont" report, published in 1948, was summed up by one sentence: "Fortunately, the human body can stand a certain amount of all toxic materials."

Committeeman John A. Gordon, seething over the group's failure to act responsibly, wrote Gibson a fiery dissent, claiming he had just witnessed "one of the most subtle, vicious, cunning, diabolical and dangerous attacks upon the great fundamental principle of workmen's compensation laws ever known to the people of Vermont."

*T*hough workplace diseases were a common lot for the employed in Vermont, the fate of the unemployed was often worse. It was the poor farm.

When I was a boy, parents often fired the fantasies of lazy kids with the warning: "Watch it now, or it's off to the poor farm with ya!" Part of every one-room schoolhouse education had been the dictum: "A reverence for God, the hope of heaven, and a fear of the poorhouse."

From a distance the poor farm seemed equivalent to falling into the black lagoon your uncle had told you was in the dark woods at the end of the lake. You never came back. Monsters there. Cripples, the deformed, the maimed, the poor who wasted their entire lives away.

It wasn't that bad. But then the myths and realities of the poor farm system in Vermont have never been finely examined. Poverty in America has never attracted the prolonged attention of the ambitious, nor, except possibly during the Great Depression, gathered much sympathy from the public. Being poor or moronic or sinister doesn't fit into the pull-myself-up-by-the-bootstraps American tradition that Vermont personified longer than most states.

In 1947 Governor Gibson did manage to reorganize Vermont's system, separating for the first time those in need of help, such as the elderly and the blind, from the mentally ill who required long-term care. By then, poor farms had started to become dumping grounds. The reorganization was a humane gesture in a state still given to an almost Dark Ages view of mental health.

One thing the changes didn't reduce much was the power of the overseer of the poor. An overseer worked for a town or for several villages who handled their poor collectively. He typically made arrangements for so-called "temporaries," people short on cash or down on their luck, to receive things like groceries and medical care until they got back on their feet. If getting back on your feet seemed unlikely, you got moved to the poor farm. There you worked and improved or became "a permanent."

The powers of overseers were legendary. When questions of discipline and authority arose, an overseer was both judge and jury, warden and gang boss. By law he needn't consult the selectmen or the courts, only his own conscience. An overseer could be kind and humane or abusive and arrogant. Whatever his make-up, he ruled his own little kingdom of the impoverished and the strange.

The History of Public Welfare in Vermont, a study by Lorenzo D'Agostino published in 1948 (Governor Gibson wrote the foreword), traced the history of public welfare legislation in the state. The book's intent was to enlighten, to demonstrate how government's concern for an underclass had gradually broadened over time, and to imply, with the very momentum of its argument, that such concern needed to continue broadening. Some of the reading is pretty scary.

In the early nineteenth century in Vermont, for instance, you got tossed into jail with real criminals if you didn't pay your debts. Every year several thousand Vermonters did a little jail time for lack of cash or easy credit. Part of the humiliation was the taking of the "Pauper's Oath," a pledge you muttered to assure the authorities that all your earthly possessions didn't exceed twenty dollars, excluding the clothes on your back and bedding for you and your family. Taking the oath set you free. Your goods, presuming you had any above the twenty-dollar limit, were auctioned off to pay your debts.

The pauper's oath was still required of the down-and-out when Gibson was pushing for change as governor, but the list of things creditors couldn't seize had grown. It included firearms, furniture, tools needed for your work, a cow, ten sheep, ten cords of firewood (large, drafty farmhouses often burned that much, and more, each winter), ten bushels of corn, three swarms of bees, lettered gravestones, Bibles, and one pew in the church of your choice.

A lawyer or a dentist on hard times was treated a little differently, seeing as he was a professional. He got to keep two hundred dollars worth of books, presumably to help him regain his professional balance. A mechanic, on the other hand, could only keep his tool chest. A farmer, possibly put in grinding debt by his inability to refrain from buying one of those newfangled tractors with a complete set of implements, could keep one two-horse wagon with whiffletrees and neck yoke, if he hadn't sold them to an auctioneer after he'd gotten rid of his horses. At least, debt no longer meant going to jail with criminals—that had been abolished for men in 1838—and for women four years later.

D'Agostino's book dwelt at length on the blurry question of "settlement." Settlement determined which town you actually lived in and, therefore, which had responsibility for you. Settlement was a financial issue because each town paid for its poor farm and some facilities were better than others. State law defined settlement, but interpretation of its fine points varied from one town to the next. Selectmen stayed up late many nights debating whether a pauper had been in town long enough to justify care.

When the federal government passed the Social Security Act in 1935, it sounded the death knell for Vermont's method of dealing with the poor and mentally ill, but bureaucratic ripples took a long time to radiate all the way from Washington to 251 independent towns in the Green Mountains. In the late forties the poor farm system, archaic, functional, local control at both its most humane and its most frightening, kept kids and adults both from thinking poverty was any kind of easy meal ticket.

Despite his setbacks, Gibson continued his crusade for improving public health. In 1949 he prophetically told the legislature that he believed public health would become one of the greatest responsibilities of state government, and commented on the "extremely bad" condition of the average Vermonter's teeth. One can imagine some of the irate Old Guard in the legislative gallery, like old horses, grinding their molars. They were irked over the liberal governor's constant insistence that state government should stick its fingers into the lives of independent Vermonters. Into the mouths, in this instance. As far as they were concerned, that was no way to spend tax dollars.

Despite the animosity blowing through the corridors of power in Montpelier, Gibson still managed to have a little fun. "He enjoyed the combat with his political opponents," Ernest Gibson, III, said, reminiscing about his father. He followed the high school football season, attended games in Brattleboro when he could, enjoyed watching a young person's athletic skills grow. While at home the governor would occasionally plant himself on Main Street in downtown Brattleboro, just to talk to people. In Montpelier he had Representative Reid LeFevre of Manchester (when not a lawmaker LeFevre toured the LeFevre Circus in the northeast) perform carnival acts in the Morgan Room of the popular Tavern, where many legislators boarded. An old photograph shows the room filled with men in suits, ladies in hats, and children in ties and white blouses, watching an acrobat do a handstand on rings secured to the ceiling. Large carnival posters—a monkey driving a sportscar, an Indian dancing by a fire— decorate the walls, and a country and western band, wearing cowboy hats, boots and yoked shirts are taking a break behind a WCAX-radio microphone, their eyes on the bare-chested performer from the LeFevre Circus.

Governor Gibson kept in touch, sometimes daily, with Senator Aiken, who supported his initiatives from Washington. But the conservatives wore Gibson down. The short arc of his enlightened concern burned out before he completed his second term. In the fall of 1949 President Harry Truman called Gibson down to the White House and asked him a question: "Who would you recommend for a federal judgship?"

"Me."

Unable to gain real control of his party, and somewhat disgusted by its shortsightedness, Gibson accepted Truman's appointment as a federal judge. He resigned as governor, leaving behind the flimsy beginnings of a state social services network, a broken mountain rule, and a fractured Republican party.

THE ROAD TAKEN

He had traveled the valley road for years.
On foot, on horseback, in all kinds of wagons;
Then on a bicycle and now in an automobile.
He'd known every foot of the highway intimately
And yet, somehow, this morning it was different.
—*Walter Hard, "The Valley Road"*

*P*inned to a wall by my desk I have a brittle, old road map of Vermont and New Hampshire. It was printed around 1950. All the paved roads in Vermont are solid red lines. There are not many solid red lines on the map. There is a spider web of other colors, though, crisscrossing the state with improved roads (gravel, stone, topsoil-sand/clay), graded roads (drained and maintained), and dirt roads (unimproved). In the 1990s we would call the improved roads dirt roads, the graded roads poor dirt roads, and many of the dirt roads off-road loops for mountain bikes. When copies of the map were occupying dash compartments in travelers' cars, the entire Northeast Kingdom had only two paved roads, Routes 5 and 105, running through it. Inside the rough triangle formed by the points of Burlington, Montpelier, and Rutland, there were six miles of paved road; they linked Waitsfield to Moretown. In southern Vermont, in a rectangle cornered by Bennington and Brattleboro in the south, and by Manchester Center and Rockingham in the north, there were no paved roads. Route 100 began near Ludlow and ended at the Canadian border. Approximately seventy-five miles of its 150-mile length was hard surfaced.

In those days if you wanted to drive north through Vermont and stay on pavement, you figuratively navigated along the siderails and rungs of a cockeyed ladder: Routes 7 and 5 ran north and south; Routes 9, 4, 2, and 105 formed the horizontal rungs, zigging and zagging up and over the Green Mountains. Branching off those main roads were hundreds of the less desirable gravel and dirt-surfaced ones, which led practically everywhere, serving not only the new car culture but those still getting around by horse and buggy.

A few "Points of Interest" on my map, which I can't find on more recent maps published by the Vermont Travel Division, are Hamilton Falls between Jamaica and South Windham, Cavendish Forge and Eureka Cave between Proctorsville and Cavendish, the slate quarries in Poultney, the site of the 1789 Indian massacre near Royalton, and Devil's Gulch north of Butternut Mountain. Traveling in Vermont then was often a serendipitous event, a blend of thrills, calm, and frustration. A motorized jaunt might start out in the misty morning past farms and through villages—some peaceful and quiet, others loud with slamming looms weaving cloth—include an exhilerating roller coaster ride on a smooth dirt road with steep descents and sudden crests, as well as plenty of drifts on gravel corners, and end in a sudden shower, your new DeSoto bogged down to the differential in mud beside a gorged brook locals knew better than to pass during a downpour because it always overflowed its banks.

As cars demanded gas to go, the new car culture needed asphalt to ride on. Vermont's motley roads, with their wooden bridges and varied surfaces and limited connections with the expanding web of new highways in southern New England and New York State, kept the Green Mountain State a secondary destination for most auto travelers. Vermont continued to draw fishermen, hikers, and summer people, as it had since the turn of the century, and the expanding ski areas, including Stowe, Mad River Glen, and Mount Bromley, lured thousands more into the heretofore ignored mountain towns during the winter months. But because of the roads, tourism and recreation remained low key.

In the fall of 1954 an Army veteran from St. Albans, an Irishman named John Finn, began barnstorming over Vermont's roads, with their dust and potholes, stopping occasionally for clanging bells and flashing red lights at railroad crossings. Finn was the front man for a Fairfield farmer named E. Frank Branon. For the first time in decades the Democrats figured they had a good chance to put their candidate, the rawboned Branon, a fellow who had a vague resemblance to Abe Lincoln, in the governor's chair. Two years previous, in 1952, they had won more seats in the legislature than ever before. Now Gibson was history, the Republicans were fractious and vulnerable, and interparty squabbles for power were further weakening the Old Guard. Mill closings (in Quechee, for instance, the Harrison and Emery Woolen Mill shut down, the dye kettles, looms, and cards were auctioned off for scrap, and a hulking vacant building sat quiet in the center of a despondent village) and farm foreclosures further eroded the faith of their constituency.

Lee Emerson, a lawyer from Barton, had succeeded Gibson. But Emerson spent more energy trying to undo the things Gibson had done than he did on positive change. In 1954 Joseph Johnson, a broad-faced, white-haired Springfield industrialist who had been general manager of the Bryant Chucking Grinder Company, intended to replace Emerson. Gibson may have mortally wounded the mountain rule, but the Republicans were trying to revive it. Both Emerson and Johnson had served as lieutenant governors, came from opposite sides of the Green Mountains, and Emerson had served two two-year terms. Meanwhile, the exodus of the young and the talented continued. Their prospects in Vermont, instead of improving, had gotten worse. There was no industrial development and little political leadership. Economically, the state was floundering.

Factories that had stayed in business after the war, firms made profitable by cheap labor and a captive work force, finally got caught by their own inefficiencies and failures to invest in new machines, plants, and management. When a factory closed in a town whose economy had depended heavily on it, times got pretty grim. For example, when the Atlas Plywood Company closed its doors in the border town of Richford in 1957, putting several hundred people out of work, its demise kicked off a series of closings: stores, the movie theater, and businesses folded. People left. Property values declined.

One region that did prosper was the "Precision Valley" and its two towns of Windsor and Springfield. Unlike in Vermont, across many regions of America, economies were booming. New factories in the South and the Midwest, in particular, needed tools and machines to make cars, refrigerators, televisions, and dozens of other products Americans were buying. Vermont's machine-tool factories supplied hundreds of these factories with lathes, grinders, and tools. Joseph Johnson cited the success of Springfield as an example of the way more of Vermont could be. People needed to hear that, because across practically all of the state the times were bleak. Even the Central Vermont Railroad, which had thrived during and after the war, was in decline and cutting back in St. Albans and White River Junction, where sprawling yards covered acres with tracks and spurs and buildings. Many of those frustrated with the lack of opportunities in Vermont rode through the two shrinking rail centers on the way to Hartford, Boston, and New York, where they hoped to find good jobs.

All in all, Vermont was ripe for dissent.

Ever since John Finn had returned home from the war, he had been stirring that dissent. Determined to get ahead, Finn had gone to Norwich University on the GI Bill and involved himself with school politics. He was elected an officer of the Norwich University Veterans Association, handled negotiations between the administration and the veterans, learned that the administrators "didn't have the first idea how to deal with older people. They had dealt with students, seventeen, eighteen, twenty for too long."

After graduating Finn worked as a deputy for his father, the sheriff of Franklin County, in St. Albans. But by 1954, when he began barnstorming for Branon, Finn was a frustrated twenty-nine-year-old between jobs. He had left the deputy post to be a reporter. He worked for several newspapers, including the liberal *Swanton Courier,* a weekly published by fellow Irishman Bun O'Shea and his wife Sheila. But now barnstorming for Brannon seemed the most promising thing he could do to move Vermont forward.

Finn and John Bouchard of Enosburg Falls, who was the driver, hauled a twenty-four-foot mobile home filled with fliers and campaign literature, speakers mounted on its roof, from one end of the state to the other.

"I was Frank's voice," Finn said.

He and Bouchard pulled the trailer with a big Oldsmobile 98 that a sympathetic car dealer in Rutland had donated to the Democratic party. "It was exciting," Finn recalled some thirty-five years later. He and Bouchard had gotten run out of a few towns. "The constables came and chased us out because we did not have a parade permit. There were a couple of towns up in the Northeast Kingdom where we got chased out. We had records on. We played this stirring national music as we drove through, into the center of town. That's a parade. And then I'd pitch whatever Frank's pitch was going to be for that town. By the time I got around the state, I knew every one of the speeches by heart."

After Finn had stirred up the voters with music and rote oratory, Branon appeared. He talked about the loss of farms, the loss of young people, the lack of roads and political leadership. Many folks in villages and small towns could relate to Branon. He had a farmer's way about him. He had the "big work-hardened hands," Finn remembered, "with fingers that looked like they'd spent time pulling tits and handling shovels." This was low-cost, by-the-seat-of-the-pants politicking, face-to-face: Democrats invading the Main Streets of small-town Republican Vermont.

In the enemy's territory some rallies fizzled. They turned into meetings between Finn, Branon, Bouchard, and a few loyal Democrats: a huddle of aliens near a Five and Dime Department Store, or beneath the awning of a Rexall drugstore probably owned by a suspicious Republican who kept an eye on what was going on outside his front window. In many towns no Democratic organization whatsoever existed. In others the faithful some-times offered their homes as "safe houses" for the daring strangers who had appeared in their big Olds hauling the dusty trailer.

But in larger, working-class towns, in Winooski with its French Canadian and Irish mill workers, in Barre with its Italian quarrymen and stonecutters, in Rutland with its Italian, Irish and French neighborhoods—

all places where the Democratic party was growing in strength—the rallies drew crowds. Among ethnic groups whose lives were linked to a withering industrial base, Yankee Vermont, with its WASP mentality and narrow-minded politicians, seemed coldly apathetic towards their plight.

Many rural Republicans resented the Democrats and their pushy demands for change. If real change came, they knew it might mean reapportionment of the legislature, giving one man/one vote representation rather than what was in effect: one town/one vote—a government based on property rather than on population. Reapportionment would mean small towns losing their seats in Montpelier. This fear, heightened by decades of preconceptions about Democrats as New Dealers who would rob Vermont of its independence and do away with the poor farm—which scared the bejesus out of the lackadaisical, thank you, so they found work instead of climbing on the hand-out wagon—kept the Republicans motivated.

In 1954 they didn't have to worry. Not yet. Johnson, who became known as "the great highway governor," beat Branon 59,778 votes to 54,554. A loss this close, however, inspired the Democrats. It gave them something to work for. They continued to build strength, caucusing in small towns, preaching that the Republicans didn't care about people, nor about keeping the young in Vermont, or about much of anything else, for that matter, except low taxes and staying in the driver's seat of a rural culture with which they were losing touch.

*R*epublicans and Democrats did agree on one thing: Vermont needed better roads. And more of them.

Johnson echoed this theme at his inaugural in January 1955. "I believe the state should extend a welcome hand to all corners of our nation," he said, "so that people will be encouraged to come here. These folks spend money and this money makes jobs." His administration intended to "furnish access roads to developments in which people, both from within Vermont and from outside the state, have invested money. These people need our cooperation. They have asked nothing else for their great investment in Vermont."

In particular, Johnson was talking about access roads to ski areas. Skiing, the newest branch of the tourism business, had played a significant part in the state's recent history, but support and encouragement like that proffered by the governor, along with the interstate system, would eventually make skiing an economic star.

During Vermont's troubled fifties, skiing seemed like the perfect partner for Vermont's beautiful terrain. It would simply embrace the Green Mountains after new highways had unzipped virgin contours. But there would be no penetration, no rape of the land. Skiing and Vermont would have a Platonic relationship.

The closeness of the big cities of the Northeast was seen as a plus. Cities were repositories of eager skiers, and of tourists of all types, in a decade when the family vacation, like health insurance and the car, was becoming a necessity to escape the angst of urban life. In Vermont, though political zeal for tourism grew rapidly, not everyone shared the politicians' enthusiasm for waiting on people. It could be downright humiliating. But as more independent Yankees made the crossover from the "can do" attitude of the farm to the "what can I do for you?" attitude of the service provider, the stigma lessened. Officials assured the skeptical that it was good for them to see new faces and hear new stories, as well as have jobs. They'd get out of their rut, meet some cultured people, and the kids would make contact with strangers who would help them past their greenness.

How innocent skiing and tourism seemed. Clean, healthy, and impact free, it would bring only goodness, not the smokestacks of industry or the crime of the cities. Pure as snow, so to speak, in a time when "acid rain" was falling but unnamed, and the word "pollution" most likely referred to the messy mental state of someone suspected of being a Communist, tourism took a powerful hold on many people's visions of Vermont's future.

Vermont's flirtation with the economic promise of nice strangers drawn by the mountains and the scenery, and put at ease by the willingness of a segment of the population to make their visits memorable, had actually begun in the late 1800s. Farms then covered seventy-five percent of the state. The rolling, inhabited landscape epitomized the pastoral ideal at a time when the more rugged mountains of the Adironadacks and northern New Hampshire, with their "God is in the wilderness" feel, were losing their fascination for travelers. With the ascent of the pastoral, like some bucolic Renoir, Vermont, round, soft, and voluptuous, came into its own as a romantic draw.

Vermont's Publicity Bureau, the first in America, began publishing "come hither" pamphlets in the 1890s. The pamphlets listed abandoned farms and land for sale. The Central Vermont Railroad advertised stops along its tracks for everyone, from the angler to the health seeker. St. Albans, the CVR's headquarters, was called "the gateway to the vacation land of Northern Vermont," an ideal place, as Frank C. Greene wrote then in *Picturesque St. Albans,* for "the tired and dusty traveler, just emancipated from the heat of a great city."

In the late 1920s the Vermont Commission on Country Life, made up of two hundred natives organized in sixteen committees, worked for three years on a vision for tomorrow. The result, *Rural Vermont, A Program for the Future,* published in 1932, summarized their conclusions. Prophetically, the chapter on tourism opens with the assertion that "Vermont's development as a recreational region affords the most promising opportunity for business growth in the state at the present time, and so far as can be seen, for a considerable period in the future." The commission suggested that Vermont exploit its thousand mountains over two thousand feet, its three hundred lakes and ponds, and its numerous streams because the "Vacation Idea" was sweeping America. And not only captivating the well-to-do. "The farmer, the wage earner, and the businessman operating on a limited scale are taking vacations."

The foresighted commission also mentioned something embarrassing: the "backward movement." The backward movement referred to things like some farmers not giving a damn about city slickers pulling over to snap their pictures and kids selling them baskets of raspberries with pebbles under the top layer. Possibly, when thinking about how backward types might scare away some tourists, the commissioners had talked about the recent eugenics survey sponsored by the University of Vermont. One of the survey's concerns had been the exodus of Vermont's good blood and what the loss meant to the state gene pool. One hypothesis was that the bad blood that stayed behind had a promiscuous gene or two, which explained why the white trash were breeding too much. "In its most foul manifestations," said State Archivist Sanford, "the eugenics survey was recommending sterilizations, and keeping certain types of people from breeding. It also encouraged the good stock to get out there breeding, so we could get some more good Vermont Yankee stock in here."

As a prescription for the growth of the recreation business, *Rural Vermont, A Program for the Future,* was sound, but the Depression and World War II intervened between ideas and realities. After the war the legislature seemed to have forgotten the advice of the book's authors about tourism at least until the mills and farms began to disappear in such numbers in the fifties that political careers were threatened. Then lawmakers again championed tourism, as elucidated decades before by the Commission on Country Life.

In the fifties America did its best to ignore the bad side of things. Civil rights riots, national recognition of poverty, and the construction of football stadium seats four inches wider than they had been because Americans butts were getting fat were still a decade away. So if the hopes for tourism bettering the lives of Vermonters seemed a little overblown and one-sided, which they were, they were simply keeping pace with other national delusions, such as a helicopter in every garage, healthy white bread, and safe nuclear power. At any rate, the legislature and many Vermonters saw tourism as a painless balm for the state's economic woes. After all, the reasoning went, three of the four necessary ingredients were already here: natural beauty, some tourist facilities, and tough times. The lacking ingredient was good roads. Once they were in place, tourists only wanted what Vermont had already: small towns, pretty commons, white steeples, and a bucolic atmosphere, sprinkled here and there with lakes, streams, and ski resorts. Meanwhile, the natives could continue to hunt and fish, to head to Thunder Road Raceway, a quarter-mile oval scooped out of the granite hills above Barre, where motorized mayhem soothed working-class souls, or shoot rats at the dump with .22s.

Vermont culture, riding the waves of change, was leaving behind the Walter Hard past and the kitchen tunk, a dance held in the kitchen and the parlor of a farmhouse, the fiddler seated on the wood cookstove to make more room for dancers, and getting its first strong dose of undiluted American culture over TV. Not yet a medium through which the world came into living rooms, but rather a piece of furniture with a picture in it, TV was a novelty. Vermonters clustered around their sets to watch shows that tended to portray rural living as quaint and backwards. The American Way of Life championed the urban and the suburban. The Gospel of Progress preached the value of material goods as powerfully as the older Vermont Way of Life had preached thrift and restraint and self-sufficiency. It mildly mocked the value of the handmade, the wisdom of old-timers, and, to an almost obsessive pitch, extolled in everyone the value of hard work in order to advance economically up the ladder of success.

That ladder, of course, didn't have many rungs in Vermont. What most folks began to want was for the ladder of opportunity to come here so they could climb up a rung or two.

National economic currents, which were transforming the South, for instance, putting its displaced farmers into mills and factories by the thousands, and revitalizing towns, were not lapping back and forth over Vermont. Vermont was a puddle of insignificance in the dynamic American scene. It was an anachronism, a place to talk about if you wanted to say how life used to be, not where it was going. At the same time many natives knew Vermont wasn't *that* regressive. They weren't so sentimental they didn't grumble about those damn dirt roads or blindly support regionalisms like the poll tax and the backhouse and the three-cow farm where the family always just scraped by. Yet a perceptive few also knew that the Gospel of Progress would have a downside. To claim that joy and goodness would come with progress, without sorrow and sadness as an equally right inheritance, was naive. It was like saying a garden could grow with all sun and no rain, that manure's richness didn't stink.

But the older, rooted-in-the-soil Vermonters were diminishing in number. Their random mutterings were but a quiet whistle in the wind of change. Practically the entire nation seemed to be feeling an exuberance, a momentum compounded of luck, resources, cleverness, and unquestioned faith in unlimited material weath and progress. America's economic destiny seemed clouded only by the threat of Communism.

*I*n the fall of 1956, John Finn's former boss Bun O'Shea barnstormed around Vermont. The thirty-five-year-old publisher of the *Swanton Courier* was powered by an impossible dream: defeating the venerable icon of state politics, Senator George Aiken. The Irishman usually took his two oldest boys, Kevin, nine, and Chris, six, with him in their new '56 Chevy station wagon. In the early stages of the campaign he also brought along Sheila, his wife, as well as Rossiter, their baby. But, as Chris O'Shea recalled with a roll of his eyes more than thirty years later, "My mother grew tired of it real quick."

In 1956 the idea of the unknown gadfly Bun O'Shea challenging Aiken for his U.S. Senate seat "was a total wild hair," Chris said.

"You're going to what?" awed Democrats and Republicans alike replied to Bun's declaration of intent.

But out on the road, all was glorious. Especially if you were six. In 1990, a middle-aged and feisty Chris O'Shea, who inherited his father's predilection for publishing (he ran the *County Courier,* a weekly, out of a large carriage barn behind his home in Enosburg Falls), recalled his first political campaign well. "It was real exciting," he told me. "I can remember the day we went down to Channel 3 to make a television commercial. We traveled everywhere. Bun loved it. I mean that's why he did it, just so he could go out and meet people. He just loved to go to the towns. I can remember going to the Danville Fair, the Rutland Fair, Bennington, everywhere."

For one debate, "Bun showed up late," Chris said. "He would do that, just to rankle people. It was in a barn, a great big barn somewhere—it might have been around Middlebury. And George Aiken was waiting for him on the stage. Bun got up and the first thing he said was something pretty smart. And Aiken—I never saw him, my whole life, get that steamed. Oh, he was pissed! Bun really got under his skin that day."

Aiken always shook his and Kevin's hands. To the boys, this grand old man of Vermont politics, with his white hair and glasses and kindliness, seemed like "everybody's grandfather."

The campaign was overshadowed by the Cold War and the question of whether the United Nations was going to recognize Communist China. The question bitterly divided people. O'Shea was a Quaker pacifist who endorsed non-intervention in Chinese affairs. Aiken supported the in-power regime of Chiang-Kai-Shek, which occupied Taiwan. In the debates between Aiken and the aggressive underdog O'Shea, undertones of pro-Communist and anti-Communist stirred the rhetoric. There was a lot of hatred beneath the placid surface of Vermont in the fifties. The McCarthy era, with its blacklists and witch hunts, had stained the American left a few years before and Vermont had not been spared. University of Vermont Professor Alex Novikoff lost his job in a celebrated case because of his association with the Communist Party. As the publisher of a liberal newspaper in Republican Vermont, both Bun O'Shea and his wife, who was the editor of the *Swanton Courier,* had been slandered by flag-waving locals. The O'Sheas were "reds," some of them insisted.

"I can remember my mother actually dragging out her service record and showing it to some guy in the shop," Chris said. "My mother was a lieutenant, j.g., in the Navy. So was Bun. Both had commendations during World War II. I can remember her calling the guy a 'son-of-a-bitch,' saying, 'I'm just as good an American as you are!'"

Bun O'Shea got slaughtered in the voting booths by Aiken in November of 1956. But Chris still marveled at how many people remembered Bun for taking the man on. "I was amazed at how that got his name out—just that one run. Taking on someone like Aiken, that gave him so much exposure."

And exposure with a capital "E" was exactly what the Democratic party needed. In the past they might have let Aiken go unchallenged. But now a decision had been made to field a full slate of candidates for every election. Democrats, many of whom had practically made it a tradition to vote for liberal Republicans, rather than for sure-losing Democrats, were urged to stay with the ticket. Their votes mattered. Grassroots party organizers hammered this into their constituencies. We can win, they insisted. Look how well Branon did. But we can't win if you don't support our candidates. This attitude meant that party loyalists like Bun O'Shea had to step forth and sacrifice their energy for the cause because no matter if snow didn't fall in winter and apples grew on cows' tails, George Aiken was probably going to get reelected until he died.

Two years later, in 1958, the Democrats finally got their first victory. A forester from West Rupert, William H. Meyer, won Vermont's sole Congressional seat. Meyer was Vermont's first Democrat to take the train to Washington since 1853. Another Democrat, Bernard Leddy from Burlington, almost beat Robert Stafford for governor. Leddy, a great stump speaker, lost by a slim 719 votes.

"To this day, I think that the damn town clerks messed everything up," John Finn contended. "It was so close they had a recount." Town clerks sent the ballots to the Secretary of State's office in paper bags and shoe boxes; they were supposed to arrive in locked containers. Finn had had an education in vote-counting shenanigans earlier in the fifties while running Democratic candidates for the aldermanic board in St. Albans. "Unless you stood right over the backs of these people who were counting the ballots, most of whom were Republicans, they'd miss count," he said.

Walter Hard had parodied the situation in one of his poems titled "Vote Fraud:"

> Counting the ballots dumped from the box by the Constable
> Ed Fletcher held a ballot up to get a better light on it.
> "By mighty," he said, "somebody musta made a mistake.
> "Here's a cross top o' the Democrat column."
> He passed it around and they all agreed.
> After some discussion as to the possibility
> That the action was wilful, Henry said to put it aside.
> They could get the rest done and then decide what to do.
> Pretty soon Henry stopped and looked at a ballot carefully.
> He held it out so that all could see.
> "I guess that settles it," he said
> "Here's another ballot with a cross on the Democrat column."
> He looked over his glasses.
> "Throw both o' them ballots out.
> That son-of-a-gun voted twice."

Voting fraud wasn't such a serious matter until the Democrats began to regularly contest the Republicans for public offices in the late fifties. But when they did, Vermont's vote-tallying laws had to be revised so that observers from both parties could sit in on the counting, keeping an eye on things to insure no ballots went the way of the two in Hard's poem.

Meyer's victory was undoubtedly helped by the improved system. But Republican strife—five candidates had slugged it out in their primary—played an even bigger part in his upset. As a forester, Meyer also had some crossover appeal in rural Republican strongholds. He talked, far ahead of his time, about Vermont losing its traditions and needing to preserve its forests. Once in Washington, however, taking the same tack that Bun

O'Shea had on Communist China, he got in trouble, lost all his conservative support, and was tabbed "a Commie lover." The irascible pro-mainland China congressman, whose pencil-thin moustache in the clean-shaven Eisenhower era seemed almost a radical statement, didn't win a second term. Robert Stafford, attacking his patriotism, defeated Meyer in 1960. Nevertheless, the Democrats had broken their century-long dry spell. And in Burlington that same year, Philip Hoff, a lawyer fired by the ideals of America's new president, John F. Kennedy, got elected to the Vermont legislature.

PART TWO

PHIL HOFF

You worked your ass off. You were a snowstorm; you
gave us something to work for.
—*State Senator John Finn to former Governor
Philip Hoff, 1989, recalling Hoff's 1962 campaign.*

Phil Hoff, a mill-town boy from Turners Falls,
Massachusetts, moved to Burlington in 1951, fresh out of Cornell Law
School. He became involved in local politics ("My parents being rock-ribbed
Republicans," he said, "naturally I became a Democrat"), and ran for an
alderman's seat on the City Council in 1958. He lost, despite, as he recalled
years later, "a hell of a campaign. That night we had a big party at our house
for all these people who worked so hard. The mayor of Burlington was
there. I said that some time I'd like to represent Burlington in the Vermont
legislature. 'Well, maybe that can be arranged,' he said. What I didn't know
was that they were looking for a candidate."

In 1960 Hoff won Burlington's seat in the Vermont House. One of forty-
six Democrats, he sat through the long session beside William Jay Smith, a
poet from Pownal. Smith later wrote about what it was like being a Democrat
in the 246-member body. He called his experience, "My Poetic Career in
Vermont Politics."

In the memoir Smith marveled at the make-up of the group he and Hoff
had joined. First off, it was not at all democratic. Hoff, for instance,
representing Burlington, with a population of thirty-five thousand, had one
vote, just like Miss Eddy of Stratton, who sat behind and to the right of the
poet and future governor. Miss Eddy's vote, equivalent to Hoff's on the
floor, represented twenty-four people.

The League of Women Voters, Smith told readers, had recently tried
to get the legislators interested in changing this, but only encountered
"supreme indifference." Senator Asa Bloomer, President Pro Tem of the

Senate, advised the ladies to forget about lawmaking and to start worrying about the pornography their children were probably looking through at home because their moms were elsewhere.

One hundred and thirty-two of his fellow representatives were over sixty, Smith wrote. Only two were under thirty. One of the latter was "affectionately known to many of his colleagues as Cornwallis, because of the fact that he frequently appeared on the floor wearing a defiant red blazer." There were so many old fogies in the House, the poet added, because Vermont was a state of old fogies. Yet they weren't easy to peg politically just because they were old. "Many of the young fogies, of which Cornwallis did not happen to be one," Smith observed, "did more to prevent the enactment of sensible legislation than some of their older colleagues."

What should a good legislator have been like? The Vermont constitution is vague on the question, Smith noted. The terse document recommends that persons "most noted for wisdom and virtue" get their town's nod, although the interpretation given to the word "wisdom" seems to have been an expansive one. "It has been said that in many of the small towns," Smith wrote, "the standard procedure over the years has been to take one of its older citizens who had been on town relief, buy him a suit of clothes, and send him up to Montpelier, where the state would look after him and keep him warm." That no longer seemed the case in 1961, Smith said. Male members, prodded to higher standards of sartorial splendor than in the past because of the increasing number of female legislators, often favored "extremely broad and bright neckties that sometimes flashed across the room during debate with the full effulgence of diplomatic sashes."

"I look up to my elders," Smith continued wryly, "and I found it often restful and reassuring to gaze out on the white and nodding heads that gave the chamber an appearance not unlike that of a wintry Vermont slope."

Turning serious, the poet noted that in 1961 the average Vermonter had the second-lowest personal income in America, and the third-highest tax rate per capita. Vermont, he felt, "had illusions of grandeur." Illusions perpetuated by a legislature that was supposed to be egalitarian, but in fact was closer to "a rural aristocracy."

"Being in the Vermont House was for me like a journey back into the eighteenth century, when one had to own land to vote," the poet concluded. "Our representation is, in essence, based not on population but on acreage. The Vermont House is our House of Lords."

Shaking the lords up a bit that session was the rugged, heavy-smoking blonde beside him. Phil Hoff introduced a record number of bills. Young and old fogies alike soon knew who he was. Hoff and ten other first-term legislators, eight Republicans and three Democrats, managed to create a refreshing atmosphere. Dubbed the "Young Turks," the group also included future Speaker of the House, Woodstock Republican Franklin Billings, Jr., who was the son of a former governor, Franklin S. Billings, and Fairlee Republican Richard Mallary, who later became an avowed political enemy of Hoff.

In 1962, after his single term, Hoff had established himself as the Democrat's fresh young hopeful. That fall he faced off against incumbent Keyser in a long-shot campaign for the governorship. It was a long shot because no Democrat had ever been elected governor of Vermont before.

F. Ray Keyser, Jr., thirty-four, was the youngest governor in the history of the state. He sat atop a melting glacier of political power, around the base of which Democrats and wayward Republicans were lighting fires. Brash and cocky, Keyser didn't seem to notice. He stayed busy offending friend and foe alike. One senator he had unwisely irked was Asa Bloomer. Deane C. Davis, a Superior Court judge during that time, remembered "Ace" Bloomer as "an individualist if there ever was one. A powerful guy, a good thinker, a canny thinker." But a politician who "could hate people worse than any single individual I ever knew. And once he decided to hate someone, he did it thoroughly."

Bloomer hated Keyser. The aging senator and the "just a kid" governor, as Davis called him, had banged heads until July during the previous legislative session, turning it into the longest in Vermont history. Why they banged heads, Davis couldn't remember, although he thought "it was just on general principles." The protracted stupidity of the session further eroded Keyser's support.

Nevertheless, in the classic mountain rule manner, he ran for a second term. Taking him on, Hoff was slow getting started. Initially, his campaign seemed like it might join the long parade of Democratic stillbirths. Accompanied by his wife Joan, who showed she was as dogged a campaigner as he was, Hoff tramped through Vermont's small Republican-held towns. He went into stores, talked to folks on sidewalks, leaned into cars. Rural Vermonters were lukewarm towards the blonde upstart and his peppy wife. Hoff's "bold new approach" sounded short on specifics. The thirty-eight-year-old also had a mild but troublesome phobia for a politician; it made him nervous to approach a complete stranger and shake hands.

The campaign took on new life when Philip Savory, a former Army intelligence officer and chief of the Morning Press Bureau in Montpelier, a news office run cooperatively by the *Burlington Free Press* and *The Rutland Herald,* came aboard as campaign manager. Savory knew Vermont politics. He had a keen sensitivity for Keyser's weaknesses and he exploited them in the press. Savory also helped convince Woodstock newspaperman

Walter Paine, who published the *Valley News* in West Lebanon, New Hampshire, to bankroll Hoff's campaign with twenty thousand dollars. After that the cocky Keyser was in trouble.

Over lunch in Burlington in August 1989 I talked to Phil Hoff about the campaign. Hoff was accompanied by Senator John Finn, the long-time Democratic workhorse. Warming to the subject of F. Ray Keyser, Hoff said, "He helped me a lot. Actually, Ray Keyser, in those days, wasn't a bad governor. But he listened to nobody. He wouldn't even go through the motions." Keyser also got some egg on his tie when he tried, as Hoff put it, "to turn a deficit into a surplus by not paying the state's bills."

Ultimately, two members of Keyser's own party, Lou Crispe and T. Gary Buckley, did him in. They founded an Independent party so that die-hard Republicans, who would rather have dropped dead at the polling place than inscribe an X anywhere near the Democrat column, could vote for Hoff. He won by a margin of 1,348 votes out of the total of 121,000 cast. Three thousand Independents voted for him. Hoff downplayed his upset victory, citing the growth of the Democratic party in Vermont during the fifties and the political rise of John F. Kennedy as finally having turned things around. "The time had come," he said bluntly.

"You worked your ass off," Finn interjected. The Irishman had been listening pretty quietly but Hoff's show of modesty was too much. "You were a snowstorm. You gave us something to work for."

Hoff cracked a worn smile. He and Finn exchanged glances: two old allies: Kennedy liberals whose dreams had faded. "In Franklin County," Hoff said in a lighter tone, "John and I stayed overnight in the jail. John was the sheriff."

Those days were long gone, along with much of Hoff's optimism about Vermont's future. He was presently crusading for a moratorium on development—the kind of development his administration encouraged from 1963 to 1969. "Developers are bleeding Vermont," Hoff lamented.

The Democrats, who had drifted to the safe middle ground as Republicans had gone further to the right, weren't doing anything about the problem because they had lost their taste for risk, he said. "I see this tendency to favor team players. It's the antithesis of traditional Vermont."

That hadn't been true in 1962. As the underdogs, the Democrats had to take risks, had to favor the mercurial over the cooperative.

"Something else has happened," Hoff added, "I think we're showing all the tendencies of the Roman Empire."

"Really?"

"Oh yes, it's almost an exact parallel." The old Clydesdale, as some folks described Hoff because of his faded blonde mane and rugged bearing, mentioned America's obsessions: flesh, mindless TV programming, violence. "It's scary," he said.

"Has all that stuff reached Vermont?"

"It's getting here."

It was election night 1962.

Returns poured in. Thousands of expectant Democrats, some curious Republicans, and a few newly-minted Independents milled around the streets of Winooski. The bulky silhouette of the closed Champlain Woolen Mill loomed stark and quiet by the riverside. Men in brimmed hats and women in shawls joined the crowd, along with young guys sporting DA's (a haircut called a "duck's ass"), bandanas around their necks, their girlfriends in skirts, saddle shoes, and bobby socks. Everyone was waiting to hear if Hoff had beaten Keyser. Hoff, with his family and some campaign staff, listened to the returns at his Burlington home. The vote remained close until midnight. Winooski, in the classic political tactic the city had used in 1946 with Gibson, withheld the winning tally, 1,768 votes for Hoff, and 188 for Keyser, until it tipped the scales.

Hoff drove to Winooski with Joan. They led a jubilant, congratulatory parade through the streets. Spirits soared and spirits flowed. His hair ruffled, a crown on his head, riding in an open convertible, Hoff kept shouting to the crowd, "A hundred years of bondage broken! A hundred years of bondage broken!"

The Democrats had ended the longest run of one-party control in American history. A coalition had done it: working-town Irish and French, burnt-out farmers, the poor and the angry, veterans still waiting for Colonel Gibson's dream to bloom, and urban newcomers to Vermont who had brought their Democratic loyalties with them. And, of course, the Republicans had helped, jumping on the bandwagon the way the Democrats used to jump on theirs, because they sensed the tide had changed, the pendulum had swung, the mountain rule was once and for all dead.

One central reality made Hoff's victory possible: a majority of Vermonters finally acknowledged their plight and accepted they needed new, spirited leadership to do something about it. Government, they hoped, as preached by idealists like President Kennedy, New York Mayor John Lindsay, and their governor-elect Phil Hoff, could make their lives better.

Stunned Republicans finally realized the backbone of their constituency, the farm population, had shrunk like the spine of a 109-year-old man. They had to regroup.

When Hoff took office in late 1962, JFK occupied the White House. The "twist," a dance craze rooted in black soul music, was sweeping the nation. Just the year before a New York Yankee outfielder named Roger Maris had hit sixty-one home runs, breaking Babe Ruth's record, and a New Hampshire native, Navy Captain Alan B. Shepard, had become America's first man in space. Following a hundred-mile-high parabola ride into the stratosphere, Shepard had splashed down into the Atlantic 302 miles away, and had been plucked up by a helicopter from the aircraft carrier *Lake Champlain*. Meanwhile, in Vermont, mud season and maple syrup remained more important than Sputnik I, the Russian's first earth-orbiting satellite, and Chubby Checker. The population, 389,000 in 1960, was climbing fast. Chittenden County, Hoff's home turf, had almost seventy-five thousand residents, along with Vermont's only industrial juggernaut, IBM, which had located in Essex Junction in 1957 and was a major force behind the increase in people and in regional prosperity.

Although major changes were buffeting Vermont, it remained for most Americans a kind of fairy-tale place where you went to get away from real life. When they thought of Vermont, they didn't think of Phil Hoff with his hands full, or of the death of the mountain rule, or of IBM. They thought of Stowe and steeples and stereotypes: a farmer in rubber boots, one hand on a hip and the other fingering his chin, telling some city slicker, "You can't git thar from here."

To his credit, once in office Hoff didn't attempt, like a prince in a pastoral fairy tale, to transform his kingdom overnight. He was astute enough, as Steve Terry, a journalist for the *Rutland Herald* pointed out in "The Hoff Era," a series he wrote near the end of Hoff's third term, to accept the fact he didn't know much about governing Vermont. And that there were a lot of forces in place that didn't want him to learn.

Actually, Hoff had never been in the governor's office until the day he was inaugurated. When he did set foot in there, he was in for a shock: all the filing cabinets were gone; the Republicans had yanked them.

"And I'll never forget the budget hearings that I held before the inauguration," Hoff told Terry. "I didn't have a single person I could rely on, except Phil Savory. I went into the hearings and asked for a ten-year projection, and they looked at me in complete bafflement and said that they didn't have that. So I said I'd like a five-year projection, and they looked at me in absolute bafflement again. Finally I said: 'Well, how about a projection for this coming year?' and they said they didn't have that either.

I was flabbergasted. I didn't know what in hell I was going to do."

Some of the outmoded institutions Hoff inherited included the aristocratic legislature, the archaic poll tax, which had to be paid if you wanted to vote in local elections, the outmoded poor farm system, and an administrative department that didn't have the economic apparatus in place, Hoff said, "to run a child's lemonade stand." Yet possibly his biggest headache, as Terry pointed out, was the Vermont state constitution. The 4,840-word document may have been a radical statement in 1777, but by 1962 its Jeffersonian idealism, which viewed government as a necessary evil in which power should reside in the hands of the legislature, which was broadly representative, and not in the hands of the executive branch, which might overextend the control of one man, was out of touch with changing times.

And change now had Vermont powerfully in its grip. Interstates 89 and 91 were being built. IBM continued its unprecedented growth in Essex Junction, drawing other high-tech manufacturers into Chittenden County. IBM was significant because in a matter of a few years it had become the state's largest employer, demonstrating that Vermont was fertile ground for high technology. Lured to Essex Junction by the Greater Burlington Industrial Corporation (an organization formed to attract manufacturing businesses and increase employment opportunities in the area), IBM initially had leased a twenty thousand-square foot building on twenty acres and hired 445 people in 1957 to make wire contact relays for room-sized computers. By late 1965, IBM employed twenty-five hundred, occupied 390,000 square feet, and made "chips"—half-inch-square pieces of ceramic that reduced computers to the size of file cabinets. In the mountains you could see from the growing IBM parking lots, the ski resorts were attracting more skiers, ski bums, and small businesses.

Yet the biggest change of all was not something you could see, such as the trails of a new ski area draped over the summit of a mountain, or measure, like the additional acreage IBM had optioned for another anticipated addition, but rather something intrinsic to the way Vermonters viewed their world. That change had to do with how the average Vermonter perceived government's place in his/her life. Traditionally, that place had been extremely limited, and only begrudgingly acknowledged. But the decline of the farm, where independence had allowed the freedom to ignore government, and the gradual growth of small cities, where liberal newcomers tended to make their homes, were having a marked impact. Hoff's ascent to power was a barometer of just how marked. Ambivalence about change was giving way to acceptance and even enthusiasm. Instead of fighting it, Vermonters seemed willing, at least for a while, to go with the irresistable tug of the American Century. They were just climbing on board sixty years late.

People were willing to give in to government programs because they had lost faith in the ability of local officials to solve their problems. It was time, they thought, to let the state take a whack at it. Yet there was a problem, and it would plague government's efforts to change traditional ways in Vermont. The problem was that many Vermonters remained infatuated with the concept of local control and with the belief they still held the reins. The reality of the power shift initiated in 1962 with the election of Hoff made local control the "big lie." This would take several decades to sink in. And for many Vermonters, it never would sink in.

The concept of local control remained a deep taproot of some kind of psychic power people invested in Vermont. You could sense that, particularly in newcomers who had left the alienation and ennui of city living and longed for a voice in what was going on in their new communities, as well as in some natives. During the next decades, many of these people simply refused to accept that local control had slipped away, leaving them little but the annual Town Meeting, where they could exercise an old-fashioned ritual of democracy, New England style, spew some rhetoric, and, in some instances, applaud jingoism wrapped up in often blurry history epitomized by the mythic individualism of Ethan Allen and the Green Mountain Boys (they wouldn't have stood for all this land regulation!). For these folks, despite the realities of state control and centralization initiated in the sixties, and perpetuated thereafter, local control was no cliché, but rather the wellspring of why they lived here. Illusory or not, it so satisfied a thirst their minds had that they couldn't let it go without a struggle.

At any rate, when Hoff took the helm in Vermont's bastion of hands-off Republicanism, he symbolized the new force of powerful centralized government. A JFK archetype in rural Vermont, the young crusader talked about government bettering lives, promoted the dream that idealistic individuals could make it happen, and put his faith in a steady stream of federal cash—as Kennedy had.

Throughout the sixties the new politics of social concern and centralization frequently were initiated in Washington, passed through Montpelier, and then splayed, like a prism-shattered beam, off the golden dome towards the villages and towns. They came with new names: the New Frontier and the Great Society. They brought money to improve education, expand social services, stimulate economic growth, and extend civil rights. They shoved local control deep in the state's shadow.

To get such a system going in Vermont, however, was not simple. Hoff, at first, didn't have much power. Nor did he have a cooperative legislature, heavy still with the conservatives he had badgered, charmed, cajoled, and impressed during his stint in their somnolent chamber. Nor did he have the hard data that could be converted into the "bureaucratese" needed to get Vermont lots of federal money. To give himself a power base, his first year in office Hoff appointed more than five hundred citizens to task forces to investigate everything from highways to hatcheries, from classrooms to performance. And he spent a lot of time talking to the enemy, demonstrating he was human. They had concerns in common, he told the Republicans. He crossed party lines to gather support among the liberal and moderate Republicans. He could often be found sparring with the opposition in the bars and restaurants of Montpelier in the evening, a drink in one hand to ease the inner tension the basically shy man always felt in hostile terrain, and a cigarette in his lips. To folks who complained that he was moving too slowly, Hoff, smoke rising past eyes a bit weary from lack of sleep, would sometimes reply: "I'm the only Democrat in my administration, you know."

*L*arge, unpredictable, divided by deep distrust between farmer members and business members, the Vermont legislature stood in the way of major reform. Notoriously cheap and doggedly allied to Thoreau's credo "That government that governs least governs best," its rural members liked to martyr themselves as saviors of taxpayers' money. Their common viewpoint seemed to be: To hell with what goes on outside of my town; we don't need it if it costs money.

As for the power of the chief executive, the Little Hoover Commission, headed by Deane C. Davis in the late 1950s, had already shown how impotent the governor was. Department heads had the power in Vermont's decentralized system. "Gee, a governor went in there," Davis noted years later about the situation, "and he didn't meet some of those people during his whole term." That was because 152 department heads, commissioners, and officers reported to the governor, the Little Hoover Commission discovered.

The quintessential department head was an affable, ski-loving fellow named Perry Merrill. For years Merrill had been Vermont's State Forester, and under Hoff had a bigger title, Commissioner of Forests and Parks, but a little less power because the new regime kept an eye on him. Phil Hoff was the nineteenth governor under whom Merrill had served.

"Pretty damned near a czar" was how Davis described his old friend Merrill, a bureaucrat who typically began "three times as many projects as the legislature would authorize money for," Steve Terry reported. Merrill always had "dozens of half-finished projects scattered throughout the state," Terry said, "and he used them as effective levers for prying more money out of the Appropriations Committee ('We sure would like to finish up that project in your town, Harry, but you're going to have to give us more money.')"

Any way Hoff looked at the system he inherited, he saw that to change it, first he had to change the legislature. It was the bottleneck, one that seldom initiated new laws—that was the governor's job—but through which every law had to pass, or get killed.

Historically, strong governors like Aiken and Gibson had managed to push legislation through. But they had been Republicans. By the time Hoff tried it, working with the Senate was different than working with the House. The Senate was more liberal, urban, and formal. Senators knew each other and usually had decided which way they were going to vote on issues before the vote was called. The House, on the other hand, was volatile, conservative, the landed aristocracy poet Smith had labeled it. Persuasive orators could swing votes in the House. Wheeling and dealing went on in the hallways and corridors. Yet bills seemed to pile up until the last days of each session, creating confusion, hasty decisions, and exasperation. In the hectic, end-of-the-session atmosphere, it was possible for any committee chairman to kill a bill and for twenty-five percent of either the Senate or the House to stall a bill because of procedural rules. Thus the legislature often killed a bill even when a distinct majority wanted it passed.

All in all, the legislature frequently found itself at cross purposes both with itself and with the governor. Add to that an impossibly broad chain of command and you had an apparatus that was wasteful because departments duplicated work, that communicated poorly both within its own framework and without, and that repeatedly squandered energy and money on turf battles, rather than coordinating its efforts for the good of Vermonters.

Although many old-timers romanticized the flaws and snags in Vermont's out-of-whack political system, the public had elected Hoff to do something about them. They gave the bold youngster a mandate to kick Vermont politics out of the barn. Once Hoff had digested his task force reports, gained a broader base of support in the legislature, and won re-election in 1964 by soundly trouncing Ralph Foote, 106,000 to 57,000, the U.S. Supreme Court lent him a hand. It ruled that Vermont was violating the fourteenth amendment to the U.S. Constitution and had to reapportion its legislature.

The vote on reapportionment occurred on May 14, 1965. From the balcony at the rear of the General Assembly, Hoff looked at the representatives. Few of their heads were nodding on this momentous day. W. Clark Hutchinson, a Republican from Rochester, refrained from chaining himself to his seat as he had threatened to do if the bill passed. Frank A. Hutchins of Stannard, a sixty-six-year-old farmer, just let his tears flow. The final vote, 163 for reapportionment and 62 against it, brought a weary smile to Hoff's face. After four months of often emotional debate, the House had finally voted to reduce its size from 246 to 150, and to elect those 150 based on population, not geography. The tyranny of small-town rule was over.

There followed the predictable denunciations, the assertions that city ways were taking over rural Vermont, that things would never be the same. Resentment edged the voices of bitter representatives whose individual villages would no longer have a say in Montpelier.

A special election was held in the fall of 1965. The House elected its redistricted body. The Senate, redistricted geographically, stayed the same size, thirty members. After the election the trimmed 1966 legislature seemed infused with liberal light. Though still solidly Republican three to one, the representatives gave Hoff his way. The poll tax was repealed. Urban renewal projects, including the ones that changed the faces of Burlington, Winooski, and Rutland, got the easy go-ahead. Vermont's prison system, with its toss-em-in-and-throw-away-the-key attitude ("My husband had his soul ripped out of him in there," one inmate's wife said about Windsor Prison) initiated rehabilitation programs. Ever since Hoff had made a hard but unsuccessful push in 1964 to regionalize Vermont's school districts, reducing 254 of them to twelve, education had been on many representatives' minds. Now some towns voluntarily joined together and formed union high schools. Additional state aid for education was passed.

"Eyeballs really began to pop," Steve Terry wrote in "The Hoff Era," when the legislature passed control of the deer herd over to the Fish & Game Board. The move left long-time observers of the Montpelier scene scratching their heads—the legislature had always guarded its right to determine the deer kill like a sow bear protecting her cubs.

Several Hoff initiatives did get killed, including the fair housing bill, which would have eliminated housing discrimination, and the Canadian power bill, which would have established a non-profit corporation to import power from Canada. Both bills resurfaced and were passed later, fair housing the following year and Canadian power in the early eighties under Governor Richard Snelling.

At the end of his second term Hoff considered calling it quits. In retrospect, he should have. Politics drained him. He drank and smoked a lot to handle the strain. But he did run, beating Snelling, a Shelburne industrialist and legislator who said Hoff had rammed social programs down Vermonters' throats and who wanted a sales tax to lighten the increasing burden being carried by property owners to support education.

*P*hil Hoff's political career seems to have ridden national waves as much as it reacted to state needs. He was a man for a particular time, a more-government-is-better moment that echoed FDR's New Deal and that had as its spokesman a man of galvanizing appeal, JFK. Few times in American history had the young felt such power as they did under a president who was not only the nation's youngest ever, but who told Americans they were getting fat, ought to put out for their country before they put out for themselves, and owed a sense of responsibility toward those less well-off than they were.

Hoff, following Kennedy's example, forged a cadre of the so-called "best and the brightest" in Vermont. His cadre was heavy with former reporters. Hoff liked the press. He confided in, relied on, and debated with journalists. His campaign manager in 1962, Philip Savory, had been a reporter. William Kearns, who had also worked for the Morning Press Bureau, and Ben Collins, a former reporter for the *Burlington Free Press,* were key members of the 1964 campaign team. Kearns was Hoff's administration commissioner and Collins was his Secretary of Civil and Military Affairs. Arthur Ristau of the Associated Press became a special assistant to Hoff. Vic Maerki, a political writer for the *Burlington Free Press* and a man with considerable influence over Hoff, didn't jump ranks, but often consulted with the governor.

That so many journalists took the walk from the newsroom to the governor's staff (and have continued to take the walk for other governors) may have helped Hoff, but harmed reportage, particularly since some of the best reporters joined the governor's team. From the governor's point of view, the newsroom as a bullpen for pitchers of press pronouncements and advice made great sense. It also dulled political analysis and criticism, and co-opted institutional memory.

Hoff played straight with the working press, many of whom knew their contemporaries the governor had hired. He grasped how strategically important they were to him, the leader of a minority regime. He several times went directly to them when the legislature stonewalled initiatives and got reporters to pen columns that helped get the public writing letters and calling representatives to urge support of a bill.

Hoff's first term, like some of his dealings with reporters, had a strategy. It educated him. His second term made Hoff arguably the most influential governor in the history of Vermont. His third hurt.

Help for the poor, civil rights for minorities, and equal education for all had been on Hoff's agenda. Federal funds, as well as a national mood of concern during Hoff's first two terms, had helped persuade the conservative majority in Montpelier to vote yes for more centralized government, voluntary union schools, and the war on poverty. Familiar bastions of power, such as the overseers of the poor and the village school boards, had lost strength. But then 1967 and 1968 turned mean and ugly. People started taking sides over Vietnam. Civil rights riots rocked Detroit and Newark. Closer to home, after Martin Luther King was killed in Memphis in April of 1968, a state of emergency mobilized the National Guard in Hartford, Connecticut. Hoff's civil rights efforts placed Vermont in the riotous national current and demonstrated, much to his chagrin (Hoff later said publicly that his liberal stance on civil rights alienated many Vermonters and probably cost him higher office after three terms as governor) that the tolerant Vermonter of myth could be as bigoted as his big city cousin—he just hadn't had as good a chance to show it before.

The Vermont and New York Youth Project, a joint effort by Hoff and New York Mayor John Lindsay, brought black city kids to the whitest state in the union for a kind of sixties nouveau-CCC experience—not to build state parks or ski trails as the CCC camps had, but to foster some racial understanding. "The camps were controversial as hell," Steve Terry told me. The Youth Project had worked on one level, Terry said, as some kids became friends. But a few black adults thought the black kids were being used as sacrificial lambs to help white kids get over their prejudices. And lots of white Vermonters discovered they had little interest in getting over their prejudices. "The reality of seeing a thousand black faces in these lily white towns—that created quite a stir," Terry recalled. "It just brought out a lot of latent racism."

Then came the infamous Irasburg Affair. On July 19, 1968, Reverend David Johnson, a black preacher who had moved to Irasburg from California, was sitting in his front parlor when his house was shot at by a nightrider. Reverend Johnson grabbed his German Luger and returned the fire. In the subsequent investigation, state police seemed to get the victim and the villain confused. Reverend Johnson was charged with adultery, allegedly having been caught on his couch with a white woman by a trooper who was supposed to be protecting the black man's house from further attacks. The story was featured in *Life* magazine, where its humorous side was aired. "Out here in California, especially among young people," said a West Coast attorney contacted about possible extradition proceedings for witnesses, "adultery is considered not a crime but a popular hobby." The miscarriage of justice smacked of rural bigotry when the identified nightrider pleaded "no contest" and went free.

An indignant Phil Hoff ordered an independent investigation, which former governor Gibson chaired. It was learned that the state police had the name of the nightrider within twenty-four hours of the shooting, but had not pursued him. In the end Vermont's Public Safety Commissioner, E. A. Alexander, refused to discipline his troops, and Hoff learned just how powerful Alexander was—the governor couldn't touch him.

It was only weeks after the shooting in Irasburg that Hoff found himself projected into the national spotlight at the 1968 Democratic National Convention in Chicago. The previous March Hoff had been the first Democratic governor to break with President Lyndon B. Johnson and to jump to the camp of Bobby Kennedy, who was making a run for the Democratic nomination. Then Hoff had stirred up the party at the national governors' convention in July, a month after he had eulogized Kennedy in a sad and painful address before the General Assembly in Montpelier. Hoff accused his fellow governors of failing to have acted quickly enough in the wake of the riots rampaging through American cities. Now, at the Democratic convention, with LBJ out of the running, Bobby Kennedy dead, and with Chicago Mayor Richard Daley's police beating and tear-gassing Vietnam protesters in the streets, a haggard, angry, and frustrated Hoff found his name bantered about as a prospect for vice president. Looking for the "protest candidate," as the media called Hoff, CBS reporter Dan Rather shoved through the delegates. Hoff, however, didn't join the ticket. He never gathered enough support. Senator Edmund Muskie of Maine became the vice presidential candidate, with Senator Hubert Humphrey as the presidential nominee.

One of the repercussions from Hoff's defection from the LBJ camp, his open criticism of the Democratic party, and his anti-war sentiments was a division of loyalty among the Democrats in Vermont. Many of them lost faith in Hoff. His support in the legislature, always a cobbled together alliance, fell apart. As Emory Hebard, a representative from Glover, put it in late 1968, "I'm not concerned with what a peacenik lame-duck governor has to say."

In January 1969 Hoff left office. He was embittered. His momentum had stalled, his drinking had worsened, his energy was sapped. Some observers blamed his problems on the wrong newspapermen getting his ear, which had resulted in spur-of-the-moment decision-making, and too little reflection about the long-term consequences of certain actions. But more importantly, the national current upon which Hoff had ridden quite masterfully had turned. In 1970 he would again seek public office, running for the U.S. Senate against incumbent Republican Winston Prouty, and get beaten badly. In 1968, however, on the state level, the new kid on the block was an older man: former judge, retired business executive, longtime behind-the-scenes Republican power broker Deane C. Davis. Davis was a man who, in the words of Steve Terry, "understood the rural mind, understood the Vermont mind."

SKIING

*Everybody in those days looked up at the ski bums—
like sometimes, in your secret dreams, you'd say, "I
wish I'd done that."*

—*Charlie Brown, ski bum, reflecting on "the golden
age" of skiing, 1965–1975*

One thing is certain: if you want to find the
seedbed of the tangled thicket of modern Vermont, take a long hard look
at the sixties, with a little spillover into both the late fifties and the early
seventies. Not only Phil Hoff and the Democrats emerged to change things.
Communes, ski bums, and rock 'n roll arrived as well. The idea of
independent political parties became popular in limited circles. The first so-
called "super agencies" appeared, swirling control toward the golden dome
of the State House in Montpelier like a tornado with bureaucrats at the
center. Interstates 89 and 91 continued opening the Green Mountains,
environmentalism became de rigueur, and the not-so-subtle transformation
of the fundamental nature of the Vermonter continued.

Despite some internal turmoil, such as the Irasburg Affair, to most
observers Vermont remained an innocent place with an almost fairy-tale
aura, however. Every year the state attracted more and more pioneer types
who rejected the American Way of Life and its Gospel of Progress and
embraced the Vermont Way of Life, which, ironically, many natives wanted
to leave behind. For them, the agrarian dream had soured, mill towns had
become vacant riverside clusters of brick mills inhabited by pigeons, and
skis were expensive toys.

In this crucible of change, skiing was a powerful catalyst. The antithesis
of politics, with its laws and authority, skiing represented unhindered
liberty, an exhilarating sweep down a snowy mountainside in the eye-
watering cold. Every year more young, desk-bound, upper-middle-class
whites from New York, Boston, and elsewhere took the new interstates to

the ski areas to try the sport. Thousands, as opposed to hundreds in the 1950s, became weekenders, enduring the long drive to Vermont and back every Friday and Sunday. Never mind that the trails were sometimes sheets of ice (snowmaking in the sixties was primitive at best), or that driving in bad weather on Sunday got you back in Manhattan with just enough time for a shower and coffee before heading to the office on Monday: Vermont was where the action was. Hundreds quit the rat race altogether. They dropped out and became ski bums. College degrees were shoved back in the closet, ambition took a sabbatical, and the newcomers waited tables, washed dishes, and plowed snow.

In 1966 I dropped out of college to be a ski bum. The first winter I was the pearl diver (dishwasher) at the Windbeam on the access road to the Sugarbush Valley ski area. The next year I tended bar, then I joined the ski patrol. The Windbeam, where I lived during those winters, was built not by a Swiss emigrant, as a glance at its soaring silhouette and overhanging eaves suggested, but by a narcotics agent and a telephone company executive, both of whom were from New York City. Although the famous "jet set" era at Sugarbush was winding down, it remained an exotic place. Instructors from Norway and Austria, with names like Ud, Inar, Thor, and Helli lived at the inns to give the sport an added flavor for the guests. Stein Erikson, an Olympic gold-medal winner and a kind of Norse god of the snow, directed the ski school, did flips off jumps, and handstands on the counter at a local ski shop. Characters with names like Hook, Pig, Fitzy, Tiny, Big John, and Tap—ne'er-do-wells, rich kids on a lark, city boys who hated the snow—passed through Sugarbush. A few, like storms, staying only a few days. Others a season. A few settled and bought land.

Life at Sugarbush was a lot different than life in nearby Montpelier. It was often frivolous, inane, and juvenile. Ski bums worked hard to keep it that way, for many of us were rejecting responsibility and involvement as zealously as the eager types in the capital were thirsting for it. We rendezvoused late at night at the Blue Tooth, a bar. The bar scene was new to Vermont, and the ski-area bars, like "the Tooth," the Wobbly Barn at Killington Basin, and the Five Flies in Manchester Center, functioned as a sixties nexus, a string of lively spots where ski bums, hippies, weekenders, real estate agents, locals, and anyone else with fifty cents for a draft beer could mingle and even talk when the music wasn't too loud.

When I think back on my carefree years at Sugarbush, the thing I remember most vividly is burning boxes. That was one of the pearl diver's jobs, taking the boxes the food came in, lugging them to the rear of the Windbeam, stuffing them into an incinerator, and watching them burn. Usually I burned boxes at twilight. Billowing orange and yellow flames hissed upward as I flung big boxes redolent of chicken fat and steak fat and vegetable oil onto the flames. What I loved most, and recall with the lucidity of a dream, were the times it was snowing. Big fat white flakes drifted down as the flames leaped high. Shadows from the flames danced in the falling snow. Flakes hit the dancing tongues and, like magic, were gone. Behind me, looming four stories, its eaves hanging with yard-long icicles, its windows warm with yellow light in the storm, stood the snug Windbeam, smoke drifting lazily from its chimney.

If this sounds romanticized, I guess it is. Being a ski bum was romantic. Frankly, I didn't even know Phil Hoff was governor. I skied as much as possible, partied a lot, and generally forgot about the world at large.

A popular novel of that period was *The Ski Bum* by Romain Gary, a Frenchman. The book did a pretty good job describing the ski bum's fixation on a mountainside life to the exclusion of everything normal and conventional below a certain altitude. But otherwise, its setting in the Alps and existential romantic angle had little to do with the Vermont ski bum experience I knew. The romance at Sugarbush for me was not so much with women, as it was with the snow and the woods and the cold of winter, elements I had cherished in my boyhood but had grown distant from as a young man. And with the challenge of learning how to ski well.

On my very first run (it was Christmas Day 1966, following a miraculous storm on Christmas Eve) the essence of the ski bum experience, risk and beauty in equal proportions, was brought home to me. Three-quarters of the way down the trail I buried my ski tips beneath a hidden log, landed on my face, and thought, I've busted my leg. By the time I had limped around enough to know only my ankle was sprained, I spotted an incredibly graceful skier carving turns down through the powder. He schussed to a stop.

"Vat's da matter?"

It was the Norse god, Stein Erikson, out for an early run. Unlashing his long thongs, he helped me look for my skis, neither of which I had found in my daze. Soon Erikson found one. The turntable and attached long thong had disappeared. Little ragged holes plugged with snow showed where the screws holding the turntable had been. A little bewildered, I muttered something to the effect, "Where the hell's my binding?"

"Der," Erikson said, pointing a gloved finger.

It was aimed at my new four-buckle Henke boot. The long thong was wrapped around it. A turntable, like a weird eastern stirrup, jutted out from my heel. No wonder my ankle hurt. I checked the other heel. The same thing. The impact of the fall had torn both my bindings right out of my new skis.

I rode down in a ski patrol toboggan. That evening, a little embarrassed, I limped to the dish-washing machine in the kitchen of the Windbeam. Hazel Smith, the wise, white-haired cook, just smiled understandably.

*O*f the varied cast of characters around Sugarbush in those days, two who stood out were Charlie Brown, a.k.a. Albert Feldman, a dropout who changed his name to a cartoon character and never looked back (in 1991, Brown was a professional photographer living three minutes from the Sugarbush Valley gondola), and Hap Gaylord, a local Vermonter who capitalized on "stretch pants hill," as he called it, to share in some of the ski resort bounty, most of which ended up in the hands of out-of-staters.

Brown had moved to Sugarbush from Philadelphia, via Florida, where he was doing consulting work. "I was dealing with the presidents and vice presidents of all these companies," he once told me, "and the next year I was up here washing dishes. I thought that was probably a much saner position; the dishes never talked back to you." Gaylord, a farmer in the fifties, was that rare breed: a Vermonter who took advantage of rapid change.

On a sunny August morning in 1989, I visited the wiry-thin, hawk-nosed Hap Gaylord in the front parlor of his house next to his Texaco Flying-A service station, a local landmark midway between Waitsfield and Warren on Route 100. Across from the station Hap had erected several eye-catching signs over the years, including "Welcome to Sugarbush: You are Now Leaving Vermont" and "Keep the Canal: Give 'Em Carter!" Today no roadside commentary was in sight, but a cone-shaped pile of sweet corn decorated Hap's lawn, a "For Sale" sign by it. A seasoned raconteur, Hap had a captivating delivery. He often smiled to himself, touched his fingers lightly to his forehead, as though feeling for memories, murmured, "What's his name?" more to himself than to me, then glanced up and said, "Dead and gone." He ended a couple anecdotes with a long-drawn out, "Maaannn." After another memory, he said shrilly, a twinkle in narrowed eyes, "Oh Jesus, you wouldn't believe it!"

In 1958, the year both Killington Basin and Sugarbush Valley opened, Hap Gaylord had gone into business. "I took a look at the whole thing," he recalled of his start-up. "I took a couple of runs from here to Rutland. There was no service station open after five or six o'clock."

Once he opened Hap towed the stuck out of snow banks at 3 A.M., occasionally refused to let cars with summer tires on leave his station in a storm, and on Friday nights during the ski season watched "an endless stream of cars rolling in." Hap pumped gas regularly for the likes of conductor Leonard Bernstein, TV personality Faye Emerson, jazzman Skitch Henderson, and New York restaurateur Ormando Orsini. "What a piece of work he was!" Hap said of Orsini, who opened a rustic version of his Manhattan eatery in a renovated barn just off the Sugarbush access road. "Hey, got out of a car with a chauffeur driving. And he looked like the Italian count from Monte Cristo."

Recounting his own origins, Hap said in a burst, "I was born with a silver spoon in my mouth and a golden harp in my hand, down on the banks of the enraged Mad River at my father's place on Route 100. I was born in 1924. That's the score." And "the biggest quagmire I ever got involved in," he added, was the blizzard of 1969:

"It turned to thirty-five or thirty-six below zero, and it stayed that way for five or six days straight. I had a 1942 Mack wrecker, with a hand-crank boom set-up on it, and a winch on the back. The wind blew so bad, and the roads were in such terrible shape despite the plows, in ten minutes the road would be filled in again, here and there, and it was so cold the cars wouldn't start.

"I started in on a Tuesday morning. I had a portable starting unit. I was coming out of Sugarbush, one car on the hook, one hitched to the car behind the car on the hook, with a driver in it, with his head out the window freezing to death. And me and the Mack pushing one ahead. So I was coming in with three cars all the time. This is when they had automatic transmissions. I was throwing raw ether right into the carburetors.

"I remember I come down by Little John's and the Sugarbush Inn, and there were nine girls right at the Blue Tooth, standing right across the road. They saw me comin' with my light on, and the wind blowing hell and it was thirty below zero. And there was a hood up there, and there was a '57 Ford sitting there. So I stopped. And the car I had rolled down into the little gully there. The cars behind me were right there. So I left the emergency brake on, took the starting unit—it was a portable; I could pick it right up, a Briggs and Stratton rig, and it had an alternator in it, a super alternator. I tapped that onto that battery, got one of the girls in there, with the thing in park, and I said, 'I'm going to set this car afire—you aren't going to believe it! I'm gonna throw the ether in there and I'm gonna throw a match right in behind it. You got it all flooded, the battery's flat. This thing may start; we better hope it will. And it it doesn't, it may blow up.'

"Well, it started. Backfired and got rid of the loaded gas. They jumped up and down and had a real dance there. They asked, 'How much is it?" 'Well,' I said, 'it's worth about five hundred dollars to pull that kind of a stunt—the insurance man saw it, he'd cut my insurance right off, I wouldn't have anything.' I don't know, they gave me fifty bucks just to start it, and I said, 'Don't ever shut it off! Leave it running night and day. I mean it.' 'My mechanic says you got to shut them off.' 'Your mechanic is not up here. He's never seen this. You got to keep it running. . . . The roads are plugged. They can't keep them open. The thruways are all screwed up. The wind's blowing so bad you can't see at all. It's dangerous.'

"We stayed open twenty-four hours a day, from that Tuesday right through to the next Wednesday. Nobody could ski because you couldn't run the lifts. The wind was howling. I would stand inside that garage and I couldn't even see the gas pumps—it was so bad! I didn't pump a drop of gas. All my volunteers did the pumping of the gas. They kept coming. They wanted to do something. And the yard was full. And every five minutes we were shoving cars in and out of two bays. And over at the dairy barn I had outside outlets, so I had portable electric units working. I even had those kerosene type heaters that will warm up an engine. We put them right underneath the engine. We dumped the kerosene right in with the diesel— it lightens up the diesel and it burns better. I remember one bus driver from New Jersey. They called up and said, 'Oh, you can't put kerosene in our buses.' 'Tell the guy to get lost, he doesn't know what he's talking about; he's never seen anything like this. We know what we're doing. It's going to start.' And it started. 'Don't shut it off! Leave it runnin! Don't shut those buses off! Can't start em with dynamite! The batteries aren't big enough!'

"Whhhyyyy I never came home to sleep, night or day, until the Friday afternoon following that Tuesday. Night and day I was driving that wrecker. All I was eating was hot sandwiches and coffee and everything I could git into me to keep me going."

Finally he couldn't stay awake. "I drove into the yard over here. I attempted to get out of that '42 Mack. I fell right out onto the ground. I couldn't stand up. I'd had it. Big Boyce Lamphear worked for me. Weighed over two hundred. He came out and picked me up and he said, 'Boss, I think you've had it. I'm taking you home. You're going to bed.' So he picked me right up in his arms and brought me back over here, and the wife met him at the door. 'Where do you want him?' 'Right in the bedroom, lay him on the bed. I'll strip him and put him to bed. He's had the cookie.' I couldn't even walk. I'd had it. No sleep. Out of my boots! Out of my underwear! In my pockets, over three thousand dollars in cash!

"And the cars—we had to have a bucket loader come in and plow off the lawn and out in the field and across the road. We lost track of it all.

"Three weeks later people were calling up from New Canaan, Connecticut, downtown Boston, New York, and New Jersey. 'You got my car—is it ready to go?' 'Yes indeed, it's ready to go.' "

In the sixties the ski business seemed populated by pranksters—lodge and bar owners who didn't take the weather, the ups and downs of the trade, or themselves, quite as seriously as their successors would. Ski area administrators with college degrees in hotel management and artificial snow manufacturing were far in the future. The lightheartedness had something to do with the nature of the risk-takers themselves, with the kind of people who chanced their livelihoods on something as fickle as Vermont weather, and on the adolescence of the ski business—that brief era before explosive popularity, litigation, and plastics totally redefined the skiing experience.

But regardless of who you were—Hap Gaylord, Fred Pabst, Jr., at Big Bromley, or ski bum Charlie Brown—there was one man, more than any one else, to whom you owed a debt. That was Perry Merrill, "the patron saint" of skiing in Vermont, as an editorial in the *Rutland Herald* described him in 1966 when he retired. Merrill was "the guiding light of the multi-million dollar Vermont ski industry," the editorial continued, "the man who preached its economic potential and used his power to nurture it when other Vermonters thought skiing, at least the downhill kind, was for show-offs, sissies, and flatlanders."

Merrill had gotten interested in skiing as a boy, back in the 1890s. He lived in Westport, New York, and his dad often told young Perry tales about a famous folk hero of the Sierra Nevadas, a bigger-than-life Norwegian from Telemark named Snowshoe Thompson. Thompson had come to California at age ten, in an era when the word "snowshoe" was a synonym for ski. Snowshoe Thompson was, in fact, Ski Thompson. He delivered the mail from Placerville, California, to Carson Valley, in the Utah territory, a distance of ninety miles, on so-called "gliding skis," which he made himself out of oak. Lugging forty pounds of mail across snow often fifty feet deep, Thompson made hundreds of three-day trips, going straight through without sleeping. The stars guided him on his ten-foot oak skis. For recreation, the redoubtable mailman used to schuss down mountainsides, leaping off the roofs of trappers' cabins buried in drifts, executing 360-degree turns (a century later they were called "helicopters"). He died in 1876 at the age of forty-nine. He'd caught pneumonia.

With visions of Snowshoe Thompson dancing in his head, young Perry had gone to the barn in Westport one winter's day, knocked a vinegar barrel apart, selected two staves, cut a little leather from one of his father's harnesses for toe straps, and gone back outside. On a slope by the barn he'd strapped on his homemade skis.

"They worked excellently," Merrill wrote years later in his book, *Vermont Skiing*. But his brother had decided he wanted a pair of skis, too. "Everything went well until my father harnessed up the team and found that the reins were short for driving."

His father's surprise notwithstanding, Perry kept his skis. And kept skiing in mind. He became a state forester in Vermont after World War I and spent a year abroad in Sweden as a visiting forester in the early twenties. Though skiing was practically unheard of in America, the Swedes loved it. Perry Merrill returned home with the idea of starting ski areas in Vermont. He hoped to use profits from their operations to acquire state forest land and to build state parks. But, as he wrote in his autobiography, *The Making of a Forester*, "How quickly I learned that having a good idea in no way assured its acceptance by those who must approve and fund a project. It was soon clear that success required one to think fast, to think ahead, to have documented justification for a proposal, and that being a bit of a politician certainly didn't hurt."

His opportunity finally came along in the thirties, with FDR's New Deal allotments for Civilian Conservation Corps projects. "I hightailed it to Washington," Merrill said. "I was just looking for interesting things."

Between 1933 and 1941 he sited twenty-nine CCC camps around the state with federal funds. Overseers of the poor sent raw-boned, would-be farmers and the unemployed young to the camps, where they built roads and picnic areas, fire control projects, dams and ski trails. Siting the camps, "I did all the dealing," Merrill said. "I had in the back of my mind a park system. I'd traveled all over the United States as a forester, and I'd seen a lot of things we didn't have."

One of those things Vermont didn't have, of course, was ski areas. But Merrill, as Vermont's head forester, placed CCC crews at Jay Peak, Burke Mountain, Ascutney Mountain, Okemo Mountain, and Killington Peak. State parks were designated and lodges built. Two decades later, some of these lodges became the terminuses of networks of ski trails.

When the CCC crew had started swinging axes and picks on the top of the Nose Dive on Mount Mansfield in 1934, hikers peered down the pitch and told foreman Charlie Lord, "Gawd, anybody goes down through there, they're crazy—it'll kill them." Lord was Merrill's "trail design master." Fifty-six years later, Lord, eighty-seven, lived in an historic log cabin in Stowe. He had a good view out the kitchen window of some of his handiwork below the Chin, a conspicuous outcrop on top of Mount Mansfield. When I asked how he had become Vermont's foremost ski trail designer, he said, "I had a knack for lining up towers."

Like his old boss Perry Merrill, Charlie Lord said that he had enjoyed the snow as a boy growing up in Groton, Vermont. He sledded on "jumpers," or "jump jacks," a ski with a seat on it, which you steered down the nearest slope, avoiding trees and barbed wire fences. When he ran the Mount Mansfield CCC, Lord said, the Taft Lodge, a rough-hewn summer cabin, offered hikers overnight shelter beneath the Chin. In those late Depression era years, skiers coming to Stowe rode trains from Boston and New York, took taxis or a bus from Waterbury, and boarded in farmhouses or rustic lodges. They climbed the mountain with sealskins over their skis and usually made one run a day.

Lord's "pick-and-shovel artists" left a trail surface rougher than what you find today. Design was handled a little differently, too. After looking at maps and drainage patterns, Lord relied for his final decision on what he called "some foot exploring." Ultimately, his guiding principle was simple: "Maybe we could ski on them. That was about it."

In 1947, on the invitation of Roland Palmedo, Lord had traveled thirty miles south from Stowe, where he had taken a job designing trails for C. V. Starr, a rich insurance man who had big plans for Mount Mansfield, down to General Stark Mountain in Fayston. There Roland Palmedo wanted Lord to lay out a single chairlift and a few trails for a ski area to be called Mad River Glen. In those days Route 100 was paved between Stowe and Duxbury, but after that Lord drove on dirt, except for a six-mile stretch of pavement north of Waitsfield. He followed a twisty, steep lane called the McCullough Turnpike up to the lower slopes of General Stark Mountain, whose elevation was 3,585 feet and whose flanks created a natural snow basin. Palmedo, his temporary boss, "was a bit of an adventurer," Lord recalled. "He had skied down Kilimanjaro."

A New York investment banker, Palmedo had also been, back in the thirties, a founder and president of the New York Amateur Ski Club. Later he helped start Stowe's first ski patrol. He was also the driving force behind Vermont's first chairlift, which Charlie Lord strung up on Mount Mansfield in 1938. There are conflicting stories of why Palmedo wanted a chairlift after years of hiking up the trails on skins. One claims he was simply getting old, as were his skiing buddies, and they didn't want to hike anymore. Another was that the women's Olympic Ski Team complained about being too tired after they hiked up the practice trails to race back down well. Palmedo, recalled Alice D. Kiaer, manager of the women's team, "cut through all the complicated red tape, raised money—above all, he had just that enthusiasm and tact which make people eager to do things with him and for him." After World War II Palmedo had a falling out with C. V. Starr, who envisioned Stowe becoming the ski capital of the East. Starr's vision of Mount Mansfield's future irked Palmedo, who loved skiing as sport, not commerce. Palmedo soon divorced himself from Stowe's future, climbed into his plane, and began some reconnaissance flights to the south. General Stark Mountain and its protected snow bowl caught his eye. He bought more than fifteen hundred acres of mostly steep, forested terrain from the Ward Lumber Company.

Palmedo and his friends, who would make up the original Mad River Glen faithful, loved tree skiing and abhorred fall lines. So the trails Charlie Lord designed followed the natural swoops and curves of the mountain. They included glades. The idea was to make skiing a happy interaction with the mountain. They had to wait several years to really get a feel for that, however, because so much snow fell in the fall of '47, when they were erecting the lift, they couldn't finish it. The next three winters, with Mad River open, snowfall was poor.

Most skiers now drove to Vermont rather than take the train. A favorite meeting spot for the New York crowd was the George Washington Bridge. From there, the drivers headed up the Taconic Parkway, then took different routes, depending on whether they wanted to ski Big Bromley or Mad River or Stowe.

For New Yorkers, with their skyscrapers, subways, and suburbia, it was terra incognita once they got to Vermont. They drove along winding roads, crossed ice-gloved streams, passed through villages where blue woodsmoke curled from chimneys, and where kids hanging out by the general store would usually wave, or at least nod, and where there was very little traffic, some of it still horse-drawn. Vermont was not yet four-season resorts and smiling innkeepers, but mostly a few simple lodges and farmhouses with guest rooms that were cheap. Ski-area help usually lived in the nearest village. Most of them were pretty glad to have a job. Some spoke a Vermont argot. Many New Yorkers had only a hazy idea of what in the world they were saying.

In those days trail maintenance meant foot packing after a big storm. Ski clothes tended towards the loose and blousy. Khaki was always popular. Bogner didn't introduce stretch-pant fabric until the middle of the fifties; and buckle boots, like my terrible-fitting Henkes, were still a decade away. You laced up your boots, tight; you lashed on your skis, your toes in bear traps; you skied in big gliding turns, khakis flapping.

One of the young go-getters who fell in love with skiing in the early fifties was a fellow named Jim Boyce, the business manager at ABC Productions in New York in the years before Vermont even had a television station (WCAX-TV, channel 3, went on the air in Burlington in 1954). Once Boyce had decided to try skiing, he had gone to the exclusive Abercrombie and Fitch store in Manhattan to buy his gear. "That's where the social set headquartered in New York," he recalled almost forty years later over lunch at the Trapp Family Lodge in Stowe, where he was director of group sales. "It was just like buying things for white hunters."

Following his first ski trip to Dorset in 1951, Boyce got hooked. "It was the most beautiful thing I'd ever seen in my life," he remembered excitedly. "I got ski sick! I got caught, absolutely caught!" He became a weekend regular. "I bought my first pair of skis at Bromley. Thirty-five dollars." He laughed. "Dartmouths!"

Skiing changed his life, Boyce added seriously. In New York he started seeing "the concrete jungle." He began thinking he was "all mixed up." He told himself, "You better go up and take a rest up in Vermont.

"So I took a year off up here. I did nothing. I was trying to get my head together. But I just loved it, I loved it so much! I did all the things I had never got around to do. I learned how to ride a horse, I did some drinking."

One year became two, became three. Boyce lived in Manchester. "*Nothing* like today. It was beautiful. The Equinox Hotel mesmerized me." When he ran short of money, his father warned him, "Jim, you just don't retire at thirty-eight without portfolio."

"And he was right," Boyce added. "Absolutely right! But I was trying to find my soul."

The search transformed Boyce into one of Vermont's first ski bums. He waited on tables at The Inn in Weston and drove the dirt roads to Bromley to ski. Others like Boyce were being drawn to Stowe and Mad River Glen, then to Killington Basin, Jay Peak, and Sugarbush as they opened.

Most of the major ski areas carried the stamp of a single man's vision. At Stowe it was Starr's. At Mad River Palmedo's. Preston Smith, a driven man in his twenties, brought Killington into being. Damon Gadd, an aristocratic gentleman who moved in the world of the very well-off, conceived Sugarbush. But no matter who the man, or where in Vermont he had in mind, first he had to get together with State Forester Perry Merrill and iron out details like an access road and where the lifts went in.

Working out the details wasn't always easy. For instance, when Preston Smith keyed in on Killington Basin in 1954, Merrill sent Charlie Lord down there to check out the wilderness site. "You couldn't even drive anywhere near the base," Lord remembered. So he and some others climbed, sealskins on, to where Smith imagined slopes, lifts, and lodges. "It's a good favorable spot," Lord reported to Merrill. "But someone has to build a road."

Although Merrill got behind it, the Vermont Highway Department did not. Officials, reluctant to lay down asphalt five miles up a rugged climb to the base of what was reputedly an undercapitalized project, kept putting Killington's access road off. Years of delays, with the money earmarked for the road going elsewhere—once for Jay Peak's equally formidable Route 242, for example—ended in 1958. Soon Killington was advertising the highest skiing in New England in a natural basin whose development potential the original lifts barely touched.

During the next three decades, Snowdon Mountain, Rams Head Mountain, Skye Peak, Bear Mountain, and Sunrise Mountain linked up with the original Killington Peak. A web of crissing-and- crossing trails, with signs at their junctions to help you figure out just where you were, made Killington the biggest ski area in the East. A gondola picked up skiers almost ten miles, by car, from the original base lodge. In the late eighties bumper stickers opposing Killington's gargantuan sprawl across tens of thousands of acres and its scheme to make snow from treated wastewater read "Where the affluent meet the effluent." The mountain's management wanted to further expand snow-making, potentially draining several of the watershed's streams to do it. Conservationists wanted Killington's suburban ski sprawl to stop.

In thirty years Killington had come a long way from the days my buddies and I rode a bumpy, curvy Route 4 up to the access road, passed a handful of lodges and the Wobbly Barn to load onto the cold and seemingly endless single chair, deep in private thoughts, football robes wrapped tightly around us to keep warm, and skied our hearts out.

By 1990, though, an industry that began as an embraced savior was perceived a lot differently than when Perry Merrill and Charlie Lord were spry and wielding power. Some saw it as an octopus with ever-thirsty, growing tentacles that drove wildlife from its habitat, dried up watersheds for artificial snow-making, and sent surrounding real estate prices into the polluted stratosphere, killing native Vermonters' chances to stay where they had lived for decades—in villages in the mountains. Others claimed it was a relatively benign economic motor that ran on "white gold" and brought skiers who, in 1988, spent around a billion dollars here.

The afternoon I talked with trail designer Charlie Lord, he urged that my book take a tolerant view of how skiing had changed since the fifties and sixties, when there was little opposition to it. Skip over the conflicts, he said. "Everything's that new has some opposition, some problems. They tend to smooth out in the long run."

I thought about this afterwards. About tolerance, one of those traditions the Vermonter of old was said to possess in abundance. When Lord had first hiked the slopes of Mt. Mansfield in the 1930s and Merrill's directives to him were summed up in one sentence: "If you lay out a trail, I'll see that it's cut," skiing was primarily escapism for Ivy League purists who could afford it. The bread lines, hopelessness, and despair of the

Depression got left behind in New York or Boston. You climbed aboard the ski train and partied until Waterbury. A half century later, skiing was big business, but hopelessness and despair still occupied many nooks and crannies in Vermont. A sport, with repercussions that have been documented as insensitive toward people at the lower end of the economic scale—loss of housing, seasonal employment, high rents, loss of identity—had evolved into a force that needed the very reins put on it that Merrill cut off his father's harnesses almost a century ago.

Whether you were a tourist or a first-time skier about to savor the joys of frostbite and narrow trails, you probably came to Vermont via Interstates 89 and 91. The interstates and the new ski areas they served changed the face of Vermont more than anything had since the Ice Age.

Eventually, Vermont built 391 miles of interstates in a giant Y-shape running north alongside the Connecticut River to White River Junction, then branching northwestward towards Montpelier and Burlington, as well as continuing northward towards St. Johnsbury and Newport. The mileage and costs did not exactly fit into the state's tradition of frugality. Three hundred and ninety-one miles averaged out to three times as many miles of four-lane interstate per resident than the other New England states were building.

The new highways got their one-two push in the mid-fifties from the National Highway Act, a trust fund established by the U.S. Congress to crisscross the country with interstates, and from Governor Joseph Johnson and the Vermont legislature. Before construction began, rights-of-way were negotiated. Judges had to deal with recalcitrant landowners who didn't care if the future economic livelihood of the world depended on it, they wanted to keep their land. Surveyors sighted through dozens of transits, and engineers laid out the superhighways on paper. The bulldozers finally got rolling in the late fifties. Drilling rigs that looked like giant scorpions, dust billowing all around them, bored deep holes in granite hills. Dynamite blasted hills into pieces that bulldozers pushed around and steam shovels dumped into huge trucks. The trucks churned to gullies and valleys on giant tires, their loads gradually filling in vast open spaces. Long steel bridges on tall pylons began to span the White River, the Black River, the Winooski River. Construction went forward piecemeal and continued through the sixties and into the seventies. The first finished section of I-91 connected Brattleboro to the Massachusetts border and I-89 linked Burlington to Montpelier. The roads were an engineering marvel, one of those protracted displays of cooperation, labor, and ingenuity that America prided itself in.

The new highways benefited skiers, tourists, and second-home owners immediately, but the impact of the roads on the lives of the average Vermonter took a while to register. As Ben Huffman, a lawyer for the Vermont Legislative Council, pointed out in his 1974 study of the interstates, *Getting Around Vermont* (published by the Environmental Program at University of Vermont), the highways initially served more as a "bridge" for people and goods passing through than for Vermonters' daily use. Promised manufacturing jobs, which had helped win taxpayer approval, didn't materialize. Yet the share of the costs paid by Vermonters was high. By 1972, that share had become $178 million, or twenty-six percent of a total cost of $670 million.

Traditionally, Vermont had funded highway construction by the "pay-as-you-go" method. But expenses of the magnitude associated with interstate building, even with all the federal aid (the typical interstate deal between the federal government and state governments called for a nine-to-one split of the construction costs), required big loans. The Highway Department and its supporters argued persuasively that the interstates justified such an "investment-in-the-future" method of funding; they claimed that highway-user taxes, in the form of licensing fees and gasoline taxes, would pay much of Vermont's ten percent share of the costs.

It didn't work out that way. For one thing, the oil crises of the seventies reduced traffic ("The transportation situation in Vermont last winter was unnerving," Huffman wrote in his introduction, dated December 1974), and revenues also dropped at first because there were fewer visitors. Yet even without the crises, Huffman claimed, the interstates far exceeded Vermont's needs. In effect, the roads were mute testimonials to the power of the car culture and to highway building. They symbolized the titan-like presence of the Highway Department in Montpelier. Secondary roads, which Vermonters did use a lot, also got upgraded, "gravel gaps" got paved, and highway construction jobs became available, so some benefits were visible. But the big loser, as Huffman made clear, was public transportation. And it was sorely needed in a state where nearly a quarter of the adults didn't own cars.

By this time the car's main competitors, the railroads, were practically dead on their rusted tracks. Once the economic arteries of the state, like railroads nationwide, Vermont's were decrepit.

For a century, ever since the Rutland and Burlington Railroad had celebrated the completion of its route across the state in 1849 at Mount Holly, southeast of Rutland, the railroads had been a power. A barrage of initials—the B&M, the P&O, the St. J. and L.C., the B&L being just a few of them—had excited boys in small towns, challenging them to memorize the more than two dozen carriers serving the state. When I was around ten or eleven, during the middle of the Eisenhower administration and the Cold War, my mother put me on notice about just how crucial the White River Junction railhead was to the safety of America from Communism. "There's an atomic bomb attack," she told me, "White River's a target."

Having seen the Central Vermont Railroad's turnaround in what was to me a vast spider web of tracks, I knew she spoke the truth. White River was a key to the defense of New England. That was why the civil defense folks had built a cinderblock bunker in the park in Lebanon, New Hampshire, where we now lived—so families could duplicate its construction in their basements and be ready for the elimination of White River Junction from the face of the earth—an annihilation we, who had a little stone niche in our cellar, into which I occasionally crawled, imagining a tremendous gray mushroom over White River, hoped to escape. The reason White River Junction was a railhead of unusual importance was, I figured, because it was where locomotives got swung by monstrously powerful machinery so they could head back from whence they had come. Like some gigantic watch with one hand stretching all across the dial, the turnaround was the most awesome piece of machinery I had ever seen.

In Vermont in the fifties, railroads still competed as a way to get around. Down in Vernon, you could board and ride to Brattleboro for ten cents. Up in Richford, you could climb aboard either the *Redwing* or the *Alouette,* two crack Canadian trains, and clickety click to Montreal, and from there clear on to Vancouver if you wanted. But the train era was only a vestige of its former self. The Woodstock Railroad, for instance, a so-called "short-line" operation that had served the woolen mills in Hartford, Quechee, and Woodstock, and traveled over a wooden trestle bridge that practically filled Quechee Gorge with supporting timbers, had succumbed to the competition of trucks in 1933. Two branches of the St. Johnsbury and Lamoille County Railroad, which served northern Vermont, lived on only in the minds of old-timers. One of them, the Victory Branch or, as it was sometimes called, the Moose River Branch, had stopped hauling timber out of the Northeast Kingdom at the turn of the last century. The Hardwick and Woodbury Railroad, which had maneuvered around some of the tightest curves and climbed some of the steepest grades in the eastern United States while carrying granite from quarries in Woodbury to mills in Hardwick, had its roadbed demolished in 1940. The St. J. and L.C. continued through the fifties and even into the seventies serving Vermont industries. It carried the talc used in baby powder from a lode at the Eastern Magnesia Talc Company mines in Johnson, as well as asbestos, which until recently was innocently used for insulation of all kinds, from the Rubberoid Corporation mine in Lowell to connecting tracks in St. Albans and St. Johnsbury.

But people didn't ride the trains anymore. Or very few did, that is, acrophobes mainly, folks afraid to head up into the sky aboard a big silver bird. Most Americans, Vermonters included, wanted to fly or drive. They didn't want to arrive anyplace on the cross-country equivalent of the "Slow, Jerky, and Long Coming," as the St. J. and L.C. was nicknamed by some wag, shuffling off with a few other passengers into a probably seedy station in a bad part of town.

The state got into the business of trying to extend the life of the railroads in Vermont in the seventies. That didn't work either. On the St. J. and L.C., which the state took over, there were thirty-seven derailments in one year. That must have been a record. One of them, fittingly enough, plopped a ship's turbine into the Lamoille River. When a freight car fell through the bridge spanning the Missisquoi River in Swanton, that was the end of the cross-state run. As for passenger service, AMTRAK, a federally financed operation, assumed command of that anachronism in the late seventies. For Vermonters, that meant one train a day, the *Montrealer*, which connected Quebec to Washington, D.C., via New York. Having ridden the *Montrealer* on several occasions, I can vouch that it was fun, but it sure was slow. Boarding in St. Albans at around 8 P.M., I would wake up red-eyed and grumpy in Grand Central Station around 7 A.M. the following morning. Taking I-89 to I-91 down through Massachusetts and Connecticut I could make New York in about half that time.

One thing the new interstates did bring Vermonters, which no statistical survey like Huffman's could gauge, was a strange sense of empowerment. I recall, back in the late sixties, cruising along the black carpet of I-89 in the moonlight, not another car in sight for miles and miles. Clouds cast shadows in the deep cuts, and the big, empty road—all that money and energy and earth-moving—filled me with a thrilling sense of promise and expectation. And I was only putting along in my Volkswagen.

*T*hroughout the sixties, across Vermont thousands of acres were changing hands. The most intense transactions took place initially near ski areas and in nearby villages, towns like West Dover, Manchester, Wilmington, Warren, Waitsfield, Stowe, Montgomery, but the real estate boom spread into towns along the interstates and into the small cities. The new real estate market proved a godsend to many natives. Marginal, hardscrabble farms on hillsides suddenly were worth something at a time when property taxes, which Richard Snelling had made his campaign theme against Hoff in 1966, were going up to pay for changes in education—many of the changes demanded by the newcomers once they settled their families into their new communities.

When a stranger knocked on the door and made an offer on the old home place, selling frequently promised to get a family not only out of "the sticks," but out of the stagnating Vermont Way of Life with its hard work and no great promise into the American Way of Life: money in the pocket, a clean, new home that was often a trailer, and no more chores. Those who sold, and their children, often filled slots in the expanding service and retail sector. They became housekeepers, lift operators, restaurant help, store clerks—seasonal, low-paying work, but with unemployment benefits. Gone for them was the hill-farm environment with its hardships and deprivations, its wisdom about the seasons and animals, its cynical view of windy promises, and its ingrained "make do" attitude.

Antiseptic homes and ski chalets shaped like rockets appeared as though from outer space in fields next to nineteenth-century farmhouses and barns filled with the sounds and smells of livestock. Newcomers and natives were curious about each other but tended to see the state from widely differing viewpoints. The new arrivals often over-romanticized things. The lives farmers led could, like the smell of manure, stir up ambiguous feelings about the truth of hill-farm life. I used to have mixed feelings myself when I visited my sister's farm in Tunbridge, up where the co-op milk truck would no longer go. On occasional trips there during the early seventies, I remained curious about the pigs, chickens, cows, chores, and venison out of season; yet I was embarrassed by Barb's lack of teeth, by her stained sneakers, by the constant buzz of flies in the kitchen. On one visit, I noticed that her big old oval kitchen table was gone—an auctioneer had made her an offer she couldn't refuse. In the back of my heart I had wanted it, too. It was beautiful. So it was not only the newcomers, but Vermonters like myself who had gone out into the world and longed to return home, who coveted the Home Comfort woodstove, the run-down farmhouse, and the rolling hillsides. The big difference between thirty years ago and 1990 was how willing old-timers were to sell and how little you had to pay.

By 1970 Sugarbush and the Mad River Valley were in the midst of an awesome transformation, as were several other regions adjoining Vermont's major ski resorts or resort complexes. In the Valley population had grown, vacation homes had sprung up along many dirt roads, the lots often sold by one-time ski bums turned real estate agents. By the mid-seventies the grand list in Warren exceeded $400 million. In 1960, it had been $6 million.

In *Time and Change in Vermont,* University of Vermont geography professor Harold E. Meeks writes: "In 1957 no 'professionals' (doctors, architects, engineers, etc.) lived in either Warren or Waitsfield. In 1976 the two towns had twenty-five firms in that category. Similarly, the number of places offering accommodations increased from five to thirty-three, restaurants from two to nineteen, building contractors and services from three to twenty-six, retail stores from fourteen to forty-nine, and gas stations from one station in Waitsfield to the present seven. Real estate offices have sprouted like weeds. In 1957, one small agency was located in Waitsfield; by 1976 there were twenty-two. In about twenty years the Valley has been changed forever. Population has doubled, the grand list has increased astronomically, and the number of commercial services has gone from twenty-eight to 210. And this action is going on in a small Vermont valley with little land that's flat, and with few native people left."

NAKED IN THE MOONLIGHT

There are vast areas of unknowns touching the manner of living practiced by these groups.
—*Major Glenn Davis, Vermont State Police, 1970*

*I*n the wake of the 1967 "Summer of Love" in San Francisco, which made "hippy" a household word, drugs an American pastime, and flowers a symbolic gun-barrel insert for peaceniks, Vermont became a geographical magnet for hippies in the Northeast. From 1967 until 1973 an estimated 100,000 rolled into the Green Mountain State, many of them in Volkswagens like mine. Both the VW "beetle," and the larger VW van were "people's cars"; that is to say, cheap, easy to repair, and with few pretentions. Occasionally painted wild psychedelic colors, these flagships of the hippy invasion sped up I-89 and I-91, veered off at various exits, and headed into the hinterland, indiscriminately carrying radical militants against the war in Vietnam, acid-tripping God seekers, college dropouts, runaway kids, body odor, marijuana, and LSD—"Hey man, you wanna get high?"

Vermont saw it all, and tolerated it all—at least for a while.

A hundred-plus communes sprang up like mushrooms, from Total Loss Farm in Guilford to Earth People's Park in Norton, with places like Hamburger Hill, Tree Frog, and Johnson Pasture in between. Still relatively cheap, beautiful, and easy to get to, Vermont seemed an ideal place for a getaway from "the system."

At its core the hippy movement, with its back-to-the-land ethic, sought escape from an America gone militaristic, greedy, and mean. On its surface, however, it was a more traditional American trip; it was middle-class white kids rejecting their parents, along with everything they stood for, from monogamy to martinis, from the "rat race" to the space race.

As Ray Mungo, one of the founders of Total Loss Farm, put it: "We were born and raised by parents who loved us at least until they lost us to a certain high-pitched whistle in the wind, which they had gotten too old to hear."

In some cases physically too old. The popular rock and roll of Jimi Hendrix, Steppenwolf, and Led Zeppelin, for instance, could send parents, like dogs pained by ear-piercing decibels, running for cover.

The rise and fall of the counterculture in America became a national phenomenon. Vermont, for once, found itself front and center. It made perfect sense, given that the dormant seeds of the first commune in the country had been lying fallow in Putney since 1847, when John Humphrey Noyes and his followers, a group called the Perfectionists, had left in a hurry. "The serpent of wife-swapping shattered their Eden," Jennison wrote in *Roadside History of Vermont.* Noyes, a Brattleboro native, Yale graduate, and cousin of Rutherford B. Hayes, a future president, had founded the Perfectionists in the late 1830s. The group strove for social, economic, and religious equality. Interestingly enough, the Perfectionists were not the first alternative living group in Windham County. A small sect called the Dorrilites, staunch vegetarians who even refused to wear clothes made from animal hides, had thrived around 1800. Then, in the fall of 1844, the Millerites, another religious group, sold everything they owned on the word of their leader, William Miller, pulled on white robes, and ascended to the hilltops of Jamaica, Vermont, where they waited and waited for the Second Coming of Christ.

The 1960s newcomers reversed the century-long exodus of the young and the restless and helped increase Vermont's population from 390,000 to 445,000, the first jump of more than five percent in one decade since the 1830s. Those who came to the Green Mountains included the ambitious (Duncan Syme, a member at Prickly Mountain in Warren, went on to cofound Vermont Castings, the woodstove manufacturing company in Randolph); the potentially political (Barbara Nalfie of the Hippy Farm in Franklin was elected to the Burlington City Council in the late 1980s); and the foolhardy (Kingman Brewster, Jr., son of the president of Yale, had a few thousand dollars he blew on fun for himself and friends in the Fairfield area before committing himself to becoming a farrier.)

The men favored bell-bottoms, beads, and T-shirts, often tie-dyed. They grew beards and sported pony tails or wild, unruly hair. Women wore overalls, dirndls, loose-flowing clothes often bought at rummage sales or flea markets. They burned their bras, like many of their beaus had burned their draft cards. They disdained make-up, let body hair grow. Communes often anchored themselves in old farmhouses, bought collectively or with money from a couple of wealthier members. But worn-out VW vans fastened to plywood sheds, lean-tos, tree houses, and old yellow school buses with stove pipes jutting through the roofs were communal headquarters as well. The hippies' dwellings looked as motley, and as unorthodox, as they did.

Hippies liked to go barefoot so they could feel the grass between their toes. They acted carefree. They were not big on work. Practically all of their communes shared the goal of being self-sufficient, so members could live apart from the American mainstream. Most communes revered nature, rejected materialism, and espoused the philosophy: "Do your own thing."

The types of communes in Vermont varied dramatically. By far the most popular was the agricultural-based. Members grew, ate, and sometimes tried to sell their natural food. There were also craft-making communes, politically conscious ones, and several with a spiritual quest as their driving force. There was even an architectural commune, Prickly Mountain in Warren.

Founded by David Sellers and Bill Reinecke, two dropouts from Yale's School of Architecture, Prickly Mountain was a place where future architects explored their design fantasies. It had started in 1965, a little in advance of the other communes, when Sellers and Reinecke decided to build a vacation home in Warren, away from the ski area yet not so far away it wasn't saleable to a second-home client. But the irrepressible Sellers got carried away. He became the guru/architect/philosopher of an experimental kingdom (Reinecke soon left) that eventually covered two hundred acres and had a master design plan along with a dozen-plus houses, none of which resembled the rectangular "box" that most Americans lived in. It was a time when the conviction that you could just go out and build yourself a house had been eclipsed from most Americans' minds by the construction industry and by building codes that had not yet made it to Vermont.

As a ski bum I occasional drove out to Prickly Mountain. There, along the base of the spine of the Green Mountains, were these magical-looking places, tall and evocative and like nothing else I had ever seen. A typical Prickly Mountain house lifted off a cement slab. It had cantilevered rooms stretching horizontally out over the hillside. Its four or five stories jutted up through the pines with an exuberant verticality. Peeking in a window once I saw a gigantic boulder in an entryway. Another time I crossed a trestle more than a hundred feet long to reach a front door. Interiors of some of the houses had been left intentionally unfinished, sheetrock joints exposed, wires visible, doors and windows untrimmed—the architectural guts on display. Rolled Plexiglass windows set into the walls suggested huge horizontal test tubes from a futuristic world. Plywood and rough-hewn lumber sheathed exteriors. The homes were heated electrically because electricity was cheap.

People buy these places, I remember thinking, amazed and delighted by that fact.

Architectural Digest, the *New York Times*, and *Life* sent writers to Warren to report back to the square world on Sellers' and Reinecke's "design/build" approach. According to the wild-haired Sellers, who was in his late twenties, everything distilled down to a simple philosophy: order your materials, get your shit together, have a design vision, and go for it.

Commenting on Sellers' home, the Bridge House, the one with the trestle walkway, *Life's* Frank Kaplan wrote: "Sellers has produced a tree-top pad whose pleasures aren't for children, the elderly or anyone who can't climb a tree. The climbing aids tend to get more Spartan and more precarious with altitude. One bedroom, just a short distance above the entrance level and reachable by a climb no steeper than Class II on the six class alpine-rating scale, has its own wash basin. This is the master bedroom."

Sellers furnished the Bridge House, which lacked traditional square corners where an owner might tuck conventional furniture, like a table or a sofa, with old machinery he had scavenged from farmers who were letting all that junk rust into oblivion. Ahead of his time, Sellers bolted tractor seats to the floor as stools, hung old saws, whiffletrees, and assorted hand tools on the walls. Staying in the Bridge House was a novel experience, said Richard "Sparky" Potter, a student from St. Lawrence University who later moved to Waitsfield and became a wooden-sign maker. "It was a rawboned house," Potter recalled, "a total experiment in plywood and Plexiglass. My marriage started in that Crow's Nest. You were caressed by the pine trees. A big wind moved the thing two or three inches—you thought you were in heaven."

Ironically, it was at Prickly Mountain, in 1970, that Vermont got its first condominium. Three dropouts from the University of Pennsylvania's School of Architecture, Bill Maclay, Jim Sanford, and Bill Travers, built the Dimetrodon, a communal space named after a dinosaur whose spine was a heat exchanger, a membrane through which blood absorbed warmth from the sun. Maclay, Sanford, and Travers built the Dimetrodon as an alternative, energy-efficient experiment before the first energy crisis. An unconstrained cluster of stacked cubes, round surfaces, and diagonal elements, it was powered by solar and wind energy, both then in their infancies as options to oil, electricity, and gas. A twelve-thousand-gallon holding tank in the cellar stored hot water. The water circulated through the stacked-cube living quarters of each owner, and also heated a common room, where meetings were held and friends could stay. When the energy crunch hit in late 1973, proving the young architects prophetic, it made the rest of the Prickly Mountain homes, most of which were completely electric, very costly to keep warm, unless you stayed in the upper reaches using the climbing aids, where the rising heat collected. Over the next few years, most were retrofited at considerable expense. Seller's Bridge House was not one of them. It unfortunately burned.

A letter from Verandah Porche, one of the founders of Total Loss Farm, to Nel, in 1969:

> Raymond, Marty (you don't know him yet), and I are all political freaks trying to be relevant, helpful, moral, revolutionary, forward-looking, virtuous, self-sacrificing, etc. (you know the scene). Anyway, I have been in the scene since grade NINE and miraculously, in spite of my most ardent efforts, the world has been getting steadily worse. . . .
>
> BUT!! WHILE Senior Citizens (anyone over thirty with many exceptions and some senior citizens underage) are dying of obesity, bad bowels, and ennui, behold there is a New Age of humanity bursting forth with cries of Oh Wow, Dies Irae, and FAR OUT! Space creatures, artsy-crafties, people who take themselves lightly and seriously, who think living is better than . . . what am I talking about, Nel—you tell me. The hippest chick I met in California was ten years old. It has a lot to do with post-psychedelic ethics—simply caring for your neighbors because there is such a tremendous universe to be lost in. It is acid consciousness but it has little to do with drugs. It's where your mind is at. But I am rambling afield. Turn on, tune in, drop into Vermont.

Total Loss Farm in Guilford, initially just another commune, soon differentiated itself. It wasn't the biggest commune, nor where the wildest orgies occurred, nor where the giant zucchini spoke to God. The focus there was on poetry, essays, and journalism. Total Loss Farm attracted writers and intellectuals. Having severed themselves physically from mainstream collegiate America (in their case, mainstream Commonwealth Avenue-America, as most of them came straight to Vermont from Boston University), the wordsmiths stayed tuned to the "straight world" via the literary marketplace and soon made their commune, in counterculture circles, famous.

Total Loss Farm began on Memorial Day weekend 1968 and still thrived in 1990 as a land trust on which several members, including Verandah Porche, who had become a poet working in Vermont schools, and Richard Wizansky, another one of the founders, still lived. Wizansky, a small, intense, polite professor (he taught English at Greenfield Commu-

nity College in Massachusetts), remembered hitchhiking to Vermont that
fateful Memorial Day weekend.

"My friend Verandah had a cape on," he said. "I had a dungaree jacket
on, and a felt hat, and a cane. And I think I was carrying a lantern, as a matter
of fact."

"Diogenes?" I asked, referring to the Greek philosopher who had
wandered with a lantern in search of an honest man.

"Yeah, Diogenes. We found out the farm was about one hundred
acres, and a barn, and a farm house, and outbuildings—all for twenty-five
thousand dollars, if you can imagine that. The moment we saw it, we
decided to do it. We got very excited."

Pooling funds, which included one member's long-hoarded bar
mitzvah money, the group, which numbered around eight, left Boston
University's graduate school, where they had been actively involved in the
war resistance movement, bought the farm, and moved in. They had two
goals, Wizansky said. First, to get out of American society, and secondly, to
become self-sufficient so they could stay out. Members remained committed to the political Left, which rampaged against the war, but the Left had
become fractured and ideological. Vermont seemed the perfect place to
regroup, far from draft-card burnings, protests, and urban riots.

In 1968 parts of Windham County and Brattleboro, the county's only
city, were enjoying an economic resurgence. I-91 had made Brattleboro a
gateway to "the beckoning country" and to ski areas in southern Vermont.
The outskirts of Brattleboro, particularly along Route 5, were being
developed. In Guilford, however, no small shopping complexes were
going in nor were many suburban ranch houses going up for young
professionals who wanted a view. They didn't have to move all the way out
there for that. In Guilford you still drove mostly on dirt roads. Packer's
Corners was an intersection of two of the roads not far from where the
Boston University dropouts settled in for a go at alternative living. The
neighborhood around the corners had a feel to it, it had a history. Packer's
Corners was where "weirdos congregated," Wizansky said with a grin.
Ghosts of black people who had lived there long ago stalked the narrow
lanes at night. Mother Honeywell had lived around there. Mother Honeywell
was a nineteenth-century spiritualist the hippies took to heart, possibly
because as Ray Mungo contended, she and her friends "also danced naked
in moonlight and swam in this pond," referring to a pond on their farm.
With Mother Honeywell having done her thing the century before, a few
dozen hippies in bell-bottoms and dirndls getting high on psylocybin, "the
champagne" of hallucinogenic drugs, skinny dipping, and traipsing
through overgrown fields and uncut meadows, caused some talk but

generally just perpetuated a tradition. It was the rednecks in downtown Brattleboro you had to watch out for, Wizansky recalled. "We avoided town a lot," he said.

No doubt, the hippies struck some Vermonters, redneck or not, as peculiar, both in looks and outlooks. Before moving to Guilford, for instance, Mungo had written: "We dreamed of a New Age born of violent insurrection. We danced on the graves of war dead in Vietnam." Mungo said the cities they had fled were "poisonous and lethal."

The lifestyle at Total Loss Farm was typical hippy. The intellectuals milked two cows. They planted a large garden. They raised chickens, fed their slops to hogs, "a kind of low maintenance animal," Professor Wizansky said, smiling with nostalgia again, an animal that "gave you a lot of meat for your money," one "you didn't have to milk." Come slaughter time, they butchered their hogs themselves. For guidance in the dying out Vermont traditions, the hippies sought advice from locals. They also ordered "how to" pamphlets—ironically, free from the federal government—on everything from candlemaking to root cellars.

Compared to most communes, Total Loss Farm stayed small. It varied from ten to seventeen members over the years. Each member had his/her own space, which was rare. And important. In more crowded quarters, not only would it have been difficult to write, but sexual tensions could literally knock the doors down. All those young bodies pulsing with hormones, often eager to mate, stoked by drugs, and, despite what the lore said, frequently as sexually competitive as any fraternity jocks at a keg party, found tight quarters, particularly in winter, tough to take. At Total Loss Farm, each member also had a special function, Wizansky said. For instance, Marty Jezer, who subsequently wrote *The Dark Ages*, a political history of the post-World War II period through the sixties, "became a wood person; he learned about trees."

In the ephemeral world of alternative living, Total Loss was exceptionally stable. "We were tight already," Wizansky explained. "We didn't have any dominant ideology. We didn't accept new people easily. We didn't have a leader."

But they did have a steady income from their published writings—another factor that set them apart. The leader of the literary pack was Mungo, a self-described "half-freaked former militant" with bad teeth and boundless energy. He banged around the back roads of Guilford in a 1959 VW. He had arrived in Guilford a little famous, having, as Wizansky mentioned, called for the impeachment of President Lyndon B. Johnson in 1967. At the time, along with Marshall Bloom, formerly the editor of *The Amherst Student*, Mungo headed the anti-establishment Liberation News

Service in Washington, D.C. The Liberation News Service was, along with the Yippies, the Students for a Democratic Society (SDS), and several other non-American Way of Life alliances of the young and vocal, intent on shaking the comfortable firmament upon which middle-class America stood, on stirring turbulence into a society just beginning to split over Vietnam. Mungo's call for President Johnson's impeachment caused ripples, both in the alternative and regular press. But soon afterwards LNS split into political factions, and Mungo, disillusioned, headed for Guilford. He set the creative pace in the drafty farmhouse. Wizansky recalled that Raymond drank coffee constantly, smoked constantly, and wrote constantly, often for long stretches late at night. "He was always getting contracts and articles and making himself famous."

Mungo's *Total Loss Farm* (an excerpt called "If Mr. Thoreau Calls, Tell Him I've Left the Country" appeared in the *Atlantic Monthly*) was published in 1970. It brought the slight, scraggly author, and the commune, national notoriety. Though longer winded and less lyrical than Richard Brautigan (he wrote *A Confederate General from Big Sur, Trout Fishing in America,* and *The Abortion,* to name three), whose domain was the West Coast, Mungo's prose had its moments. He chronicled Vermont hippydom. His readers included anxious parents who would have sold a hundred shares of blue chip stock for an insider's view of the world of their dropout kids. Mungo's view wasn't very reassuring to them. In fact, he castigated grownups for being so uptight. The wanderers and exiles of his generation weren't going to be like that. They intended to feel the wind in their hair, he wrote, listen to their hearts, know their bodies. Be free.

The famous writer was "a pretty wacky visionary," according to Fritz Hewitt, a member of the Johnson Pasture commune, which located a mile down the road in the Packer's Corners neighborhood. "And very little grounded in reality. Verandah once said that Raymond could make a walk to the beaver pond sound like a parade on the Great Wall."

To Mungo, another sixties credo, "Now is where it's at," was literary gospel. Everything in the immediate present hummed with cosmic meaning and was mythic in proportion. That included the eating of lentil soup cooked on the Home Comfort woodstove, as well as the scrutinizing of the hard, poor look of the commune farmhouse, with its pots and pans hanging from the ceiling, and its assorted dishes and cups from broken sets scattered on the big round dining-room tabletop that rested on a cider barrel. He and other members often sat in their rockers, sipping mushroom tea, talking about the psychology of Alan Watts and Wilhelm Reich, or the poetry of radicals like Allen Ginsberg. Out of the stereo speakers, a concession to technology, came classical and Middle Eastern music, as well as rock and roll (hippy writers seldom delved into the irony of the high-tech roots of the lifestyle, such as amplifiers, speakers, and laboratory-concocted drugs; they seem to have been, in retrospect, more postmodern then truly primitive, mixing the past with the future as they saw fit).

Winters were long, Wizansky admitted. But trips to Boston, visits to other communes, chores, writing—the tasks got them through. "Jesus," he said with a sudden laugh, "in the winter, that's all we did was sit around, smoke dope. We wore a lot of wool and smelled like woodsmoke and pachouli."

Wizansky, Porche, Mungo, Jezer, and the other Total Loss communards were, like the majority of hippies huddled in Vermont farmhouses, urban and suburban types who had been raised not on woodsmoke and pickled beets, but on cement sidewalks and food from the supermarket. They had memories of traffic and commuting encoded in their respective adolescences, rather than memories of roosters and the slamming looms of woolen mills. As dropouts in the country, though, they felt liberated from their collective past, which, after all, was only a recent past, a past severed from an agrarian society much like the one Vermont had perpetuated as long as any other state in America. They had traveled back to the future to get in touch with their instincts and their spontaneity, which contemporary culture, emphasizing consumption and credit and Orwellian rhetoric broadcast as truth, had prevented them from experiencing. The hippies had definite American antecedents, most notably the Hudson River School of painters and the Transcendentalist writers. Both groups had flourished a century before, when America changed from a nation of farmers to one of commerce and industry, from a place that worked the soil to one that exploited its resources. The painters, led by the English-born Thomas Cole and his pupil Frederic Church, evoked the majesty of the wilderness with big canvases suffused with the light of the Great Architect. They had thought, at least until Charles Darwin pulled mankind out of the hairy skin of the ape with the publication of *On the Origin of Species* in 1859, and the Civil War mocked the idea of a kinder America with its appalling carnage and casualty lists, that science and religion would unite to create a better world. The Transcendentalists, led by Henry David Thoreau and Ralph Waldo Emerson, though not quite so optimistic, glorified nature's elusive spirituality. Popping a tab of acid, of course, to turn leaves, ferns, and flowers into a kaleidoscope of heightened imagery, aided the hippies in feeling both godlike and a little transcendent simultaneously.

Few parents could fathom their dropout children out, however.

"Why do you want to go backwards?" Wizansky's dad once asked his son.

There was no pat answer. Twenty years later, relaxing in his comfortable home on a secluded site of Total Loss Farm circa 1990, with *Smithsonian, Harper's* and an L. L. Bean catalogue arranged neatly on a glass table by his knees, Richard Wizansky turned pensive. "Why did I want to go backwards?" he mused. "To slave, canning over a woodstove in August, canning hundreds of quarts of tomatoes, for years." He glanced at me quickly. "Not that I regret it, by the way—because I don't."

In truth, he had been swept along, a fish in a torrent, an activist in a marvelous parade. He and his peers had existed for years on a private wavelength, with their own lifestyle and spiritual wellsprings, tapped into music, high on drugs, fired by social concerns. Those times "taught American culture a lot," Wizansky said. Most hippies he knew had seen themselves as risk takers with exotic tastes, he went on, as idealists with audacity. They thought for a brief shining time, for a foolish few years, they could establish a society apart from the war-mongering United States. Compared to the students he taught in 1990, "We were much more into exploring the edge of self-destruction," he said. "We were much more interested in being educated. Not necessarily a college education—but learning about who we are and where we came from, historically. We were very concerned about what it means to be a human being."

Eventually, begrudgingly, even his father had accepted Total Loss Farm. On one of his infrequent visits, the older man had lugged a pressure cooker filled with brisket up to the farmhouse through the snow, possibly right past the ghost of Mother Honeywell.

I exited I-9I on a crisp February afternoon in 1990 and drove into Brattleboro past fast-food franchises and small malls linking the interstate with downtown. On Main Street, a corridor of nineteenth-century four-story brick buildings, I passed the corner where Governor Ernest Gibson used to hang out on Saturdays once in a while, back in the forties, chatting with Windham County shoppers. Straight ahead, on the other side of the gulley carved by Whetstone Brook, I spotted Fritz Hewitt's Queen Anne style house. It was hard to miss. Three stories, pale pink, with blue and wine trim, its single turret looked back towards Brattleboro's four tall church steeples, and also had a view across the Connecticut River towards Rattlesnake Mountain in New Hampshire. Fritz Hewitt had been one of the founders of the "Johnson Pasture," as he called it.

In his apartment on the second floor Hewitt, a thin, sallow-cheeked, friendly man in his early forties, poured himself a few fingers of bourbon, took a seat beneath a big cage holding some chirping finches, their seed husks by his feet, and said he had thought that some day history might find the story of the Johnson Pasture revealing.

He had first come to Vermont, he said, as a last hurrah to a disastrous college education. He'd been kicked out of Yale, quit the New School in New York, then failed a last try at organized learning at Mark Hopkins College—"a fraud, a waste of Dad's money," he called it—in Brattleboro. "But I didn't care about his money at the time. I went for one semester and then quit."

But before he quit, Hewitt and a couple of buddies from the "so-called college" rented a farmhouse in Guilford. They didn't call it a "commune." The word hadn't come in vogue yet. "We took in a couple of real hippies, Michael and Annie Carpenter. Michael didn't bathe at all. And he wouldn't cut his fingernails—never mind his hair. He knew about astrology, he knew about the Tarot—all those arcane sciences. We were all quite thrilled by him."

Michael Carpenter was twenty-three, Annie was pregnant. She and Michael wanted to have the child at the farm, in a manger. The delivery got complicated, though. Luckily, a doctor was visiting his literary friends at Total Loss Farm nearby. He drove over and delivered Red Pony, as the Carpenters eventually named their baby. They didn't name him Red Pony at first, Hewitt said; they wanted Red Pony to name himself. Michael and Annie soon learned, however, that it would have been a while before the child could do that.

Following the birth of Red Pony the farmhouse in Guilford became known as the Baby Farm. But Hewitt, the Carpenters, Red Pony, and the others, all wanted a commune. And fate cooperated: Michael Carpenter inherited some money. With it, the new dad bought a hundred acres of meadow and woods a mile from Total Loss Farm.

"We took a great acid trip on the new land on Groundhog Day," Hewitt said with a smile. "We wandered all over, each going our separate ways. We might run across each other and hang out a few minutes, smoke a joint, and go off in different directions again, climbing around, sliding on the snow."

Hewitt sat up sharply and grinned at me. His bourbon was gone. "Now I hold down four jobs!" He was part-owner of Colors, a gay bar in Brattleboro, the property manager for the Brattleboro Area Community Land Trust, which provided people with low-cost apartments, and occasionally did counter work at a local grocery. He never mentioned the fourth. "Paying for it!" he declared, "paying for those days!" He eased backwards, looked around at his hippyish decor of rugs and thrift-shop furniture, photos and exposed studs in a partially removed wall, a globe and a mask hung as decorations. "Well, it's okay. They were worth it. It might have been the last acid trip I ever took. But it was just beautiful. We did feel godlike that day. There was a thick crust on several feet of snow. We were three or four feet above the earth."

That spring they left the Baby Farm behind. "I will tell you I was the first to spend a night at the Johnson Pasture. Our little house was getting packed with all these people I didn't know, so I went over and I started sleeping on *the land*."

They had a big May Day celebration and then started building a place in which to live.

"We used the materials from a barn to build our little shack. We were terrible carpenters. We didn't know shit."

Although Johnson Pasture was near Total Loss Farm, the two groups didn't mingle much. "They fancied themselves as very famous," Hewitt said. "But we didn't know who the hell they were. They were up there to get away from perhaps even the likes of us. We were acid-headed flower children."

In May 1969 the flower children moved out of the Baby Farm and into the shack they had nailed together. Hewitt kept count of newcomers. That summer about four hundred of them drifted through, mostly from Queens. "They were going to stay forever. Most of them only lasted a couple weeks."

Although Michael Carpenter had bankrolled the land buy, the new dad with the long nails and hair never assumed the posture of a guru. "He had very clear ideas of what he wanted," Hewitt said. "But he did not want to impose those ideas on other people. He wanted us to come up with the ideas he already had. He wanted somebody else to lead in his name. Actually, he wanted me to. What I think is he wanted me to lead and never have a thought of my own."

It wasn't an unusual situation. On many communes a dreamy idealism based on responsible hedonism, an oxymoron if there ever was one, quickly outpaced reality. All the dreaded standards left behind in Queens and elsewhere, the responsibilities, the decisions, the obligations, threatened to capsize a fragile rural freedom. Movement and drugs often helped stave off the facts of life. The era's carrot, the tantalizing idea that caring and cooperative people living in the country could invest their lives with joy and meaning, kept the momentum strong. The backpacks and faces changed, but what poet Gary Snyder described as the countenance of the normal hippy, "a bright and tender look; calmness and gentleness, freshness and ease of manner," seemed to remain, as did the enthusiasm, at least for a while, for the alternative living scene. Most of the newcomers at Johnson Pasture, however, curious about the communes upstate and not eager to settle down, moved along.

Merchants in most Vermont towns didn't think much of the gypsy-like wanderers, whether from Guilford or elsewhere. They spent too little money. They were absurd looking, funny smelling. The voluntary poor, they could seem demeaning to the real not-so-well-off natives who sometimes looked a little like the hippies but lacked their loose indifference to a tough economic situation. A few hippies also figured out how to take advantage of Vermont's expanding social welfare system. A couple of bra-less earthmothers collecting welfare checks while their pony-tailed boyfriends waited in battered pick-ups got the locals steaming against hippies in general. "No bare feet" signs appeared at eye level on screen doors of general stores. To some disgruntled natives the hippies were undesirable throwbacks to a Vermont they wanted to eliminate. Most hippies were anti-flag and against the war in Vietnam besides.

At Johnson Pasture, a two-storied bunkhouse, fourteen by forty-two, was finally completed in late fall of 1969. Meanwhile, "a Peter-Pan boy collective in a treehouse," as Hewitt described it, came into being in Turners Falls, Massachusetts, about fifteen miles from Guilford. New members of the Brotherhood of the Spirit, as the group of teenagers was called, signed their possessions over to their leader, a take-charge kind of guy named Matellica, whom Michael Carpenter admired.

"Michael wished he had as much will to lead as this Matellica guy," Hewitt remembered.

Within a small orbit you now had three distinctly different kinds of communes: the activist, older Total Loss Farm group, the hedonistic Johnson Pasturites, and the teenage Brotherhood of the Spirit: college grads, college drop-outs, teenage followers. They were examples of the variety of communes throughout Vermont and in western Massachusetts.

At Johnson Pasture the winter dragged on. "We froze our butts off," Hewitt said. "What we didn't know would fill a library. We didn't know about cutting your firewood and letting it dry out. We didn't know what creosote was. We were just pitifully unprepared for winter."

Their uninsulated bunkhouse was heated "by one really lousy stove, a sort of donated stove. Our firewood was cut in November, and we left it in four-foot lengths. We didn't know how to split it. It was elm! We weren't allowed to kill trees on our own land. This was a gross hypocrisy. If you stepped six feet off the place, you could kill a tree. But ours were somehow holy."

Hewitt found a job at a sawmill. He walked to work, three miles, and back, daily. "I was a good Protestant ethic kind of boy. So my sixty dollars a week supported the thing, along with a few welfare checks."

As cold penetrated the tarpaper and icy temperatures froze the few cars that had started okay in July, but which now refused to even turn over, tempers grew short. With the geese gone, the leaves down, the sky leaden, the Green Mountains could be seen in their nakedness, desirous of snow. It wasn't like summer. In the warm green months of birdsong and mist, any fool could survive, any klutzy suburban refugee could make it through the night. But Vermont became herself, bared her soul, in winter. The hippies at Johnson Pasture hung on and made it through only to have their bunkhouse burn to the ground on the night of April 16. Four people, including a sixteen-year-old runaway, died. Fire trucks bogged down in the mud trying to reach the scene.

The next day the hippies, most in their early twenties, with long dirty hair and sad eyes, stared at the smoldering remains of their showerless, electricity-free flirtation with alternative living. Reporters, police, and locals hiked toward them alongside a road of churned mud. Wisps of smoke lifted off the ashes, encircled by melted snow. There was a little half-hearted talk about starting over. Reporters, notebooks in hand, approached to ask questions. When asked about the media's preoccupation, drugs, one hippy assured the reporter from the *Brattleboro Reformer* that this group had never needed drugs. "Look at that mountain," he said, shifting his eyes. "I mean I get high just by looking out at all the beauty here."

"The fire was horrible," Hewitt concluded sadly. "But people were wonderful to us." His boss at the sawmill offered free lumber to rebuild. Other folks said they'd take a hippy in. But the short and eventful life of the Johnson Pasture commune was over. The Carpenters had already left. "The place was rudderless," Hewitt said. Long meetings and personality harangues replaced the sloppy consensus-making that had preceded the fire. No one wanted to be the leader. Meetings became ordeals between the members who now occupied a second smaller building on the site. "It got hard. We wanted to have this spontaneous tribe. A group like that is a slave to whoever talks the longest. That spring I threw up my hands and quit."

For the first time since the pastoral movement of the late-nineteenth century, Vermont found itself a national image to be desired. It also felt the grip of a paradox. Here you had thousands of idealistic young people moving to the Green Mountains to live the old-fashioned lifestyle that thousands of native Vermonters had left behind. Initially, old-time tolerance prevailed because, for one thing, the hippies reminded a lot of Vermonters, often begrudgingly, of their grandparents. But there was a glitch in the comparison: few of the hippies worked. It took a dozen or so of them to run half the farm that a couple of old-fashioned Vermonters had managed by themselves. To some folks, that validated how lazy they were. Even so, there was no law against being lazy. But there was something not quite right about how free and easy they were and what they did for work. It just didn't seem they had earned the license to do what they wanted, but had often inherited a presumptuousness that license was a God-given right.

The authorities tended to leave the communes alone. The attitude was that if the dropouts wanted to isolate themselves, and do stupid things like cut up their expensive clothes and braid them into rugs to keep their feet warm, so be it.

Talk about orgies and free love bothered some natives, too. Just grabbing anything with hair and rolling in the hay, like the hippies were said to do, smacked of moral depravity, not to mention the barnyard. And raising kids without any rules—how was that going to turn out? As for their "natural" gardening, everybody with half a brain knew you needed chemicals to keep the bugs from eating your tomatoes. Well then, maybe not if you had a half dozen people to fuss over the garden every day. But who, besides hippies, could do that?

Perceptions of hippies as lazy, loaded, and libidinous, yet earthy, old-fashioned, and non-material fueled the paradox of their coming. And the orgies popularized by the media did occur, but nowhere near as often as both hedonists and moralists thought. Drug use, though, that was a different story.

Drugs and music were the two favored teachers of this generation that had rejected the Establishment, in which college and a decent job were fundamental buttresses. Mescaline, peyote, psylocybin, LSD, and other mind-expanding and mood-altering drugs were their buttresses. Drugs, as touted by the likes of writers and artists and musicians, were seen as the doors to wisdom and insight. Getting high allowed you to transcend America's stifled spirituality. LSD in particular was the counterculture's wafer of communion, his/her transcendent religious ticket: a quick drop over the edge of reality. Possibly even a confrontation with God, whether as a human or an animal or a power. On LSD you might feel the depth of the universe, laugh from the core of your soul, watch in awe as your hands dissolved, or, if unready for the drug's power, flip out and become a basket case, psychologically unraveling like a ball of yarn terrorized by kitten paws, which then might transform into lion claws puncturing your throat. In Vermont, a few communes forbade drug use altogether. They, however, did not get much press. Marijuana—called Mary Jane, pot, dope, reefer, and a dozen other names—was usually as available as water. A few seeds tossed into the compost heap and, presto!—by fall, seven-foot plants waved in the breeze. Hippies dried their plants over their woodstoves, then rolled the marijuana into joints, baked it into brownies, steeped it in teapots.

Although the intellectual group at Total Loss Farm might devour books while sipping their tea, most hippies put music on a higher shelf than literature. They listened and swayed a lot more than they sat and read. Lyrics of some popular songs were laced with nuances only the young, having dropped out and tuned in, understood. For instance, Grace Slick of the Jefferson Airplane sang about White Rabbit from *Alice in Wonderland* and urged listeners to remember what the dormouse said: "Feed your head! Feed your head!" The Beatles sang, "Lucy in the Sky with Diamonds," a homage to LSD, initialed in the title and carried along throughout the fantasy tune with a whimsical seriousness that few adults ever deciphered. Along with the Beatles and the Jefferson Airplane, the Rolling Stones, the Who, the Byrds, the Purple Haze, the Turtles, and other groups with names that dumbfounded adults captured the attention of the young. Bob Dylan, taking his name from the Welsh poet, Dylan Thomas, was the pied piper of the hippy generation. His songs of alienation, plaintive regret, and poetic rebellion, sung in a voice that few parents would ever mistake as melodic, were counterculture anthems.

Popular songs, electrically charged and often rebellious, played on FM stations that had neither playlists nor rigid formats. Across Vermont, not only hippies listened to this music. College kids, ski bums, high school students, and young people on their way to work tuned in, too. Their parents might still be moved by Pat Boone or Frank Sinatra, but the kids longed to hear the Rolling Stones sing "Ruby Tuesday," Aretha Franklin belt out "Respect," Simon and Garfunkel do "Bridge Over Troubled Water." Lyrics often told these listeners that politicians ignored the young and supported evil causes, that they refused to listen or communicate. The group Crosby, Stills, Nash and Young turned charged rock into moving ballads that touched the nerve endings of the tumultuous times. "Letting my freak flag fly" meant not getting a haircut. "The feeling you get when looking in the mirror and seeing a police car" was paranoia.

It's probably just as well that a political manifesto called "Jamestown Seventy," written by James Blumstein and James Phelan, two Yale Law School graduates, was never put to music. If it had been, the merchants, natives, and their elected authorities across Vermont, and the hippies and their flower-power illusions, might have dropped their often strained tolerance and cordiality and gone at it.

The "Jamestown Seventy" advocated a mass migration of young people to a sparsely populated state to take it over in a conventional fashion, through the political process. Vermont, with 288,000 voters in a population of 445,000 in 1970, had 108,000 young people between the ages of eighteen and twenty-four. Therefore, it seemed like an ideal place to test the thesis. In his article, "Taking Over Vermont," which appeared in *Playboy* in April 1972, Richard Pollack posed a question prompted by "Jamestown Seventy." What if enough anti-establishment youth moved to the Green Mountains, took advantage   state's brief ninety-day residency requirement, and did usurp

Far-fetched? Probably, g   : fact the hippies were a very loose affiliation. Few communes we   litical as Total Loss Farm. But Vermont was within easy hitchhiking distance of about forty million potential drop-outs, Pollack reminded readers. In 1970 "be-ins" and anti-war rallies were routinely drawing 100,000 of the baby-boom generation.

"The goal of the takeover would be to establish a truly experimental society in which new solutions to today's problems could be tried," Blumstein and Phelan wrote.

Even if the hippies didn't all register to vote, elect one of their own as governor of Vermont, and turn the statehouse lawn in Montpelier into one big love-in, with Bob Dylan singing and Timothy Leary preaching and Raymond Mungo taking notes, many did vote later on, when they began to integrate into the towns and villages across the state. A large percentage of them had a flirtatious relationship with Vermont's Democratic party. The conservatism of the core of the Democratic organization, which for one thing supported the Vietnam war, alienated most of them, however. The disenchanted helped jump start several political alternatives, including the Liberty Union party, and set the stage for the ascent of an unlikely Vermont hero, a Brooklyn-born Jewish socialist named Bernard Sanders. Under the Liberty Union banner Sanders, thirty, a true believer in the potential of political change, first ran for the U.S. Congress in 1972. He got 1,571 votes. But he'd be back.

ACT 250

People all over the state were asking these environmental questions. It awakened me to a problem.
—Former Governor Deane C. Davis, in 1989, remembering the origins of Act 250

*I*n early 1969 newly elected Governor Deane Davis got a call from Bill Schmidt, the director of the Windham Regional Planning and Development Commission. Schmidt, Davis recalled, sounded like "an earnest environmentalist." He invited the governor to have breakfast with members of the Windham Commission when he came to Brattleboro for Governor's Day. They wanted to talk to the governor about growth and development.

Deane Davis was not an environmentalist. Not yet anyhow. If pinned down, the shrewd, big-eared country lawyer probably would have labeled himself "an outdoorsman" or "a sportsman." He had fished ever since his boyhood in Barre. He liked to hunt. Or used to like to. The last few decades he had been so busy as a lawyer, judge, businessman, and Republican power broker that he didn't have much time to tramp around the woods in the fall with a rifle. During his recent race for governor, however, traveling around to Vermont's towns and villages on a low-budget campaign (he spent six thousand dollars in the primary, then thirty-five thousand dollars in the general election), Davis had learned something new: there were thousands of environmentalists out there. In fact, they seemed to outnumber the sportsmen. They sure seemed more vocal. And they had dozens of fledgling organizations, practically all of which were worried about growth and development, just like Bill Schmidt and the Windham Commission.

Governor's Day, during which Schmidt hoped to gain Davis's ear, was an event Davis used to vacate Montpelier and mix with the people. An old-fashioned politician, he liked to press the flesh and talk to voters. He was rare in other ways as well. Davis had never held any major elected office before being chosen governor, and he seemed to have stowed his ego somewhere besides the governor's office. He also had learned not to make too much of himself and insisted, at age sixty-nine, that he still had plenty to learn. A Governor's Day was Davis's grassroots schooling. After all the scheduled tours, the hand-shaking, and the speeches, he made sure there was ample time left over for a leisurely question and answer session. Recalling those sessons, Davis told me during several talks we had the last year of his life, "I learned more from the questions than they did from the answers, I'm sure."

As for relieving the worries of environmentalists like Bill Schmidt, on first glance Davis didn't seem like the right governor to do it. He was a lifelong conservative. He had run because "I was kind of bored [he had recently retired as president of National Life Insurance Company of Vermont]. And every man, particularly if he's bored, is a good subject for thinking he can do something good for the state." The environment had not even been on his agenda. Davis campaigned against Rutland Democrat John Daley on the old Republican standby of fiscal responsibility, lambasting welfare programs and excess spending, which had left Vermont with a seven million dollar deficit.

Once in office, Davis fooled people. He showed he had wisdom that went beyond partisan politics. In his consciousness a taproot seemed to pass back through the decades and sink directly into the populist concerns of the old liberal wing of the Republican Party, the Aiken-Gibson wing. He also knew the ins and outs of government (he had chaired the Little Hoover Commission of the late fifties, which identified administrative inefficiencies, setting the stage for the super agencies that Davis would introduce to state government during his second term). And it didn't take Davis long, after getting elected for a first term, to figure out the fundamental conflict of the times. It was not welfare or taxes or education, but rather the clash between economic growth and what he called the Vermont scene: "deer in the fields, open and beautiful countryside, the Green Mountains skyline, sunrise over Lake Memphremagog and sunset over Lake Champlain.

"The question is, my friends," as he told the legislature in 1970, "can we preserve it?"

It was a tough question.

While the hippies had been glorifying the land and the ski bums romancing the snow, a much smaller group had been turning land and snow into profits. They were the developers, opportunists both big and small who saw land and snow, made accessible by the interstates, as the ingredients of a profitable recipe. All they had to do was supply housing. Vermont's natural allure would do the rest.

Until the late sixties, before the second-home market proved it could handle big numbers, Vermont's tradition of hands off business, combined with its respect for the sanctity of private property, had allowed a land owner to do just about whatever he or she wanted with property, whether one acre or a thousand. But projects had tended to be small: a few second homes, a lodge, a restaurant. Once big operators and speculators moved in to take advantage of a growing market, things changed considerably. To many folks, and particularly to those who had come to Vermont to get away from places whose identities had changed so fast that they had felt dislocated, the boom was unsettling.

In 1968, for instance, three major development projects appeared on drawing boards in Windham County. One was Haystack Mountain, a ski area with two thousand housing units and a golf course. The second was a smoke-and-mirror scheme concocted by three guys from Connecticut who bought two thousand acres in the Whitingham area. With the consent of the selectmen and using a little false advertising (they took pictures of Harriman Reservoir in Wilmington and said their lots were on this lake), the threesome had devised a twenty-one-hundred-home development. The third project, Dover Hills—three thousand one-acre lots, a seventy-acre lake, and a golf course—came from the Cavanaugh Corporation, a major Florida real estate development firm. The Cavanaugh Corporation had bought Vermont Lumber Corporation, an entity that had little to do with chainsaws and skidders, but did own eighteen thousand acres. Five thousand of them were in West Dover, a couple of miles from Mount Snow.

Yet these three large projects paled compared to what was going on in Quechee, my old hometown. There, a combination of increasing property taxes, few jobs, and apathy had made the down-on-its-luck village so vulnerable that a developer named John Davidson systematically bought practically everything, intending to metamorphosize Quechee into a multi-million dollar second-home mecca. To his credit, Davidson, thirty-eight, acknowledged the conflict between Quechee's recent past and its envisioned future. "Instead of those Holsteins," he told a reporter from *Yankee* magazine, as they looked down at the village from a high field, "gentlemen farmers will be keeping horses. Instead of that cornfield, there'll be a lake. Which is better? I don't know."

A lot of people scattered throughout the state thought they did know. A growing number of them were waking up to Vermont's beauty, vulnerability, and destruction, and spearheading the state's environmental movement. Even more pervasively than the counterculture movement that had preceded it and from whose ranks it heavily recruited, the environmental movement became an American phenomenon that focused a disproportionate amount of attention on Vermont, a small state where conflicting values and visions grappled over the future against a picturesque backdrop of mountains and farms. Heightening the drama were low wages, limited job opportunities, and a substantial population of the not-so-well-off whose climb up the economic ladder often seemed threatened by environmental protection championed most loudly by the educated and well-off.

"The environment was certainly on people's minds," Bill Schmidt told me when we talked at his farm in Dummerston in early 1990. Back in 1968, when he had been the director of the Windham Regional Planning and Development Commission, the environmental movement had been in its infancy. Problems then, he said, "were much more black and white." They included obvious things, like sewage from badly planned septic systems seeping into streams and poorly designed roads eroding hillsides. Many of the problems were associated with big developments sited on large chunks of pastoral countryside within sight of ski trails draped over mountaintops. "There just weren't standards for developers to meet," Schmidt said. "So they took the path of least resistance and didn't do what they should have done."

Cavanaugh Corporation's Dover Hills project captured a lion's share of attention because of its size and density: three thousand lots on five thousand acres. The principals, a Florida real estate trader and a Harvard professor/land planner, had hired a sales team whose philosophy was simple: a lot was a lot—Florida, California, Vermont, it didn't matter. The sales group advertised and held parties. Prospects gathered at Holiday Inns and other hotels in the Northeast, three couples to a table, a salesperson at each table, chicken and peas and potatoes, with spumoni for dessert, wine. The wine-and-dine strategy concluded with a visit to West Dover if you were a good prospect. But none of the marketing strategy seemed to work. So the real estate trader and the professor had called Don Albano, twenty-nine, a real estate hotshot—silk suits, sunglasses, tasseled loafers—who was selling land in Florida. Lots of land. Would he go to Vermont and find out what was wrong? Albano, though raised in Springfield, Massachusetts, had never stepped foot in the neighboring state to the north. He thought of Vermont, he thought of cows. He thought of three thousand lots, he thought of peanuts. In Florida "I was used to a hundred thousand lots," he said.

But Albano took the job. He was engaged, thought it'd be different. He arrived in West Dover and lost his composure. Vermont awed him: its beauty, its people, its phone system. "I picked up the telephone and there was no direct dial," Albano remembered more than twenty years later, still sounding incredulous. "I had to introduce myself and tell them where I wanted to call. And for two months after that—you know, I have a unique voice, it has a resonance—for months after that I'd only pick up the phone and they'd say, 'Okay Don.' I mean, they recognized me! I felt like part of something. Not lost, like you did in New York and Miami, where you became a face and number.

"So I got rid of my sunglasses, I got rid of my silk suits." Yet Albano never completely adjusted. He kept his loafers, never bought any Sorels. But he had found home. "In my soul was a need to be in a rural area," he said.

Once Albano analyzed the situation at Dover Hills he reported back to Cavanaugh Corporation that the reason lots weren't selling was that they were priced from five thousand to thirteen thousand dollars each, with seventy-five percent of that attributable to cost of sales—all that chicken, spumoni, and sales talk in Holiday Inns—while you could get the same lot for between one and two thousand dollars from realtors and farmers nearby.

So there you had it: the gap in price between the big business way to do it and the old-fashioned little guy way. But the gap closed. The big guys wanted their lots to sell, so they lowered prices. The little guys, caught up in the idea (and often in the need) to capitalize on land, which was becoming a commodity instead of the life force to which their forebears had been tethered like trees to the soil, wanted to make better profits, too, as they presumed the big guys were making. So the little guys raised prices.

In some villages as developments both large and small spread down mountainsides and into commercial districts services became overloaded. Selectmen and work crews weren't used to dealing with the hurdles and challenges of rapid growth. Problem-solving took time and money. Often those who caused the problems were charming and persuasive. And there was always the old saw: "this will broaden the tax base." Common sense frequently took a back seat to legal maneuvering and a lack of specific regulations. Developers tended to do only what they had to do.

Changes in ski towns such as Stratton, Manchester, Stowe, and Waitsfield were palpable. To some people, they carried the pleasing aroma of money. To others the stink of greed. No matter how you looked at it, the great white horse of tourism and recreation, long championed as a clean and impact-free alternative to manufacturing, was romping friskily, occasionally urinating where it pleased, and growing bigger by the season as it foraged on the landscape. No place was the presence of this runaway horse felt more intensely than in Windham County, the gateway to southern Vermont and the home of a number of big ski areas and numerous speculative schemes, both grandiose and modest.

What was happening in Windham County highlighted the conflicts inherent in the cultural crossfire of rapid growth. When somebody came along, bought a house in a town from a family who had lived there for generations, then sold it for double that price a year later, it irritated folks. When newcomers who had been all gushy about how wonderful it was to move onto a dirt road complained loudly about the snowdrifts in January, snowdrifts that had collected on the same corner for as far back as the road commissioner could remember, that road commissioner could lose his patience. When an articulate new family in town praised the picturesque architecture of the village school in the fall and then criticized the weak curriculum in the spring, noting that subjects like these would never get Jeffrey into Amherst, the school board members could get a little curt. These were cultural clashes, introducing those with great expectations to those with stoic reservations about just who in the world these newcomers thought they were. For the most part town officials and boards didn't know how to mitigate problems, nor did they receive much in the way of help from the state. Neither bureaucrats nor legislators seemed willing to hobble the great white horse that was so obviously revitalizing the state's economy with its vigor and zest.

The tradeoffs for new jobs and opportunities were many. A flood of newcomers primed a town's economic pump while undermining community identity, which drew on trust, neighborliness, and collective memory. Yet the newcomers also brought money, ideas, enthusiasm. They restored barns, houses. They often infused the cynical with optimism, nudged substandard school systems towards change, supported cultural events that otherwise would never have occurred.

Many newcomers hungered for a sense of belonging to a community. Yet the very presence of too many new people like themselves made it almost impossible, at least in as short a time as they hoped it might happen. This was a second paradox of an evolving Vermont. At the very core of community life was the concept of knowing one another and one another's families and one another's churches, schools, histories. Of recalling the talk you'd had three years ago about so and so's uncle who used to be your grandfather's pal. All this invisible intertwining of social and historical webs that underlay the surface of a Vermont town, the way roots held a tree to the earth, was as real as rain but as little understood as why birds migrate. And it, more than the village green, the church spires, and the grand list, made a town what it was. Once severed, it left a place adrift, struggling for a new, and often suburban-modified, identity.

No place was there more change going on than in Windham County. And Bill Schmidt was in charge of something frightfully new there: planning. Although the hippies in Guilford might have thought that by fleeing to the Green Mountains they had left mainstream America behind, Schmidt knew better. With projects like Dover Hills, Haystack Mountain, and the fly-by-night Whitingham scheme underway, and dozens of lesser ones going forward simultaneously, real estate was hot. The situation was driving prices up, locals out, and planners like himself to distraction. The term "runaway growth" came into fashion. Relative to the dormant real estate market of the previous hundred years, what was going on did somewhat warrant the use of hyperbole.

One force Schmidt and the Windham Commission did have on their side was the Vermont Municipal Regional Planning and Development Act. Passed in 1965 by the Hoff administration, the act foresaw the need for planning to counterbalance growth. It called for, but did not mandate, regional planning and development commissions. The first regional commission was the Ottauquechee Planning and Development Commission, which eventually worked with Davidson and his Quechee Lakes project. The Windham Commission was the second. A commission's purpose was basically twofold. It advised selectmen on writing town plans, and it educated people about the value of planning, showing how developments, taxes, school growth, roads, quality of life, and a host of other variables were all interconnected.

Schmidt, a soft-spoken New Yorker who had moved to Vermont in the early sixties, worked his way up the chain of command of the Windham Commission. In 1965 he had been Putney's representative. Then he had become the commission secretary. In 1968 he was named director. Schmidt had a philosophical cast of mind and a keen feel for the erosion of such traditional Vermont benchmarks as thriftiness, which he saw becoming almost immoral in some communities, and ethics, which were becoming debatable to an alarming number of people.

At this time the development scene in Vermont looked wide open. It was populated with a wide cast of characters, from the native who didn't think any restrictions on growth should apply to him because he had lived here a long time, to the shyster who seemed to be a reincarnation of the Vegamatic salesman at the Tunbridge World's Fair, to Don Albano who soon went to bat for Act 250, Vermont's first-in-the-nation environmental control law.

When Brattleboro's Governor's Day arrived in May of 1969, Governor Davis showed up at the Theater Motel early in the morning to have breakfast as planned. "We talked to the governor for twenty minutes, half an hour," Schmidt remembered. "We had some flip charts. He started asking questions, and he had some people with him who started asking questions. He was obviously very interested. You could tell the man was doing more than just putting in an appearance. At the close of the meeting, he said, 'I'm really interested in this subject. I'd like to see these problems you're talking about. I'd like to come back in a week or two and have you take me around to Dover and Wilmington.' So two weeks later, he came back and spent a whole day with us. He met with Wilmington selectmen and listers in the morning, toured Wilmington developments, and then went to the Skyline Restaurant in Marlboro for lunch, then went through a lot of developments in Dover, and then had a big dinner gathering at the Red Mill in Wilmington."

Recalling the day more than twenty years later, Deane Davis said, "I found that these developments were being built on the most improper basis," he told me. "I mean, on hillsides where there was very fragile soil. The roads that they had to them were the kind of roads that you could never get a school bus around. And, of course, the history of second-home development is that a lot of them do come to be permanent homes, and it becomes the responsibility of the town to educate the kids, and also to keep up the roads, to plow the roads—that sort of thing. In Wilmington, I found one development where the sewage was running right onto the highway. See, in a lot of those places, you couldn't put in a septic system. In Dover, they had one development where the technique they used was to put up a lot number on each one of these acre pieces of land—189, 190 and so on. You added up these lot numbers, you would find that on that one development, if every lot was developed, there would be more houses in Dover than there were in Brattleboro."

At the Red Mill in Wilmington about a hundred people—developers, town officials, real estate brokers, planners, and interested citizens—sat down for dinner after Davis's tour, then listened to him talk.

"It was fascinating to me," Schmidt recalled. "The man just viscerally opened up. I mean, this obviously was a whole new subject to him. He wasn't aware of it at all."

Davis suggested an interim development task force to take a look at what was going on.

"So, two weeks later," Schmidt continued, "in June, when we had our annual meeting, he came back again. He announced the appointment of this task force. The first development that it would deal with would be the proposed Haystack development in Wilmington. So he, you know, was a man who listened. But he was also eager to take immediate action.

"If you want to pinpoint an origin of Act 250," Schmidt contended, referring to the major legislation that Davis would soon initiate, "it was in his visits."

*T*hat fall Davis called a statewide conference to gauge Vermonters' support for environmental legislation. Wisconsin had, in 1964, passed a one-cent-per-gallon tax on gasoline and was using the proceeds to buy wetlands and scenic areas around water and on ridges, and Vermont had, again during Hoff's administration, passed Act 3333, which eliminated billboards. But no state had yet passed a broad, visionary environmental law that recognized land, water, and natural resources as being equals of capital, progress, and change. More than five hundred people came to the statehouse for the conference at which environmental author/activist Barry Commoner spoke and out of which emerged one overriding and unifying concern: the governor should appoint a commission on the environment and hear their recommendations.

"Well, that gave me my chance," Davis said.

He issued Executive Order No. 7, which created a Commission on Environmental Control, and named Republican Arthur Gibb of Weybridge to head it. Davis appointed both liberals and conservatives to the so-called Gibb Commission with the charge that they study two specific types of environmental impacts, those that caused esthetic change and those that affected ecological balance. The former included hillside junkyards, roadside litter, slum housing, and landscape blight. The latter included chemicals and pesticides, which were washed off farmers' fields (practically all farmers now relied to some extent on commercial pesticides and fertilizers to kill pests and to supplement nutrients in soils). The commission also named goals that Vermont should strive towards, including the optimum use of resources, a plan to minimize damage from development, a statewide land use plan, and the creation of a permanent environmental agency.

That fall and winter legislators and staff of the Gibb commission traveled back and forth to the Wilmington/Dover area of Windham County. They wanted to have a look at what Vermont's future might be like if a hands-off development policy prevailed. The Gibb Commission Report, finalized before the 1970 session of the legislature, cut straight to the heart of the matter: the accelerating loss of open spaces, the health threat posed by excessive pesticides and fertilizers, and shoddy development, often by large corporations with little attachment to Vermont and with no guidelines to control them, were irreparably altering the landscape.

When the legislative session opened, an environmental control law labeled Act 250 quickly came into being. It moved through committees fast.

"That whole scene, that seventies session," Schmidt remembered "was a watershed on environmental legislation: Act 250, Act 252, the Water Quality Bill. There was a whole range of legislation. It was just amazing."

To push Act 250 through Davis did a lot of what he called "personal politicking." His assistant, Elbert "Al" Moulton, a humpty-dumptyish fellow who had emerged as a power broker in state government after having managed the Brattleboro Chamber of Commerce, been Hoff's commisioner of development for several years, and chaired the Vermont Republican State Committee, gave Davis a hand. "Al was very popular with the legislators," Davis said. "He knew practically all of them one way or the other. He was a big help, because he would normally be on the other side because of his experience as a developer." As for the opposition to the act, Davis conceded with a laugh, "I think we overwhelmed them, to be honest with you."

The first major land development control act in America, Act 250 listed ten criteria for judging the impact of a development. Nine district environmental commissions were established to apply the criteria around the state. Each district had a trained coordinator as its point man, someone who determined whether a project needed an Act 250 permit, whether the paperwork was complete, and, finally, wrote the permit if approval was forthcoming by the three-member district commission based on the ten criteria. The first criterion, air and water pollution, proved to be a major obstacle for developers. So was criterion six, which dealt with impacts on schools, criterion eight, esthetic impact, and criterion nine-B, which analyzed a project's effect on agricultural soils. If a project permit was denied on the regional level, it could be appealed before the State Environmental Board, a nine-member body made up of one representative from each of the districts.

Never very well understood by most Vermonters was the fact that a crucial part of Davis's environmental-protection vision, the statewide land use plan, never made it into law. "Here, the legislature passes the act and tells the governor to get a plan for the whole state," Davis told me with a rare touch of bitterness. "And we bring it in. And they won't pass it."

Conservative forces in the legislature, having endorsed a law that regulated development, balked at the statewide plan. Governor Davis, who had seemed downright avuncular to many legislators compared to the high-strung Phil Hoff, had momentarily disarmed them with his simple language, country wit, and charm. All during the passage of what was now a broader law than they had realized, he hadn't even seemed in a rush. But the conservatives suddenly realized they had undermined the fundamental right of being able to do what you wanted with your property. So they gulped and said hold it right here. They were vocally supported by some large landowners and by a group in the Northeast Kingdom, the Landowners Steering Committee, who had vehemently opposed Act 250 from the start. Davis and his forces countered that without the statewide plan, Act 250 would have only one leg to stand on. And with only one leg it couldn't look with balance at all regions of the state. It would limp along, applying a different yardstick to like situations in different counties. In other words, it would become too subjective. Fine with us, the conservatives replied. Let it limp. We don't want the same yardstick applied to, say, Sutton, in the Northeast Kingdom as we want applied to Stratton, one of the richest villages in Vermont.

To Schmidt, one-legged environmental legislation was a shame. For a brief time, he remembered wistfully almost two decades after Act 250 became law, the potential for statewide planning had been in place because of the newly organized central planning office that came into being. The momentum had been there, Schmidt said, the legal mechanisms in place, people eager. Back in 1970 voters' attitudes toward state initiatives had been positive, and Vermont was momentarily riding the crest of the national environmental wave. Vermonters were thinking positively about "how Vermont might grow and develop," Schmidt remembered. "With growth centers and a lot of the stuff you hear about now. So there was that kind of mentality. People thinking in statewide terms, not just piecemeal."

The statewide plan had hung on for a while. But then slowly expired, like a trout out of water, gasping futilely for air. Davis's successor, Democrat Tom Salmon, tried to revive it in 1973. He named a Commission on Land Planning. Members included Bill Schmidt, Don Albano, Leonard Wilson, who was chairman of the State Environmental Board under Salmon, environmental lawyer Jonathan Brownell, and others. By then Albano had become a developer/environmentalist. He had determined it was wiser to work with Vermont's formidable array of vocal environmentalists than to butt heads. Besides, he said, the ten criteria struck him, at least if administered sensibly, as reasonable. As the black-hat-wearing member of Salmon's Commission on Land Planning, Albano traveled with the other members to various towns, meeting the public, urging support for the statewide plan. But it was too late. Act 250 had to learn to live with its limp. The public hardly noticed. Their attention had shifted to rising oil and gas prices and to interest rates, which kept pace with prices.

The first oil crisis had hit in late 1973. If it had been twenty years earlier, most Vermonters on their farms and in their villages probably would have cut some extra firewood, canned more vegetables, and watched the rest of America get uptight. But times had changed. Few folks had chickens anymore, or woodstoves, or canned much, for that matter. The hippies, their philosophy finally born out, had fallen apart as a viable movement. People talked relentlessly about raising chickens, installing woodstoves, and buying cars that got thirty miles on a gallon. The legislature decided that environmental considerations were hurting people's pocketbooks. It sent the statewide land-use leg of Act 250 to its grave.

Over the next few years Albano's sympathy towards Act 250 gradually waned as well, not because of the criteria but because of the way they were enforced. Albano had never viewed developers as guileful cutthroats out only for a fast buck, yet acknowledged that they needed guidelines. By the mid-seventies, however, "the bureaucrats started taking over the law," he claimed. Toward the end of the decade Albano attended a meeting where the state showed a film demonstrating unscrupulous land development. To his dismay the film starred Dover Hills, his defunct project conceived by the Florida land trader and the Harvard professor/land planner. "It was a scare tactic," he said, "a disturbing trend."

I visited Don Albano in early 1990. He was no longer involved in development. A portly, middle-aged man with a resounding voice, and still wearing loafers, he published the *Deerfield Valley News*, a weekly whose offices were tucked in a little shopping strip a couple of miles from Mount Snow.

"Major developers will not come to Vermont today," he told me earnestly. Act 250 remained a sound law, but it had "become a bureaucratic administrative nightmare." Paperwork had tripled. Inexperienced personnel new to power could shut down major projects they didn't even understand. The bureaucrats had "put Vermont on a high horse coming to the rescue of the small towns, like West Dover."

Bill Schmidt was not so hard on the law, but recognized shortcomings. The biggest problem was that Act 250 became perceived as a planning law, he said, when in fact the planning leg had withered away and died. Act 250 was regulation, pure and simple. Yet, by the late 1980s, Act 250 had taken on a Big Brother image. Times had changed drastically from the days when Deane Davis came down to Brattleboro, got an earful, and responded from the heart. Suspicion towards government had become a state pastime, Schmidt said, and the broad view had narrowed. The 1990s would be a land trust movement era, he thought, because land trusts worked individually and cooperatively with landowners, rather than regulating what they could do. For the private landowner, the present reality was that he/she had lost faith in the state's ability to handle property with regulations.

Regardless, Act 250 remained Vermont's primary growth and development law. Deane Davis still saw the law associated with his name as "merely a method of reorganizing the planning function." There are always problems, he said, "when each individual's own interest conflicts with the good of all."

KILLINGS

It was colder than hell. I got called to go to Cabot.
Three bodies had been found in a house.
—*Detective Sergeant Nelson Lay recalling a 1968
homicide*

Whearen Deane Davis left office in January 1973
Vermont certainly was a much different place than it had been ten years
before. It had become desired, populated most everywhere with newcomers, aware of its preciousness, and more than ever severed from its agrarian
roots. Yet Vermont hadn't damaged its allure, its rural magic. To many
urbanites, weary of where they were and eager to live in the country,
Vermont remained a last recalcitrant rural bastion of nineteenth-century
independence, community, and integrity—in other words, the perfect place
to dream about moving to.

Understandably, few of them knew the dark side of the Vermont dream
had bloomed eerily during the flower power years, 1967 and 1968. But over
eighteen months, instead of the three, maybe four, homicides that were
normal, more than twenty had occurred. The rash of killings startled,
fascinated, and frightened people. It prompted an aside: "Just like New
York." Yet most folks looked at the violence somewhat askance, as an
aberration, a quick blip on an otherwise peaceful pastoral screen, rather
than as a symptom of a deeper malaise. The killings carried a message
nevertheless. They said that more than politics and economics in the Green
Mountains were modernizing. The Vermont psyche, the Vermont soul, the
Vermont character were being buffeted by twentieth-century forces which
previous generations, working on their isolated farms and in their mill
villages, had not been subjected to. Forces having a cumulative effect
included the pervasive counterculture, the loss of thousands of farms with
their isolation and protection, the breakdown of families, and the war in

Vietnam, which was beginning to bitterly divide generations in the same household.

The Vermont Bureau of Criminal Investigation (BCI), which handled all murders, had its hands full. "You'd get done with one," recalled former BCI Detective Sergeant Nelson Lay of Sutton, "another would pop up."

Lay had been a member of the BCI since its inception in 1959, following the murder of Orville Gibson. Gibson, a prosperous Newbury farmer, had been blackjacked while entering his barn to do chores at 4:30 A.M., dragged to a car, hog-tied and trussed, driven around in the trunk, then dumped into the Connecticut River from a bridge, wrists behind his back. Various law enforcement agencies, including the local sheriff's department, the Vermont State Police, the attorney general's office, and police from New Hampshire (they got involved because the coroner said Gibson had been breathing before he went into the river, which was in New Hampshire's domain), all descended on the scene, messing up each other's leads and bungling the case. It became a classic example of a crime in which the locals seemed to know the culprits but the authorities could get no one to talk. Although two locals were tried for the crime, neither was convicted.

After the bungled affair, which got embarrassingly broad press coverage, Vermont started the BCI to insure such debacles, hopefully, became a thing of the past. An arm of the Vermont State Police, the BCI originally numbered five plainsclothesmen, most of whom, like Nelson Lay, carried snub-nosed .38s. The officers were specially trained in such police arcana as forensics, autopsy exams, and the use of mockups to detect the most obscure clues. Members attended polygraph school in Chicago. They went to a two-week school at Harvard where the training focused on the right mindset for good murder investigating. The apropos mindset, a retired Nelson Lay told me, was one imbued with patience, keen powers of observation, and methodical stick-to-it-ness. At the two schools, he added, BCI detectives made close contacts with big-city professionals, like the chief of detectives of Chicago. "We learned a lot from being with these people who weren't small-time cops," he confessed, "like we were."

The small-time cops in Vermont put their new talents to use on limited homicides during the early and mid-sixties. The rare killings allowed most Vermonters to deal with the particulars of each case, to dwell on motives, to ultimately sympathize with the victims caught in the ripples of tragedy that always radiate from murder. But in the late sixties, when the killings suddenly quadrupled, this kind of collective and healthy grieving became a luxury of the past.

When the homicides increased, many of them seemed senseless and perverse. They frequently involved juveniles. In Rochester, for instance, in a big old house, a fifteen-year-old shot his parents as they slept in separate rooms after the family returned from the drive-in. The boy hauled both bodies up to the attic, an almost superhuman feat given his small size. BCI Detective Elton Hislop discovered them there, back beneath the eaves. "There were cobwebs and everything," Hislop said, describing what he'd seen. "It was like Frankenstein." The juvenile's motive for killing his parents? "They bugged him."

The Hipps, an elderly couple from Florida, pulled their travel trailer into a rest area by the Barre dump one afternoon in the summer of 1968. Their killer smashed both the Hipps with a hammer, slashed her throat, breasts and pubic area, then hauled the trailer, leaving the Hipps' two poodles tied to a tree in the rest area, to Calais, where police later found it, the bodies inside. No one was ever tried.

One cold morning in November 1968 Detective Lay got a call to go to Cabot. Three bodies had been discovered in a farmhouse. At the scene Lay and State Trooper Ed Fish shoved their way in. A two-year-old boy was frozen, his bloody footprints patterning the floor around the body of his mother, who was naked. Her common-law husband, a much older man with, as Lay phrased it, "a healthy criminal record," was slumped over the table. One of the man's sons had done it, "pissed off because the father had taken off with this woman," Lay said. A second son, and his girlfriend, had been accomplices. "They drove all the way up from Randolph to pull this shenanigan," Lay recalled. "They weren't drunk."

"Woodchucks," seethed Hislop, describing people who would leave a child to freeze to death. "Just didn't give a shit."

Lay, Hislop, and a third member of the BCI from that era, James Ryan, who later served as director of the state police between 1978 and 1984, blamed the increases in killings and of violent crimes in all categories, which escalated throughout the seventies in Vermont and across America, on the liberal Earl Warren-led Supreme Court and the permissiveness of the sixties. Safeguards passed by the court made criminals less afraid of getting caught, Hislop and Ryan told me on separate occasions. The safeguards included the Miranda ruling, which said a cop had to explain a suspect's rights to him immediately upon arrest, free public defenders for the poor, lighter sentences, and probable cause to justify a search warrant and seizure of property.

In the wake of the Warren court, Vermont's cops had "to live with police screw-ups in New York City," Hislop said. Yet the new rules were a consequence of urban realities, he added, not rural ones. The rules got forced on rural Vermont, undermining traditional respect for the law.

"Sure, we used to pull some stunts," Hislop, a lifetime veteran of law enforcement, admitted in the spring of 1990, when he was still doing some part-time sheriff's work in Montpelier. "But they worked. People used to have a little fear of policemen and the law."

Even the "unwashed troublemakers," as some natives began calling the hippies in the early seventies had found themselves exposed to the dark side of their Vermont pipe dream. Runaways, radicals chased by the FBI, drug use and sales, and the lifestyle in general brought increased surveillance. Earth People's Park, a sprawling commune in Norton, far up in the Northeast Kingdom, where often as many as a hundred hippies lived in all kinds of dwellings, gained a reputation for violence. There was a stabbing death there, following an argument over a tent.

The cumulative violence in many arenas of American life, from the political assassinations of the Kennedys and Martin Luther King in the sixties, to the stabbing at Altamont in California (Hell's Angels guarding the Rolling Stones during a free concert knifed a man to death as Mick Jagger sang "Sympathy for the Devil,") to the protracted slaughter of troops and noncombatants in Southeast Asia had seeped like a poison even into the counterculture camped about as far away from the establishment as you could get.

Trouble at Earth People's Park became almost as routine as dropping acid had been a few years earlier. Lay said the townspeople of Norton called the U.S. Border Patrol and the Vermont State Police regularly with complaints. He recalled going up there once and "harvesting their marijuana for them before they did it." Irate hippies tagged along with the troopers. A couple got arrested for interfering with the cops' early harvest. Others fired shots over the roofs of the police cars as they drove off with the confiscated weed.

It was in Norton that the sixties in Vermont came to their figurative close, three years after they had literally ended. The decade terminated metaphorically, with an alluring promise of camaraderie shattered by a violent note, or lack of notes, as it were. Rock bands hired to entertain thirty thousand fans at a festival abandoned the scene before even plugging in their amps because it looked like they were going to be playing for free. Only a fraction of the wild crowd, about fourteen hundred in total, ever paid to get in. Thousands crashed the flimsy fences and overran the security. The festival rapidly transformed from three days of music into mayhem. It became a parody of Woodstock, a mob scene without the love.

This happened over Labor Day weekend, 1973, a record-breaking scorcher. Swimmers flocked to Lake Champlain, and hikers ascended the cool slopes of Mount Mansfield as the multitudes on motorcycles, in cars, and crammed in VW vans ascended on Norton. Problems had been plaguing the festival organizers for weeks. Locals didn't want it. The state had threatened to use Act 250, which required a permit for such an event, to stop it. But never did. After the bandless scene self-destructed, some brazen festival-goers sent moms, and dads, and kids scattering from Lake Seymour when they stripped and dove in. Thursday, four days after the non-event, headlines in the *Burlington Free Press* read: "Salmon to View 'Carnage' Today."

By then the weather had turned cool and thunderstorm-thick, following the sweltering warm spell. Tom Salmon, a liberal young governor who had listened to his share of rock and roll music, stalked around the garbage-strewn hillside from which volunteers had hauled torched latrines, feces, abandoned clothes, discarded coolers. Around a hundred locals, a few muttering about how these festival-goers had been like animals, and some reporters and photographers gathered on the windswept field to hear Salmon give a speech. It was a photo opportunity, but not one the image makers of the state liked.

Salmon was mad. His hair occasionally lifted in the gusts as he made it clear that the beckoning country had beckoned the wrong folks. They'd left a mess, bad vibes, peeved townspeople. The governor called the whole rock festival concept "a vestige of a bygone era." Adopting a John Wayne-like manner, he said, "There are certain events that just send shivers up the spines of real men." There would be no more rock festivals in Vermont, he decreed. Never again would an unruly mob congregate in this state and leave carnage like this.

One farmer told reporters the festival had become "a battlefield." There had been guns, fights. Only memories of the recent shooting of four college students at Kent State University in Ohio had kept town officials from calling in the Vermont National Guard.

"We want to do with this what we did to motorcycle scrambling," Salmon said. That meant shut it down. Troublemakers were troublemakers; neither rock festivals nor motorcycle races, which Salmon reminded everyone were no longer welcome here either, fit the Vermont image. What did? Salmon mentioned a peaceful music festival held over the same weekend, and how successful it had been. Folk festivals were a Vermont tradition, he added, noting that the one held at Sugarbush had drawn five thousand people. It had been a nice, quiet, controlled event, the kind to be encouraged, the governor said.

Salmon's speech was the last hurrah for the flower children's sympathetic acceptance by most Vermonters. It closed out the final chapter of their tolerant hospitality towards the aborted dreams of the counterculture.

PART THREE

GOD'S COUNTRY

Let's Hear It for Manure!
—Country Journal *article, August, 1975*

*I*f the sixties had a shape, a kind of gradually rising slope of expectation and promise shouldered by Vermont politicians and newcomers concerned with change, the seventies flattened out, then became bumpy. There was Watergate, OPEC and the energy crises, twenty percent interest rates. The "mink and manure" set, made up of older, often gilt-edged refugees from affluent suburbs to the south, staked out sizable chunks of rural real estate. Artists discovered Vermont and moved here, particularly to the remote and cheap Northeast Kingdom. The middle-class, fleeing the crumbling cities later in the decade, abandoning the skyscraper-centered metropolises with their crime, drugs, and traffic, rediscovered Vermont's small cities and towns with their architectural feast of restorable buildings. The state remained a fertile place for all kinds of ideas and characters and was still relatively low cost and innocent, though not as low cost and as innocent as it had been a few years before.

This was the decade during which Vermont plunged into the economic mainstream. Or, if not exactly plunged into it, became a minor tributary into which the American mainstream had to flow if opportunities were not to dry up, if Vermonters were going to be able to heap gifts under the Christmas tree, keep thermostats at seventy degrees Fahrenheit in February, be able to jet away to Miami in March to relieve cabin fever. Manufacturing jobs, service and trade work, and construction all linked into what was going on outside the state, and particularly into what was going on in southern New England, from where economic ripples radiated, tending to hit Vermont about six months after leaving the Boston area. Regional ups and downs, as well as national ones, could not be as selectively ignored nor taken to heart, as they had been not that long ago when Vermont had been populated mostly by farmers and mill workers in self-sustaining communities.

The seventies also became the decade of *Country Journal*, a magazine that appealed to upwardly mobile back-to-the-land types whose college educations had neglected certain rural verities, things like how to can, how to erect a stone wall, and how to deal with the mid-March conviction you had screwed up royally to chase some bumpkin fantasy: living in the forever gray countryside, as Jim Boyce's father had warned the erstwhile ski bum back in the fifties, "without portfolio."

Advertisers loved the new magazine, which first appeared in May of 1974. They needed a vehicle to reach the resettlers of "God's country," the nickname given the rediscovered lake and mountain regions of many pieces of rural America. Across Vermont, well-educated and information-hungry transplants, many of whom disdained television (not that they could get it very well in most places, anyway), needed a bible for the soil, a guide to the woodstove, a knowledgeable yet informal voice of consolation ("Are you sure we're doing the right thing, Marjorie?" "Just shoot the raccoon, Tom!") that assured them it was okay to have an icemaker in the refrigerator and a good idea to put an oil furnace in the cellar as a back-up to wood heat. They needed to know more about the postmodern energy source, firewood, so *Country Journal* carried lots of ads and articles that explained things like flues, drafts, top loaders, side loaders, front loaders. There was a whole new arcane wood-burning world out there, a world populated with characters in top hats called chimney sweeps, with fancy canvas wood toters you could order from L.L. Bean, with little fans you could hang in doorways to push some of your stove's heat into the freezing room next door, with compactors to transform your Sunday *New York Times* into a perfect fireplace log, gauntlet-like gloves to save your fingers from third-degree burns, smoke detectors to save your life. An old timer happening upon an issue of *Country Journal* must have scratched his head, wondering how he'd managed all these years to get by with regular old stovepipe from the general store, simply stringing up long horizontal runs and never once buying a pair of those expensive gloves.

As for the actual getting of the firewood, that subject deserved several books, both humorous and tragic. Suffice it to say that chainsaws and axes were implements that only a small percentage of new Vermonters ought to have ever bought. Many did, though, insisting on what was perceived as a manly rural initiation. In Firewood 101, self-taught, unlimited enrollment, some degree of manual dexterity preferred, country acolytes learned that a maul bounced high off elm, that green wood was heavy, that lugging wood from the cellar up the stairs all winter was masochistic. On one of my visits to Barbara's farm I told her she had been ahead of everyone all these years because she never stopped burning wood. A couple of teeth showing, she just laughed.

Whereas the hippies had sent off for free pamphlets from the federal government in a kind of subversive learn-by-mail program that taught them things about subsistence living, *Country Journal* got delivered R.F.D. Thousands of newcomers in Vermont made the magazine compulsory reading. It was the *Time* and *U.S. News & World Report* of their rural reincarnations. It became a kind of talisman, a guide. And in the process *Country Journal* also became a runaway commercial success for two transplanted New Yorkers, Bill Blair and Richard Ketchum, who tapped into that elusive marketing entity, an identifiable consumer group as yet unexploited.

Why was the magazine so successful?

Demographics, Bill Blair answered the afternoon in February 1990 when I visited him in his sunny, high-ceilinged office in downtown Brattleboro. Simple demographics. Aided, he added, by some fundamental shifts in American habits. Habits that Blair, as the publisher, had been sharp enough to spot a little earlier than the other guys.

An Englishman, Bill Blair, now in his late seventies, I guessed, had a faint British accent and an aristocratic air. These days he used his big office part-time to tend to personal business matters. In the early seventies he had been the publisher of *Harper's*. Then he and Ketchum, who had been editor-in-chief of American Heritage Books, had decided to pool their funds, quit their jobs in New York, and move to Vermont, where they both had second homes—Blair's in Guilford, and Ketchum's in Dorset—and start a magazine. Initial circulation had been around thirty thousand, but it had grown rapidly. "There was no competition," Blair said. Circulation had reached 350,000, most of it in New England and the Northeast, by the time the two entrepreneurs sold their magazine in 1984.

Blair handed me a copy of something titled *Rural Renaissance, Recent Population and Market Trends*. He had had it prepared in the late seventies, he said, to attract advertisers. The report statistically validated the steady loss of farms in New England and across America and the shift of population from cities to the country. Income and status also meant less to many younger professionals, the report said, and clean environments meant more. Early retirement was also changing rural America, the statistics revealed, as tens of thousands of middle-aged and elderly Americans left the job market and moved to where land was cheap.

Ultimately, of course, Blair and Ketchum's *Country Journal* succeeded because people did want to learn how to grow muskmelons, how to nourish both the body and the mind in a Finnish sauna, and how to buy an old pickup. Readers were also extremely eager to validate their own experiences by reading articles with titles like "The R.F.D. Reaction." For the super flatlander, the magazine even ran an article titled, "What is a Swimming Hole?" And "Let's Hear It for Manure!" informed readers of the intrinsic value of various strains of effluent.

By 1978 double-page spreads advertising Mercedes Benz appeared regularly, suggesting who was planting those muskmelons and nourishing their bodies in a sauna. By then being rural was okay, even fashionable. There were designer jeans and cosmetics for the country man and woman. A half-dozen clones had entered the country magazine market, catering to a fundamental American concern, the worry about "doing it right." It was a sign of status to own a nineteenth-century house with a late-twentieth-century interior. If relocating to the country meant becoming more comfortable with life, more at home with yourself, many of the magazines said, why not saturate yourself with creature comforts as well? Why not marry rural with luxury?

One limit to such a marriage, a marriage that had enticed Americans ever since the Victorian era when the Gilded Age robber barons had built their "great camps," log masterpieces with every convenience of civilization in the remote Adirondacks, and their "cottages," huge ramshackle homes in Newport, Bar Harbor, and Saratoga Springs, for the summer season, was, at least in the mid-seventies, the times themselves. They did not breed confidence in tomorrow. Once OPEC, the thirteen mostly Arab countries that controlled the bulk of the world's oil reserves, got together and formed a loose cartel, instead of competing with one another, decades of cheap gas were over. Suddenly, a full tank cost twice what it had, if you could get it. Supplies dwindled during the early months of 1974. From Newport to Bennington, lines formed at service stations. A three-dollar limit was often imposed. Some ski-area managers turned livid when they heard of local station owners detouring skiers, claiming their pumps were dry, in order to hoard gas for locals who needed it to drive to work.

I recall a trip I made to Sugarbush in early 1974. The carefree ski bums of yesterday were frowning. Skiing's days were numbered, the more cynical predicted. The hippies had been right, one told me, America was out of control, veering around the economic sky with one engine out of fuel and the other almost on empty. Vermont, having boarded the jet America, was going to crash, too.

Yet Vermont rode out the crises better than most states. Smaller numbers helped, as did the fact that there was a lot of the old frugal Yankee in folks a generation or two off the farm. Life went forward, not as well lubricated with oil and cash as it had been, but forward nevertheless. The times gave Vermonters a chance to exhibit the cynicism many of them came by quite naturally.

Of course, there was a new "typical" Vermonter coming into being. An independent person, for sure, but also a more co-dependent one. His/her livelihood was linked to the new economic order. That new order made room for hippies cutting their hair and hanging up their dirndls, for ski bums knotting ties and discarding their faded jeans. The transformed took out mortgages, bought new cars, books, vacations, ski passes, boats, wine—all those material goods they couldn't afford so easily when they had waited on tables, or stabilized busted femurs in traction, or smoked pot at sunset in a treehouse. Almost all of them had college degrees, which gave them an advantage over the typical natives their age with whom they were competing for limited better-paying jobs.

All this time, one thing about Vermont didn't change at all. That was the weather. The weather remained a touchstone, as it had been for centuries, unchanging in its constant changefulness. Everyone, from the sullen punk smoking a cigarette on the corner of Church and Main in Burlington to the longest-striding backpacker, least sensitive developer, and most dutiful grandmother carrying six triangles of still warm apple pie out to her grandchildren on the home-place porch, had to deal with it. And they usually had something to say about it as well.

Tremendous, awful, delightful, unpredictable—Vermont weather was all these, from gray November twilights with gloomy clouds trailing tassels of mist up brook valleys, to bug-swollen July mornings, the birds singing in the trees, to crisp, sharp September afternoons, the ripe apples pushing their taut skins towards the cooling sunlight, to blizzards that knocked down trees and called for the services of the Hap Gaylords of Vermont.

If differences in income, background, and worldviews were shoving Vermonters further apart, the weather kept doing what it had been doing for centuries: pulling them back together. If the most retrograde hippy and the most greedy speculator found themselves stranded beneath a covered bridge during a thundershower (one had been picking berries on the brook bank, the other contemplating brook-view lots), one of them probably would have eventually, begrudgingly, muttered to the other, "Just give it a minute."

"And it'll change."

Well into the seventies Vermont also retained a purity in look, in architecture and settlement patterns, in farmscapes and open spaces between most of its villages, that few other eastern states could match. Like many aspects of Vermont that made it different, this one, too, owned much to the small population, which was 440,000 in 1970, or forty-eight people per square mile. Connecticut and Massachusetts, by way of contrast, had burgeoning populations (Connecticut with just over three million people, or 623 per square mile in the 1970 U.S. Census, and Massachusetts with 5.6 million, or 727 people per square mile) and were becoming hodgepodges of residential areas, malls, new subdivisions, and commercial strips, often surrounding village cores that retained what a tourist might call "New England charm." Precious little open space separated that charm from the new, which was seldom quite so charming. Open space was usually sold, then built on. With its loss went the historic and orderly pattern that made New England romantic and so enjoyable to look at. Strict zoning kept some places historic-looking and open, but the economics behind most such visual showcases made them the new settlements of the rich.

In Vermont the crossover of farmers and their families, who had been the primary purveyors of that look, a nineteenth-century one threaded together by roads that followed the landscape rather than reshaped it, into the new jobs springing into being, undermined the look even as photographers sought it for the state's image-making promotional campaigns. Although some new industries, restaurants, and shopkeepers renovated old factories, warehouses, barns and stores, more and more built new. The architectural antecedents of the new typically lay beyond state borders. The harmony and continuity of many villages also suffered from neglect, age, and indifference of the locals. Historical preservationists were few, architectural appreciation minimal. Inexorably, trailers, prefabricated garages and farm buildings, as well as characterless telephone company structures, U.S. post offices, and numerous one-level schools, surrounded by yellow buses, their designs determined by institutional and economic forces rather than by esthetic and historical ones, continued to punch holes in the rich visual fabric.

Barns—in the fifties they had numbered over thirty thousand—became an endangered species across much of the state. Empty of animals, which warmed their foundations, and of hay, which anchored their gray and red silhouettes in winter storms and winds, innumerable barns followed the footsteps of their last users. That is, they buckled under to pressures out of their control. Opportunists bought many of them, dismantling their huge carcasses, and, like whalers on high green seas, storing and shipping the saleable pieces—the massive, hand-hewn beams and thousands of board feet of authentic weathered sheathing—often as far as California. Folks there paid dearly for a little of the New England look. The scavenged barns, their remains either burned or left to rot, were a dramatic metaphor of change. For by this time the agrarian culture across most of Vermont had literally split apart at the seams.

Around seven thousand farmers had called it quits in the fifties, and more than five thousand more joined the exodus during the sixties. By 1970 Vermont had sixty-eight hundred farms, down from approximately twenty-four thousand immediately after World War II. During those twenty-five years since the end of the war, few writers or analysts had dealt with the issues related to this protracted drama, the most touching, painful, and socially significant event in Vermont's history. A kind of cultural amnesia gripped not only Vermont about its agricultural decline, but New England as a region and America as a whole. With no national policy for the protection of agriculture, nearly one million farms ceased operating between 1960 and 1970 alone. Average acreage of the surviving farms was up, however, from 303 acres in 1960 to 390 ten years later. New England's loss of farms during the period, from fifty-six thousand down to twenty-nine thousand, as a percentage far exceeded the national average, although again the average farm size increased from 164 acres to 198 acres.

The "who cares?" attitude about farms disappearing, at least in Vermont, if not around the country, eventually evolved into "we better care" in the late eighties. Then, subsidies were passed by the legislature to help keep the fields in hay and the pastures dotted with cows, a rural backdrop in a landscape being rapidly suburbanized.

Throughout the seventies the combination of newcomers, dying farms, ski-area growth, and speculation accelerated the changing pattern of land ownership. When the typical farmer sold, for instance, sometimes his neighboring farmer bought his land and kept it in agriculture. But more often a realtor, logger, or developer bought it. What usually happened afterwards was that the timber was cut, including the sugarbush with its century-old maples, the land was subdivided according to Act 250 and local zoning laws, if any, and the lots were sold. Buyers varied. They included young professionals, older ones, retirees, speculators, and natives anxious to own a piece of the state while they could afford it. Buying property as an escape or investment in Vermont became so popular that some landowners were the type who seldom set foot in Vermont, or if they did, came only several weeks each year. At Town Meeting you didn't have to listen to them complain about their taxes, which often were high because the listers socked it to them. Yet absentee and second-home owners had power just waiting to be organized. And, as Governor Deane Davis had pointed out, second homes tended to become permanent homes, with children who needed schooling, roads that demanded attention, and occupants who voted.

It was also in the early seventies that Vermont began to have conspicuous "have" and "have not" towns. Rising prices in one place often drove the not-so-well-off into adjoining or nearby communities. The have-not towns tended to levy high taxes, however, because of a marginal tax base and a school system overflowing with kids. The have-not towns had big houses, which didn't seem to get painted as frequently as they ought to have been, lawns that got converted into parking lots for tenants. For instance, Bellows Falls, a down-on-its-heels industrial town clinging to the side of the Connecticut River, housed poorer folks in Windham County; Moretown and Waterbury became low-rent alternatives to the Sugarbush Valley area; and Morrisville functioned in the same way for Stowe. Ski areas began to hire employees from several towns away because their wages wouldn't pay the rent in their towns. It was a spiral, with escalating prices highest at the apex. The further out from the center you went, the lower the prices. The situation was not confined to ski country. Spilling out of a growing Burlington, people looking for a deal bought in Charlotte, Hinesburg, Richmond, Jericho, Westford, Colchester, and Milton. They drove back and forth to work. The commuter had arrived, transforming the interstates into more than a bridge for strangers passing through and trucks hauling goods. Some newcomers to Vermont's scattered cities looked even further away than twenty or thirty minutes from their jobs. They thought little of the drive or compared it favorably to one they had probably made daily somewhere else, in heavy traffic. Here they had the Vermont scene to savor and thought little of a long commute—at least until it snowed.

*J*ust how much land prices had escalated came home to me when I returned to Vermont in 1972. First, I asked my sister Barbara and her husband Raymond about buying a piece of their farm in Tunbridge. They had already sold a few ten-acre lots, Barb told me, and had offers on more. Their two sons had also gotten some of the shrinking farm. The youngest, my nephew Willie, had perched a trailer a hundred yards from the farmhouse, managing somehow to get it up on a knoll so the mobile home looked as if it had been installed by a helicopter. His brother Rammie had built a small house nearby. Both boys had married girls from New York City, daughters of welfare-system families whose urban roots had snagged their country hearts.

At the time ten acres had become the magic number to keep the old-time Vermont freedom of choice—no septic system inspections, little official intrusion—despite Act 250. Legislators had slipped the ten-acre exclusion into the law to make it more palatable.

I wanted to buy fifty acres. I soon learned that what I had to spend wasn't going to buy fifty acres in Tunbridge, even if my sister would give me a deal. It wasn't going to buy fifty acres in Quechee, either, where I had often dreamed of owning property.

"They bought the whole thing," my mother told me when I mentioned the idea of being a Quechee landowner.

She was right, or almost. John Davidson's Quechee Lakes Corporation had bought over five thousand acres, including large farms, many of the nineteenth-century houses lining Main Street, the Harris and Emery Mill, the derelict Parker House that stood beside the mill, and most of the old Dewey's Mills community. And although Davidson had told one reporter, "This is—and can remain—the most beautiful valley in the country," to me, walking around the village past an ersatz new common bordered by historic houses transported from other New England towns, and through the rebuilt covered bridge (Governor Davis had attended its opening in 1970), and then up past the water tower to my old home on High Street, which was vacant, wallpaper peeling off the walls in the front parlor, plaster on the floor, the whole scene made me feel like I had walked into the "Twilight Zone." I went through the cemetery behind my old home, by the elementary school, by the little library, then between the mill and the post office above which Elmer Eaton had lived with his mother when I was a boy. The silence was spooky.

I drove along Main Street, past the steepled Congregational church, and out to the Quechee Fells Farm. Several broad ski trails cut swaths through the apple orchards below the millionaire's house, or what had been the millionaire's house in my memory. There was a golf course in the meadows alongside the Ottauquechee. Sections of the river had been broadened by the Army Corps of Engineers on both ends of the village to create the lakes needed to validate the resort's name. I had this eerie feeling about Vermont's future that day. Other people from other states had told me about their hometowns changing so much that they didn't recognize them. But this was a town of three hundred in central Vermont. My town. And it was becoming an archetype of New England packaged for visitors with cameras and for newcomers who could afford to live here, a quiet visual shell of the past drained of its rural soul.

John Davidson had shown up in Quechee at an opportune time a few years before. Progress had forgotten the mill town. It hadn't shared in the resort renaissance nor had high-tech firms located there. Nor low-tech firms, either, for that matter. The musical slamming of looms was long gone. Where men in green and black T-shirts, and women with their hair in long ponytails, both sexes smelling of lanolin, had leaned out the big windows of the Harrison and Emery Mill, watching cars and horses emerge from the covered bridge below, there was now sky. That end of the mill had been demolished. A mile downstream the little principality of Dewey's Mills had literally disappeared. Its five-storied mill that had once seemed so alive to me, the mansard-roofed office, the dormitory, and all the support buildings had been razed. What remained of a century of manufacturing shoddy was a foundation hugging the river, one house, and, high on the flat plateau overlooking the mouth of the Quechee Gorge, the home of the mill's last owner, Bill Dewey, obscured from view by the same tall hedge.

The end of Dewey's Mills had come suddenly, in 1956. Unlike the end for most of Vermont's woolen mills, it had nothing to do with economics. The federal government bought Dewey's Mills for $288,000 because it sat in the floodplain created by the Hartland Dam downstream on the Ottauquechee River. The horse-drawn carriages went to the Shelburne Museum, some machinery was salvaged, then the wrecking balls did their work.

John Davidson, however, wasn't interested in Dewey's Mills per se, nor in the old Harrison and Emery Woolen Mill. He had a bigger concept than either mill owner had ever envisioned, a paternalism on a grand scale, at least by Vermont standards. Davidson wanted to make the Kiley Report, a master plan for the development and conservation of the Ottauquechee River watershed, a profitable reality.

Laurance Rockefeller, who lived in nearby Woodstock, had paid for the Kiley Report. Quechee's natural bowl, the nearness of both I-89 and I-91, which crossed in White River Junction, the village's faded charm, and possible federal dollars were elements that had attracted Rockefeller's attention. He had dubbed his idea the "Ottauquechee Project" and hired internationally respected landscape architect Dan Kiley of Charlotte to visualize a new village and riverside. The Kiley Report, once completed, was an upscale vision of what Quechee might look like tomorrow. Though Rockefeller's project never jelled, John Davidson stepped in and inherited its potential.

Davidson said he had grown up on a farm in Massachusetts. He had a different vision of Vermont's future than other developers, he liked to remind people. In fact, he didn't even see himself as a "developer," he insisted. Yet exactly what he saw Quechee as was hard to discern. The smiling Davidson's usual response to questions from the press was "No comment."

As with most successful developments of this scale, the timing was right. Lady Bird Johnson had dedicated the North Hartland Dam in June of 1967, creating the George Perkins Marsh Lake and making the upstream shorelines of the Ottauquechee River a focus for development when federal, state, and local forces were cooperating in the name of recreation and conservation. For some time Hartford officials had been urging Governor Phil Hoff's administration to buy promontories overlooking Quechee Gorge, the community of Dewey's Mills, and other available properties between the gorge and Quechee village. Their hopes were that the state would make a park. Davidson slipped into the driver's seat of an already in-motion concept, deftly taking the wheel. He visited Governor Hoff and got him to endorse Quechee Lakes' potential. Davidson and his associate, Hollis Paige, drove around Quechee, knocking on doors, making sizable offers. Just who was backing Davidson remained a bit vague, but he paid his bills and exuded confidence and optimism, two attributes in short supply around Quechee since the mills had left. His aggressive buying made Quechee's future the focus of lengthy discussions at municipal meetings in Hartford (politically, Quechee was part of that town, as was White River Junction). The selectmen tended to see Quechee Lakes Corporation as an opportunity to broaden the tax base. Some other folks, including the listers, weren't so sure about that.

Davidson bought the five-hundred-acre Henri Dupuis farm for $180,000 and hired Henri, who also happened to be a well-liked selectman to be his real estate front man. The corporation bought the 435-acre Quechee Fells Farm, home of John Marsh, Vermont's first lieutenant governor, for $150,000. Davidson held a meeting for the locals in the barn of Marshland Farm, with its views of the Dewey's Mills pond, alongside which polo ponies would soon be galloping. Standing on a box, the short, swarthy developer told those who came what Quechee was going to be like in ten years. He assured them that property taxes, the thing most folks had said topped their concerns on a recent village survey (after taxes had come the loss of farms and a pervasive sense of apathy), would be about nil once Quechee Lakes became a reality. One of those who attended the meeting in the historic barn, Walter Spencer, had followed the woolen mills south for a few years, but then had returned to Quechee. Spencer recalled that what he heard from the talkative Davidson "sounded good on the surface. But it washed out quick."

Davidson hired some locals to work for him, including Raymond Young's brother Melvin. Melvin had been building wooden rowboats since the mills had closed. Working for Davidson he ran a crew of twenty, renovating old houses and buildings and putting up new homes and condominiums.

Despite all his negotiations and meetings and visible presence, John Davidson remained somewhat of a mystery, as did most details of his plans.

"I know these people are up there and they have said they intend to develop Quechee in the best interests of the area," reported Hartford Town Manager Ralph Lehman. "I don't know any exact details."

Ottauquechee Regional Planning and Development Commission chairman Henry T. Bourne of Woodstock claimed he was the one who had first brought Davidson to the area. To soothe worries, Bourne assured the public that he was working with Davidson to preserve open space in Quechee. "This group's coming to Quechee is the best fate that territory could have had," Bourne said. "These people have the highest possible interests and what they're doing will have a major beneficial impact on the Hartford tax rolls."

The state generally endorsed the concept, whatever the details might be. As for the citizens of Quechee, they got very little input into the future of their community.

Bill Dewey's daughter Carol moved back to her hometown in 1971. "What I heard from the beginning," she recalled, "was that the Mafia was buying up the land—who else had enough money?"

Then she met Davidson. They fell in love. The daughter of the last heir of the principality of Dewey's Mills became the wife of the new duke of development of modern Quechee. But all was not peaceful. Two years in a row on Halloween, Carol Dewey Davidson said, "Locals burned the condominiums down."

Animosity about losing the soul, the very guts of their village, whether it was down and out or not, filled some natives with hatred towards Davidson and his dream. The stranger had crammed barns with antiques bought at auctions (auctioneers gloated and bargain hunters groaned when he showed up because he bid on just about everything). He had hired locals like Melvin Young, but his relationships with them were volatile; the alliances often deteriorated when disagreements surfaced. None of this deterred Davidson. He kept adding to Quechee Lake's assets. Sales of lots, rehabilitated homes, and condos went forward under a sophisticated marketing plan. Advertisements, phone follow-ups, presentations in the homes of prospects, and trips to Quechee were elements of it. Promotional materials and salesmen, of course, never mentioned the fact the locals might despise you if you moved here.

Then, in 1973, something happened. "John was not a businessman, really," Carol Dewey Davidson told me. Others claimed John Davidson got squeezed out. But in 1973, due to financial and managerial pressures, Davidson sold Quechee Lakes to CNA Financial Corporation in Chicago, with the agreement he would stay on as manager. But CNA hired the Larwyn Development Group to handle sales.

"They were California people who had no idea what a New England village should look like," Carol Dewey Davidson said. "John didn't get along with them."

He quit.

So, six years after its conception, the conservation/recreation development vision of my boyhood home, a vision that had taken seed in the fertile mind of Laurance Rockefeller, been fleshed out by the visionary eye of Dan Kiley, and been brought to early fruition by Massachusetts mini-tycoon John Davidson, was in the hands of a corporation whose managers didn't know what a New England village looked like. The Larwyn Development Group was based in California and had several former Boise Cascade Corporation recreational community salesmen on its payroll. Larwyn had hired the salesmen after Boise Cascade dissolved its recreation communities marketing force in 1971 and 1972. Walter Henson, a big, muscular bartender I had known at Sugarbush, became one of the Larwyn Group salesmen. Before moving to Vermont, Henson had sold real estate in Ocean City, New Jersey. A few other former ski bums from Sugarbush, a little older now, ambition chafing at the frayed collars of their blue denim workshirts, also joined the marketing team. By then Al Moulton had come on board at Quechee Lakes Corporation as vice president in charge of just about everything. The former political insider had not retained his clout in Governor Thomas Salmon's regime, but he remained a strong link between development and the legislature. He still knew most of the members personally. Moulton also knew what a New England village was supposed to look like.

Thirteen salesmen, working out of the Parker House, sold the look. Several of them commuted daily from Sugarbush Valley. The marketing strategy was an updated version of what had failed at Dover Hills for Don Albano and his bosses five years before. But times had changed. Strategies had been refined. More customers were now armchair, country home shoppers. There was less competition from fewer farmers sticking signs that read "Land for Sale, Cheap" by the ends of driveways. Quechee Lakes had several off-site offices that fielded queries from ads. Following up on queries, "off-site reps would do a home sit," Henson explained in sales lingo, "and try to generate the people up to Quechee for a weekend." Prospects often stayed at the refurbished Hotel Coolidge in White River

Junction, which had been bought by a buddy of Davidson's. Sales were brisk. The basic selling unit was the one-acre lot. But there were also five-acre lots and farmsteads as large as ten acres. The plans for Quechee Lakes, endorsed by the state and approved by HUD, called for two thousand homesites and five hundred condos, surrounded by a greenbelt.

Though it was initially viewed as a prototype for Vermont's future, Quechee Lakes prompted a number of questions. Some of them related to turnover. John Davidson may have had a vision, as well as some sensitivity to the village's past. He was a hands-on developer. He may not have agreed with you, locals confessed, but at least you could talk to him since he was there. Subsequent owners (CNA sold the resort community in 1979 to David La Roche from Rhode Island, and in 1989 La Roche sold it to NECO Enterprises, Inc., a utility-holding company with some real estate ventures) were not so easy to look in the eye. They had managers on site, not principals. Quechee became less a village than a fifty-five-hundred-acre commodity, albeit one with a cleaned up river and a rebuilt water-driven turbine in the old Harrison and Emery Woolen Mill where a glass blower had set up shop.

A more perplexing question involved the whole idea of development on such a scale. Development, no matter how you dressed it up, meant cultural change. And cultural change of this magnitude both dwarfed a town's past and yet somehow tried to freeze-dry its look for perpetuity. In other words, it embalmed the place. But then, with its master plan, state approval, and Vermont "look," Quechee Lakes Corporation had done everything right. But an embalmed community? Just driving through it sometimes gave me the creeps. My childhood home came to epitomize a dilemma: where had the soul of this place gone now that the natives had sold out? Where were their children supposed to live as housing prices eliminated any chance of staying here? Should condominiums overlook the graves of your parents, like they did mine?

I stared down at the river from the covered bridge, imagined my sisters as young girls swimming in the deep water above the dam, us kids threading our way through the dozens of workers pouring out the mill at the end of the first shift, the looms that are so ingrained in my memory singing overhead out the big open windows. Even by 1972 Quechee had become no place for the likes of me. I soon headed further north, where land was cheaper. I eventually found myself close to Canada and still unable to buy fifty acres. I settled on thirty-six, in partnership with a friend. The land had brook frontage, a collapsing sugarhouse, and cost a little over three hundred dollars an acre. I never met the fellow who sold it to us. He had a Connecticut address, a Bermuda phone number, and apparently had never visited the land because thousands of balsam and Scotch pine Christmas trees, planted in the mid-sixties, were coming to maturity on eight acres. Their harvest paid about half the mortgage.

This was in the far northern tip of the Green Mountains, in Montgomery, a town of six hundred tucked into the western slope of the state's geological spine. Twelve miles from Jay Peak ski area, Montgomery had been changed by the resort, but nowhere near as dramatically as Warren and Waitsfield had been by their nearby ski mountains. Montgomery didn't have any gift shops, wasn't cute yet, and seemed likely to remain relatively untouched for some time because of its distance from an interstate and its location in the far north.

The attitude my wife Maggie and I adopted once we moved to Montgomery in July 1973 had a little of the Vermont Way of Life in it. We kept expenses down, refrained from credit, made friends. Although we never thought of ourselves as hippies—I had been a vice president of marketing in Los Angeles—some locals seemed to see us that way. Living in a teepee, which we had hauled across country from Idaho, along with a dozen fourteen-foot poles (talk about a dangerous way to drive, those poles sticking of the roof of your car and back to the roof of the U-Haul), my having long hair, and driving an old Volvo qualified us.

The teepee burned in early October while drying after a downpour. Maggie had a fire going inside and a gallon of Coleman fuel ignited, turning the canvas into a glowing mantle that vaporized our possessions. We moved into a cold, waterless shed alongside a medieval-like stone castle/restaurant built by an artist/musician named Charlie Trois. Trois had come to Vermont after reading the futurist Edgar Cayce. Cayce had predicted a flood that convinced Trois, who had eight gold records from a brief musical career (Trois had been a member of the Soul Survivors, a group that had a number one hit with "Expressway to My Heart" in the late sixties) to settle in Avery's Gore, an elevated slice of wilderness separating Montgomery from Belvidere. By winter, however, Maggie and I had left Trois's cold castle and rented a milkhouse alongside an empty barn about a quarter-mile from Montgomery's most famous attraction, Zack's On the Rocks, a restaurant known for the effusiveness of its owner, Jon Zachadnyk, and for its decor, a cross between the glitz of Las Vegas and the sumptuousness of the hideaway of the Marquis de Sade. Maggie waitressed for Zack and I harvested Christmas trees, including ours, for a forester named Galen Huchinson who had a bluegrass singer's nasal twang, liked to work until "dark thirty," and referred to his father as "the master of the universe."

It was a strange time in the hills. Interesting characters abounded. If there was one thing I noticed that had been lost since the mid-sixties, it was innocence. The surviving farmers in particular were no longer willing to open the screen door to anyone with dollar signs in his or her eyes. Like the rest of America, farmers had televisions now, telephones, even credit cards. They knew "the land" was worth something. Vermont had joined the twentieth century and there was no going backwards.

THE GREEN MOUNTAIN FUEL-LINE BLUES

We're now getting seventeen miles per gallon in the big bad Ford Lincoln . . . pretty darn good!
—*Governor Tom Salmon, 1973*

I laid eyes on Thomas Salmon only once while he was governor. It was during a brief bicentennial ceremony in the early summer of 1976.

A lanky, big-striding man with a full head of hair, his aide hustling to keep up with him, Salmon crossed Route 118 by the Montgomery General Store, a bulky, columned, porched landmark with just enough room for two cars to park between the steps and the highway. He joined two selectmen, a few members of our Montgomery Bicentennial Committee, and some locals in the village common, a small green triangle shaded by maples and embraced by a sampler of nineteenth-century architecture: a brick Greek Revival church, a Queen Anne style home with a corner tower, a Carpenter Gothic cottage, a rambling two-story Victorian in which an elderly lady who often navigated the common with two ski poles lived with folks older than she was (she took care of them), and a Gothic Revival style church with a slightly leaning bell tower. The Episcopalians had recently sold the Gothic Revival church to a hastily organized Montgomery Historical Society for a dollar; otherwise it would have been razed. What I remember best about the ceremony in our common was the contrast between the restless young governor and our two selectmen.

One of the selectmen, Harry Dutchburn, had something wrong with his back. Harry was bent at the waist, jackknifed right over. His fingertips seemed to be grazing in the grass. In his other hand was a cane.

Harry and his brother Mike, who was not at the ceremony, were Vermonters of another era. People called them "the Dutchburn boys," though boyhood was far behind them. Mike and Harry spent countless hours in their barn. They milked at odd hours. Strangers entering the barn sometimes found them seated between stanchioned cows, both boys fast asleep, their heads against cows' flanks. For this special occasion Harry had not gotten carried away over his outfit. He wore barn clothes and barn odor. A cap on his head, he twisted his grizzled face sideways, like a caterpillar, to get a look at Governor Salmon when they were introduced. Merrill "Billy" Cabana, the other selectman, was a bachelor who lived with his parents. A reluctant farmer who once told me he had gone five years in a row without missing a single milking, Billy beamed and shifted his shoulders around, as though he were wearing wool underwear that itched, then thrust out his hand like a nervous schoolboy.

Governor Salmon said a few words. It occurred to me that the governor and Harry Dutchburn, who rested both gnarled hands on his cane and stared in the direction of the speaker's shoes, might as well have been from different planets. Tom Salmon, about to run for one of Vermont's U.S. Senate seats, had his eyes on Washington. God only knows what Harry had his eyes on—certainly not on a brutal night a decade in the future, when three strangers would break into his farmhouse, beat him and Mike senseless, steal their money (since the Depression the Dutchburn boys had carried wads of cash in their pockets, afraid of the banks, a fact that prompted police to put out an advisory: anybody receiving any hundred dollar bills that smell like manure, please report them) and leave the boys, then both in their seventies, for dead. Salmon lost his race for the U.S. Senate in November 1976 to the Republican incumbent Robert Stafford. The defeat ended his political career at the relatively young age of forty-four.

A native of Ohio, Salmon had first moved to Vermont in 1958 to practice law in Bellows Falls. In 1965 he had been elected to the House from Rockingham. Liberal and ambitious, he rose through the Democratic ranks fast. His 1972 gubernatorial victory over Republican Luther Hackett was a major upset, given the outgoing Deane Davis's popularity. Once in office, however, unlike Phil Hoff, who had ridden the wild crest of the political wave of the sixties, or Davis, who had gracefully allowed himself to be swept along by the tug of environmentalism, Salmon, like his namesake, often seemed to be swimming upstream against powerful social and economic currents. Salmon was young, though, and strong. He logged seventeen-hour workdays. While campaigning, he had frequently hit the trail without other Democratic hopefuls along because they slowed him down. On one occasion Salmon had even boasted he had shaken the hand of every workman at a factory entrance in twenty minutes, rather than the forty allotted by his staff. Moving around Vermont like a dervish, Salmon seemed not unlike the long-legged Texan, former president Lyndon B. Johnson, whom he admired. He certainly stalked around with a gait similar to the one Johnson had made his trademark.

Though not as big an upset as Johnson had pulled in his infamous 1948 victory over "Mr. Texas," Coke Stevenson, a victory for which Johnson lied and bought votes, Salmon's win in 1972 startled folks. It demonstrated conclusively that in Vermont voters were more in tune with the themes and ideals of their candidates than with their party labels. Hackett, a former majority leader of the House, wrapped himself in the Republican banner and looked at first like a shoo-in. Yet without party labels identifying who was who, it was Salmon who looked like Davis's natural successor. Hackett's Achilles heel proved to be television advertising. He never launched a decent media campaign on the tube in an age when TV created instant personalities. Salmon did. Using lots of short ads, Salmon told voters repeatedly that Vermont was for Vermonters, not for out-of-staters, and that the state needed to tax developers.

Ironically, it had been Deane Davis (he endorsed Hackett) who had demonstrated TV's power to sway an election only two years before. In 1970 Davis had been in trouble with voters because of his new three percent sales tax. Never mind he had pushed it through to pay Hoff's deficit; his name got attached to the tax. Looking like a sure loser against Leo O'Brien of Burlington, Davis had gotten creative. He made the "boat ad."

"The most corny piece of political advertising you could ever hope for," he called it during one of our talks, laughing to himself. "But, the most successful."

Davis said the ad was conceived by "a very high-principled guy named Sam Miller—he was a freelancer, a young man of twenty-eight, or something like that." Al Moulton, then Davis's assistant, had gotten his boss and Miller together. A meeting was necessary because, Moulton had informed an impressed Davis, "You know, this fella doesn't take any political retainers until he's spent a whole day with the candidate and comes to the conclusion that he ought to be elected."

"Alright, bring him up here," Davis had replied.

Miller spent the whole day with the governor. He went to every conference, stayed a couple hours at the house, went out to the barn where Davis kept his horses. Then Miller wrote the earthy, symbolic ad that changed political advertising in Vermont forever.

The boat ad was shot on Lake Champlain in South Hero. "They had an old scow out there," Davis said. "They had *Vermont* painted on it, in big letters. I was bailing away there, and they had all this high-pressure camera stuff in another boat. They told me to start bailing, and I was pointed in the other direction—so, I couldn't see what they were doing. Apparently, they had some equipment problem . . . but they didn't bother to tell me. I went on for twenty-five minutes, bailing that damn boat! I was exhausted."

An exhausted sixty-nine-year-old, his pants rolled up, scooping out a scow, caught people's attention. As soon as the ad aired, folks on the street grinned when they saw Davis. "Keep bailing, Governor!" some called out good-naturedly. The TV ad had done the trick; it showed that Davis's sales tax had bailed Vermont out of a sinking financial situation.

Tom Salmon, once he was elected with the help of television, appeared on the medium before taking the oath of office and told everyone he was closing Vermont down as "the beckoning country." But then, hardly had he settled his big frame into the vacated governor's chair, when he had his rude awakening. President Nixon, in his inaugural speech in January 1973, informed the nation that federal funds for state programs were going to be cut, welfare rolls trimmed, attitudes changed. The next morning Salmon told reporters that Nixon's speech "sounded to me like the death knell of the programs of the Great Society."

It was. Helping the poor, integrating blacks into a white-dominated society, and improving social injustices were about to go to the end of the line. Nevertheless, in Vermont, Salmon pushed his liberal social agenda. He called for property tax reform and tried to get the second leg, the land-use planning one, under the much-maligned Act 250. Neither effort went very far. Property tax reform simply was never initiated, and the land-use plan became an albatross that plagued Salmon for years.

Basically, he got elected too late for what he wanted to do. National forces, and then international ones, started shoving Vermont around only months after he took office. Salmon gathered key lawmakers in Montpelier to discuss some conservation measures to combat high energy prices, but after the meetings he told reporters "the American public and the average Vermonter do not believe the energy crisis exists." He tried to stay cool about it, didn't want to incite "tourism-crippling publicity." For the holiday season in 1973, Salmon dimmed the statehouse lights, eliminated the Christmas bulbs on the state tree, and told Vermonters that these were the types of belt-tightening measures they ought to be ready for. The warning fell mostly on deaf ears. One reason, in addition to the fact, as Salmon had said, that people simply didn't believe the dire predictions, was Watergate. Across America, everyone was absorbed by the scandal that would eventually usher President Nixon out of the White House. Some soothing experts also insisted that OPEC wouldn't keep its act together, its members would start undercutting each other's prices, and pump prices would drop.

It didn't happen. A besieged Richard Nixon hung on for months. As for oil, even before the new year, State Senator Russell Niquette, a Democrat from Chittenden County, warned that the black gold "might reach thirty-five cents a gallon." Taking a different tack, Speaker of the House, Walter "Peanut" Kennedy of Chelsea, when asked about a possible postponement of the upcoming session, said sarcastically, "I think a lot of hot air generated up here will help to relieve the energy crisis."

As the 1974 session opened, the Republicans had the Democrats, like OPEC had the world, over a barrel. Ever since the 1970 elections, when the Democrats had lost all the important political seats despite running their best hopes (Hoff against Winston Prouty for the U.S. Senate and Leo O'Brien against Davis for governor), party unity had been unraveling. Now state revenues were down, ski area owners were crying because they saw empty chairlifts all over their mountains, and Salmon was blithely bragging about how more efficient his chauffeur-driven Lincoln was at fifty miles per hour than at seventy. "We're now getting seventeen miles per gallon in the big bad Ford Lincoln . . . pretty darn good!" he told reporters. Then oil prices soared. The ski areas lobbied for more gas for Vermont. They didn't get it. Some poorer Vermonters wondered where they were going to find their next three bucks to wait in line at the local fuel pump, and many of them hauled old woodstoves out of the barn, ran some pipe up through the roof, and cut some firewood.

In Montpelier, fitfully overseeing the mayhem, was the Republican-controlled legislature. Robert V. Daniels, a University of Vermont history professor who had been elected from Chittenden County in 1972, was one of the seven Democrats in the thirty-seat Senate. The senior house "turned out to be an Ivy League social club," Daniels told me. But the big problem facing the Democrats back then, he continued, even though they had almost gained parity in the House, was the fact they lacked the unity they had briefly forged in the early sixties. Party work at the grassroots level had waned (a fact Hoff paid little attention to in 1970, and which, according to Daniels, contributed to his loss to Prouty). Then, in 1972, the nomination of anti-war candidate and party outsider, George McGovern, for president, had put the old-time Democrats at odds with many young, liberal newcomers to Vermont. The newcomers wanted to support the party, Daniels said, but not a conservative branch of it that did not oppose the war in Vietnam or believe in continued funding of social programs. Thus, some desperately needed new blood was turned off by staunch conservatism. The Democratic party became rent by factionalism, over which the fast-moving Tom Salmon tried, with only marginal success, to reign.

An entrenched core of Democrats, Daniels said, "more interested in controlling what they had than winning anything bigger," alienated and frustrated younger people so much that many of them rejected the party altogether. They looked around, seeking what Daniels called "uncontaminated alternatives," and helped found Vermont's independent and progressive party movements. What had begun as a revolt within the party itself undermined its power and nourished the growth of the third party system. One of the stalwarts of the alternative system was an abrasive, wooly-haired socialist named Bernie Sanders. Sanders' name first appeared on the ballot in 1972, when the unknown ran for the U.S. Congress on the Liberty Union ticket.

After all this, in the mid-seventies, the alienated Democrats of the anti-war McGovern camp, and the old-timers, never fused behind Tom Salmon or his land-use plan nor his proposed increase in the sales tax, which he called for to offset the declining tourist revenues. Salmon did enjoy some victories, however. Making good on his promise to tax development, he originated Vermont's land-gains tax; it put the bite on exorbitant profits speculators made with rapid turnovers of land by taxing capital gains on a declining scale, thus discouraging the buying of land for quick sales. Salmon ushered in the bottle bill. The nickel deposit became mandatory in July 1973, despite hard lobbying against it by the U.S. Brewers Association. A bill prohibiting the use of phosphates, which rob streams of oxygen and kill plants and fish, also became law. But otherwise, as Tom Slayton, a reporter for the Barre *Times Argus*, put it, "the juice kind of ran out of the environmental movement."

The legislature had gone along with the smooth, avuncular Deane Davis during the creation of Vermont's pace-setting environmental laws, but once a liberal Democrat, a fellow who had hitchhiked to his own wedding (Salmon told the legislators this when he asked them to repeal a state ban on hitchhiking in 1973), who endorsed the decriminalization of marijuana ("I just don't think that possession of small quantities of marijuana is a serious crime," he said at a press conference), and who often chastised the elected representatives of the people for lack of vision, tried to enlist their cooperation, they shied away. Salmon's four years as governor certainly had a complex and contradictory nature. He was a man in a hurry during a slow-down. He found himself heading a liberal party that refused to build bridges toward fresh visions. As a leader, Salmon's rhetoric often seemed contradicted by his actions. Maybe it had to do with how long he had lived here, but Salmon, the fast-moving flatlander whose heart seemed in the right place, gradually perfected the knack of making the flawed symbolic gesture. When he pulled the plug on the state Christmas tree as a symbol of cutting back on energy use, it seemed a move insensitive to the fact that Christmas lights, really, at their essence, were for kids or for the kid in all of us. When he canceled the inaugural ball after his reelection, he could have made a stronger statement by riding to the affair in a crowded old Valiant, say, and maybe moving everything outdoors to a cleared lake in the moonlight, with bonfires—in effect, still celebrating, but in a refreshingly Vermont way, instead of taking all the fun out of it. After all, Vermonters had created their own sense of fun under trying conditions ever since the late 1700s. To think they couldn't do it for the want of a little gasoline seemed to deny the very ingenuity and spiritedness of state legend.

In 1974 Salmon's reelection campaign against Speaker of the House "Peanut" Kennedy turned nasty. Kennedy slammed Salmon for having introduced communist-like attitudes with his administration. An angry Salmon accused Kennedy of using Hitler-like tactics. Salmon's campaign poster, printed in sepia tones, showed a smiling forty-two-year-old in a kind of a haze. According to Neil Davis, a reporter for the *Burlington Free Press* who covered the political beat, Salmon retained strong support among female voters, lost that of many men, and ran more on charisma than on issues.

One of Salmon's successes came on the final day of the 1975 legislative session. A fifth superagency, the Transportation Agency, was formed. It brought highways, motor vehicles, railroads, waterways, and public transit all under one department. The Transportation Agency joined four other superagencies: Human Services, Administration, Development and Community Affairs, and Environmental Conservation, which Davis's administration had begotten, and perpetuated the centralization of state government.

*D*uring the 1960s, according to a study by G. Ross Stephens published in the *Journal of Politics* in 1974, Vermont had become one of the three most centralized states in America. The other two were Hawaii and Alaska. Stephens, a political science professor at the University of Missouri, claimed that large states, like California and New York, had been going the other way, decentralizing their control and power. Stephens, in a conclusion that should have startled absolutely no one, determined that the more federal money a state received, the more autonomy it gave up, and that the more state money a locality received, the more autonomy it gave up. During the sixties in Vermont, of course, with Phil Hoff at the wheel, and with the big Y of interstates being laid down, the state got a sizeable chunk of federal aid and the towns got their share of it from the state. According to State Archivist Gregory Sanford, Vermont's drift towards this monolithic form of government headquartered in Montpelier, with long bureaucratic arms and fingers into every city, gore, and township, was nothing new; it had been going on for the last hundred years.

"One of the great mystiques of Vermont," Sanford explained, "is that here is a loosely-knit central government overseeing a series of independent fiefdoms: each town. The reality is something completely different. By the 1890s Vermont is in the vanguard of centralized government. We're among the first states to create a statewide highway commission. We're among the first states to set up a public service board. We're among the first states to become involved in publicity for tourism. So, behind that mythology is this growing mood of putting more and more responsibility and authority in Montpelier."

Around the axiom of greater efficiency in a centralized government, a kind of political Holy Grail, elusive but majestic, surely there but just around the next corner or beyond the next law, state government consolidated its powers. An oxymoron to some, as improbable as "hedonistic responsibility" or "impact-free tourism" to others, "efficient government" nevertheless set the tenor of Vermont politics, especially after World War II. Historically, with its long Republican heritage, and with its locally elected selectmen, locally run poor farms, and locally directed schools, Vermont had been a synonym for efficiency. In the late 1940s Ernest Gibson, Jr.'s initiatives in education and health care had not gotten very far because most legislators equated increased spending, with a long-term goal of improving minds and bodies, with an inefficient use of tax dollars; to them, shortsightedness was efficient. In the late fifties, the Little Hoover Commission, charged with finding out whether the organization of government itself contributed to inefficiency or not, discovered that at the top, in the Vermont legislature and in the governor's office, there had always been talk about efficiency, and at the bottom, in the voting booths where Vermonters checked their ballots, they opted for politicians who promised efficiency; yet, in between, where most things political and bureaucratic got done, inefficiency, in truth, ruled. Substance and surface, the commission's report revealed, had become separated. Vermont's 152 department chiefs, commission chairpersons, and committee heads who answered—or were supposed to answer—directly to the governor, were about twenty times the number of subordinates a fine-tuned span-of-control encouraged. They were squandering their potential internally: wasting time, seldom establishing clear directions, and failing to communicate.

The sixties became a decade of consolidation of political power in Montpelier in the name of efficiency, first under Phil Hoff, then under Deane Davis. As in the federal government, it was an era that marked the rise in power of the executive branch and the diminution of power in both the legislative and judicial branches of government. This fundamental shift reflected America's growing infatuation with big business, with its CEOs, presidents, and executives who ramroded through change and made stockholders happy no matter what. Government became perceived more as a business, with certain departments responsible for "product" and "profit"—social, educational, and so on. In Montpelier, as a realigned government placed more power in the hands of the governor, and in the legislature as well, where power also increased, even if disproportionately compared to the governor's office, local control became a myth perpetuated at Town Meetings and bantered around by office seekers more attuned to folklore than to reality, or at least attuned to the reality that many voters still believed the folklore—far be it for most elected officials to upset their constituents with the truth.

Of course, once the superagencies were in place, a growing bureaucracy often waylaid visions of potentially powerful governors as effectively as 152 department heads had back in the fifties. There was one big difference, however. A department head could be talked to, whereas bureaucracy had a kind of elusiveness. Dealing with bureaucracy could often seem akin to wrestling with a lump in a waterbed.

KING RICHARD

A powerful incumbent who intimidates aspirants for his job tends to assume an exaggerated view of his importance in the political system.

—Burlington Free Press *editorial about Governor Richard Snelling, May 16, 1978*

*T*he election of Republican Richard Snelling as governor in 1976 signaled the ascent of the efficient business mentality to the top of the heap in Vermont politics. A self-made millionaire from Shelburne, Snelling was a bright, arrogant, and often intimidating leader with a "one man" managerial style. Though Snelling had lost his first round for the governorship against Hoff in 1966, this time he soundly trounced the Democratic hopeful, former State Treasurer Stella Hackell, who further weakened her party's already fractured unity with an anti-welfare stance. Hackell also had a hard time explaining away the deficit Salmon was leaving behind.

Once in Montpelier Snelling was high on development, tight-fisted management, and a thinned-down bureaucracy. He was not so high on the environment, on dealing candidly with the legislature, or on reporters, whom he seemed to view as royal stenographers. Not one to suffer a slight graciously, the governor had a habit of sending press clippings he didn't like to the reporters who had written them, underlining in red the parts they had gotten wrong. Snelling's business savvy, however, made "King Richard" popular with the voters. So popular they reelected him three times: in 1978, in 1980, and in 1982, always by sizable margins.

Snelling's first year in Montpelier was a tough one. He inherited the energy crisis from Salmon, America was in a recession, inflation was bad, interest rates high, and unemployment figures daunting. Fortunately, Americans still wanted to ski. They *needed* vacations. As a result, state revenues proved unexpectedly good, and Snelling was able to reduce taxes and to soon boast he had turned the state deficit into a surplus. This warmed the hearts of a cynical electorate that was still feeling the fuel blues and not exactly elated over newly elected President Jimmy Carter's inability to boost the national economy. The nation was in the process of learning a hard lesson: it was not immune from worldwide inflation fanned by OPEC, nor independent of the floundering world economy. Ironically, though, Vermont was finding that recreation, long thought of as a kind of luxury and as an economic force directly related to people's excess disposable incomes, was now a must in many people's minds. They needed escapes in an era still heavily shadowed by Vietnam, soured politically by the bitter aftermath of Watergate, and divided over issues of equality for women and minorities, and over the danger of environmental hazards. Who, for instance, besides a science fiction writer, could have imagined a few years before that a harmless inert gas fizzed out of aerosol spray cans could drift fifteen miles into the stratosphere, eat away at a protective layer of air you couldn't even see—called the ozone—and slowly expose you to the perils of ultraviolet light, causing skin cancer?

In any event, the tourists, as well as the flatlanders (a pejorative label that grew in popularity during Snelling's first two terms), continued to come to Vermont, priming the economic pump. Those moving up full-time put continual pressures on limited job opportunities and rising housing and land costs. The state as a whole, though, enjoyed a series of good years as revenues stayed high, establishing Snelling's reputation as a capable administrator and financial officer, until the early eighties when the national economy went into another sharp tailspin, taking Vermont down with it.

Snelling's most ambitious idea was a statewide property tax. The measure promised to better fund ever-increasing education costs and spread out the tax bite between the rich and poor towns, both of which had to meet the same state-mandated education requirements. The tax would eliminate some of the inequities of the existing system, which had been designed when Vermont was a state of hill farms and small towns, with some disparity between them, for sure, but with nothing like the economic disparities of the mid-seventies. There was already a mechanism in place called the state aid-to-education formula, which annually shuffled money around from town to town, compensating somewhat for the uneven distribution of wealth and varying growth patterns. But, basically, Vermont was strapped with a nineteenth-century property tax system and using it to fund late-twentieth-century education complications. Those complications included more and more kids needing mental and emotional help before they could even focus on a page of writing or a few math problems. High divorce rates, working families with no parent home after school (what would Senator Asa Bloomer have said about the eighties?), the absence of any spiritual grounding in many families, and the constant cultural bombardment from television and the media, all working in synergy, made the minds and hearts of many kids a kind of educational battleground.

Snelling failed to get the legislature behind his statewide property tax. No other governor, before him or after, fared any better. The rich towns didn't want it because they would have to pay more, but the poorer towns didn't want it either. They didn't want to give up setting and collecting their own taxes, a last vestige of local control. And the disparities, as certain towns continued to get richer, and others poorer, increased, putting greater stress on the education formula, as well as on local school boards and town budgets, which, in the eighties, irate taxpayers would start to vote down regularly. Though motivated by a fine ideal—that children, whether they attended a one-room school in Walden, a three-teacher school in Westfield, or a school with a gym, library, and shop in Bennington, should have an equal opportunity at learning—Vermont's way of paying for it always seemed to be struggling to catch up, and, if voters had anything to say about it, falling further behind every year. Declining national test scores, distressing reports from the workplace of high school graduates who couldn't read or write or add, never mind identify California as the big state on the west coast of America, along with rising teachers' salaries across the state throughout the decade, only exacerbated the dilemma. So did the 1984 Vermont School Approval Standards, which were additional legislative mandates—gyms, libraries, guidance counselors, and coordinated curriculums being a few of them—but without the money earmarked to pay for them nor any yardsticks to determine how well they worked.

In the late seventies, Snelling had better luck reducing state bureaucracy than he did changing the way education was paid for. Following his 1978 reelection, Snelling told the legislature at his inaugural, "After decades of incessant growth of the bureaucracy, we have, together, reasserted the people's determination to keep government in its place." About his government of limits, he continued, "I believe that we can see clearly now that when government feels compelled to fund every program, the total burden of taxes will inevitably make it impossible for our citizens to afford their own personal programs." In addition to curbing the growth, at least temporarily, of state government, Snelling also managed to write a much-needed state energy policy. It included a Hydro-Quebec deal that guaranteed Vermonters years of low-cost electricity from Canada but ignored the environmental destruction going on in James Bay in northern Quebec, where huge dams, some of them causing rivers to reverse their directions, were being built in order to sell power to New England and the Northeast.

All through his eight years as chief executive of the state, Snelling was dogged by two questions. Did this capable administrator have any vision of what Vermont should be? And why the constant round of controversies inflamed by his arrogance and temper? His well-documented arrogance divided loyalties towards him, alienated the press ("We would go to his barbecues," recalled one scribe who covered all four of Snelling's terms, referring to the cookouts the governor had at his Shelburne home for the media, "eat his steaks, and be plotting malice in our hearts all the time"), but may also have been exaggerated on occasion. Stephen Morse, Speaker of the House during Snelling's third and fourth terms, and a Democrat, insisted, "He's such a principled guy, it often got seen as ego or arrogance."

Whether from arrogance or principle, Snelling wasted tremendous energy on controversies that stemmed from an attitude of superiority, a lack of trust in subordinates, and a disinclination to compromise. The so-called "drill bit affair" in 1979 was a case in point. The drill bit affair was a nasty spin-off of a much-resisted reorganization of the state police, which Snelling supported, in the wake of years of sloppily handled internal problems. The governor soon got into a head-to-head with Public Safety Commissioner Francis E. Lynch, whom he had brought in to improve the state police. Lynch, in the words of Stephen Morse, "turned out to be a real para-military cowboy who just wouldn't quit." And worse, in Snelling's mind, just wouldn't cooperate. One of the things he wouldn't cooperate with was an investigation into the theft of some drill bits, allegedly by state troopers, in St. Johnsbury. Once the press put the pressure on, trooper Howard Gould of St. Johnsbury got so depressed over feeling he was being fingered that he shot himself behind the statehouse and left Dick Snelling, whom he blamed for ruining his reputation, an embarrassing note: "I hope you sleep well at night."

The year before, during the fall of 1978, Snelling had gotten into a wrangle with House Appropriations chairperson Madeleine Kunin. Kunin was running against Snelling's favorite, Peter Smith, for lieutenant governor. Their to-do centered on differing interpretations of the word "trust." Kunin told the press she was confused about the governor's use of the word, but that she had kept her word to everybody, him included. Snelling brushed the incident off by saying he didn't mean he didn't trust Kunin, he just trusted Peter Smith more. The exchange of broadsides in the press (Kunin beat Smith at the polls) only hinted at the depth of enmity separating the governor in power and the one to be. Subsequently, Snelling excluded Lieutenant Governor Kunin from his cabinet meetings. When I interviewed Governor Kunin in the late summer of 1990, she said about her former adversary: "I found him unapproachable."

Probably the murkiest controversy of Snelling's first eight years as governor occurred near the end of his fourth term. After some agonizing over the decision, on June 22, 1984, he ordered a predawn raid of the Northeast Kingdom Community Church in Island Pond. One hundred and twelve children and one hundred and ten church members were rounded up by ninety state police wearing bullet-proof vests and by fifty social workers. Hardly had the authorities placed the children in custody, when Vermont Superior Court Judge Frank Mahady ruled that the state had overstepped its constitutional power. Because several children allegedly had endured long disciplinary sessions in the name of the Lord didn't mean totalitarian tactics were an appropriate response, Mahady decided, especially since the state had little hard evidence of the abuse. "In our society, people are not pieces of evidence," Mahady said. He ordered that the children, who were being held under a blanket detention order so they could be questioned, be released. Snelling was livid.

*T*he raid on the Northeast Kingdom Community Church was one of the more bizarre episodes in recent Vermont history. It was notorious not only because of the rationale behind the unconstitutional sweep and Judge Frank Mahady's response to it, despite the fact the governor and the Attorney General John Easton, Jr., had approved it, but because of the role the press played, first as a beacon exposing the almost pagan rituals of the sect and its approximately three hundred members, and then as a shield so the raid could go forward secretly.

The church certainly captured its share of attention in the land of white steeples and a tradition of religious tolerance. It had an elusive leader, the thrice-married, Bible-quoting, charismatic Elbert Eugene Spriggs, Jr., a native of Chattanooga, Tennessee. Spriggs had advised his flock, before they moved to Vermont in 1978, that "child training begins at birth." Don't wait "till the child can 'reason' before disciplining," Spriggs told the church elders, a group of twelve men he selected. "The rod produces proper reasoning."

As *Burlington Free Press* reporter John Donnelley described Spriggs in a riveting series of articles in October of 1983, the zealot had coal black eyes, a mustache and beard, and as many addresses as a carny barker; in fact, Donnelley reported, Spriggs had once *been* a carny barker—his wife, his second, had had the bear act in a traveling show. But this had been before Spriggs found God. The self-ordained preacher relocated his church to Island Pond because of a Vermonter named Andre Masse. Masse urged Spriggs to move his flock there after members had worn out their welcome in Chattanooga. In Island Pond Spriggs once disciplined Masse before the congregation for having fondled a girl, going so far as to raise an ax to cut off Masse's guilty hand.

At first most folks in town tolerated the church. They discounted the weird rumors about whippings and brainwashings. The church bought houses, businesses, and a restaurant it operated twenty-four hours a day. Trouble started when authorities got wind that church doctors practiced without medical licenses and didn't bother to register either births or deaths. Following several infant deaths that did come to light, the FBI and the U.S. Border Patrol began to investigate the church.

At the time—1982–1983—when the woman's movement in Vermont was gaining support, the bandana-wearing, docile, and submissive womenfolk of the Northeast Kingdom Community Church seemed of an earlier era, the Puritan period, possibly, or the days of the Salem witch hunts. "Being submissive to men is a way to restore women to their rightful position," a member, a woman, told Donnelley.

Word also got around that the children of the Northeast Kingdom Community Church bore welts on their backs and bitterness in their hearts to serve the elders' sense of righteousness, a righteousness rooted in Proverbs, including chapter thirteen, verse twenty-four ("He who spares his rod hates his son, but he who loves him disciplines him diligently") and chapter twenty-two, verse fifteen ("Foolishness is bound up in the heart of a child: the rod of discipline will remove it from him"). The most publicized incident involved a pubescent girl who leaned against a windowsill in a room that was about forty degrees while Sprigg's right-hand man, an elder named Eddie Wiseman, striped her back, legs, and heels with a thin wooden rod. All the while, Wiseman, in the name of God, lectured her about righteousness. The girl's parents stood by, mute, watching. She had on nothing but her underwear. The session lasted for hours.

At the time the word "cult" made flatlander seem like a compliment. Cults were portrayed in the media as satanic. A weird church was one thing, but when the Island Pond Church was referred to as a cult, folks flashed on Charles Manson, the devil-worshipping leader of a small clique of followers who had butchered the pregnant actress Sharon Tate and several of her friends in California. More recently there had been the cult in Jonestown, Guiana. There the Reverend Jim Jones had ordered hundreds of his faithful to drink cyanide-laced Kool-Aid. And they did. Of course, most Vermonters could chalk those two cults up to the fact they had been seeded in California, where anything could happen. But a cult in Vermont?

In the fall of 1983, when Donnelley told Vermonters all about the church, from its day-long Sunday "celebrations," its vows of renunciation of material goods, its cheap labor force that made church businesses very competitive, and its run-ins with deprogrammers, trained professionals who focused for days, and sometimes weeks, on members of cults in an effort to crack the mindset and allegiance they fostered (members were often kidnapped, or "rescued," as their abductors put it, so the programmer could confront them), the reporter also described an exchange he had with Spriggs. The leader suddenly appeared, a Jesus-like figure, with shoulder-length hair streaked with gray, his face aged and lined for only forty-six. Spriggs laid hands on Donnelley, members of the congregation encircling them, and thanked the notebook-bearing scribe for doing a story. Spriggs assured Donnelley, somewhat humorously it seemed, "Even a reporter can be saved."

Spriggs had just shown up. He'd been traveling with a former church member's wife, now renamed Hanna Newsong, and Lydia, her four-and-a-half-year-old who believed Spriggs was her daddy. They'd been in Europe, at the church's chateau in France, then in Nova Scotia, on Sable Island, where a sixty-foot steel "ark" was being built to ferry the righteous back and forth across the Atlantic.

In the Northeast Kingdom, where times were tough, the church and Eugene Spriggs elicited some begrudging admiration. Not that it was shared by local law enforcers.

"How to hell are you going to serve papers on these people?" asked Sten Lium, a former Essex County States Attorney involved in the inquest of the unexplained infant deaths. "We didn't even know who they were."

But they were learning.

Said Lium: "Spriggs is a dictator."

Said church defector Naomi Kelley Goss about the church's "one mind": "Actually, what they have is the mind of Christ as interpreted by Gene Spriggs."

Said Charles Pope, founder and director of a rescue mission in Santa Barbara, California, where Spriggs worked after his initial religious conversion in 1971: "I believe Gene got away from the truth in the Scripture . . . He finally got on top, with people looking up to him, and I think he forgot the weight of the purpose that Christ served him for."

Said defector Larry Davis, a former elder: "It's not a mindless obedience. You're not a brick in God's building. You're a living stone that's unique."

Said an old friend from Sprigg's pre-conversion days in Chattanooga: "He was the wildest of us all."

Said Spriggs, about the children: "We discipline them because we love them."

A major investigation was initiated under the direction of Attorney General Easton. Officers traveled to nine states and Canada to talk to defectors. Then, on June 22nd, the state troopers and social workers swooped into the houses owned by the church and confiscated the children, based on testimonies under oath from several dozen excommunicants who had convinced authorities of the church's wicked ways. The problem, Mahady ruled, was that no laws had been broken. Or if they had been, those responsible had not been identified and arrested for their indiscretions.

Constitutional questions swirled around the raid like mist around a river valley on a cold June morning after a day of warm rain. The state defended its actions as the only means of rescuing brutalized children. But the children went back to their parents.

For the state's two biggest newspapers, the *Burlington Free Press* and the *Rutland Herald* whose editors had quashed the story because of political pressures, the questions of responsible journalism and of whether they had conducted themselves responsibly in the circumstances remained troublesome. Were the two largest papers in the state, both of which had sent reporters to the scene before the raid, but who only reported it after the fact, cowering to power? Or were they, as contended, protecting the children, too?

Steve Terry, editor of the Rutland daily at the time of the raid,, remembered it with mixed emotions. "If I had to do it over again," he said, "I wouldn't do what I did. I had been led to believe—and I think somewhat quite disingenuously now, that there were some real bad things being done to those kids up there. And I'm not so sure about that now. But I was persuaded. And then I helped persuade the *Free Press.*"

That Snelling muscled the press came as no surprise to long-time observers of the governor's methods. Nor did the fact that collusion between the press and politics had facilitated an unconstitutional roundup redolent of fascism in the name of justice. After all, it was 1984.

*J*ust where Vermont was headed during the late seventies and early eighties was a puzzle. The "vision thing" hung awkwardly around Snelling, like a cheap suit. The industrialist's concept of Vermont's future seemed to be a kind of Massachusetts North, but with higher mountains and less welfare. Of course, vision was not a word synonymous with the late seventies. Surviving was most folks' goal. Keeping debt low, staying employed, going to the disco where you could dance to the hypnotic beat of "Shame, Shame, Shame" by Shirley and Company, or to the pounding rhythm of KC and the Sunshine Band's "That's the Way I Like It." Disco seemed symbolic of a kind of insidious and infectious zoning out of more complicated realities, realities many people did not want to hear about. Sex, power, and an ominous rhythm often charted by a computer mated to a synthesizer radiated from the new music, offending old rock and rollers. "Disco sucks," they sneered.

New York City tottered on the edge of bankruptcy, America-at-large seemed to be suffering from a low-grade malaise, and the middle-class hungered for a lost sense of belonging to a place. They hungered, in the words of Frank Bryan, a political science professor then at St. Michael's College, for "the community axiom." The community axiom promised a "return to the good old days, to traditional American values, to a simple life of interpersonal relations where individuals still control events in society generally and in the government as well." Unfortunately, Bryan warned, if they moved to Vermont they were going to be sorely disappointed. That was because "the system axiom" now predominated, the professor said. The system axiom saw community as a myth of the quickly disappearing past.

Bryan published his often brilliant and generally persuasive argument about the nature of change in Vermont in 1974. The heart of it was contained in the now well-known chapter six, "Political Life in a Rural Technopolity," in his book, *Yankee Politics in Rural Vermont*. If your true interest was in interpersonal enrichment, Bryan advised, try Baltimore, or the Bunker Hill area of Boston. Not the rural byways of the Green Mountains. The administrative state was taking over here, he said quite correctly. Efficient and bureaucratic, it conducted decision-making in a centralized location called Montpelier and disdained Town Meeting as a quaint ritual to placate the community types.

Bryan was no apologist for the future he saw coming at Vermonters. And he spelled out what it would be like: heavily taxed, isolated by choice, and spiteful towards additional outsiders because too many of them would ruin the view. Life in God's country, or the "back beyond," as he liked to call it, had already become so desirable, even by the mid-seventies, that those already here were willing to pay large taxes to keep it untainted. The old willingness to tolerate newcomers had already started to wither, Bryan insisted. Zoning and regulations were thriving. Status was the modern carrot that enticed the technocrat. Rural living in a high-tech mode, with your *Country Journal* close by, horses in the barn, your twenty or thirty or two hundred acres protecting you from all encroachments, conferred status of a kind that population pressures elsewhere only heightened.

Forming the system axiom so dramatically transforming Vermont, according to Bryan, were three layers of humanity. One layer was the technocratic elite; well-educated escapees from urbania who now they had their rural paradise damn well meant to keep it. A second was the middle-class operatives who labored beneath, and usually for, the elite, carrying out their decisions and cashing their paychecks. The third group was the one Bryan loved to talk about: farmers.

Vermont farmers were the ultimate technocrats, Bryan wrote. They were not only willing to escape the interpersonal past, but had become leaders in its dissolution. "Technocrats to the core," he called them. "They understand that their survival depends on a political system geared to the language of science and process—in a word efficiency. It is not the lifestyle of farming they are interested in, it is the economics of agriculture." More than anyone else, Bryan said, farmers, once such an independent, can-do group, had their lives run by outside decision-makers who determined how much they got paid, and for what, and relied on technological innovations in machinery and science to stay competitive.

Bryan didn't blame the future he foresaw on newcomers, however. They weren't ruining Vermont traditions. Urbanism didn't transfer here well at all, he insisted. Urban values—anonymity, the status of material goods and position, impersonal relationships—could be seeded, but they wouldn't grow. Many newcomers wanted to jettison those values anyway, right off the bat getting to know everybody on their dirt road.

What would grow, Bryan predicted, was something he called "a rural technocracy." A rural technocracy was a twenty-first-century place in which technology, traditional rural values, and the scientific method fused into a system, a lifestyle, much of it electronically plugged into the world-at-large, but run by old-fashioned values. The "immersion of the individual in a sophisticated life pattern anchored in technology" was going to determine the future in the Green Mountains, Bryan wrote, not a second-hand blooming of "urbanism [that] has gone stale."

It sounded not all that bad, except for the death of community part. Bryan's discussion of how rural types were different from urban brought to mind something a friend of mine had once told me: "You bump into somebody in the city, they get offended. Bump into somebody in the country, they remember you for the rest of their life."

The cracks in Bryan's arguments, it seemed to me, had to do with the "traditional rural values" part of his technocracy trinity. What were traditional rural values? Physical labor was certainly one. Self-sufficiency was another. A third was the powerful desire to be modern, to leave traditions behind. A fourth was neighborliness. Fifth, a belief in God.

Networking and FAXing and constantly using the telephone, dominant features of the near-future technocracy that would suffuse the back roads and the villages, making them electronic fast lanes and optic-fiber commons of the eighties, didn't lead, as far as I could see, to labor, self-sufficiency, or neighborliness. They did lead towards the new and the modern, and had as much spirituality invested in them as those New Age users wanted to put in. But also very important, and something that technocracy didn't mention, was what to do about the resentment bubbling up in natives pushed aside by the new technocrats, and the failure of politics to build bridges connecting the old values and hopes with the new technical realities and high I.Q.s.

Nevertheless, Frank Bryan had the kind of futuristic vision no politician had made his/her domain. On the rear jacket of the book was the author himself, a model of the brainy technocrat of Vermont's future, a boyish-looking fellow in unlaced barn boots and a dark T-shirt, tugging the head of an ox into a yoke. "His oxen, Mickey and Joe, placed first in the under-2500 pound class at the Orleans County fair in 1973," the blurb read in part. "Helping their owner cut wood and haul it for the previous winter's supply undoubtedly contributed to their success."

On the farms, as Bryan predicted, things kept going high- tech. Farmers continued trading in the bull for sperm kept alive in liquid hydrogen and implanted by the long arm of the local artificial inseminator. They bought bigger tractors, taller Harvestore silos, and more sophisticated vacuum-powered pipeline systems to get the white cash crop from the cow's fluid outlets to the stainless steel bulk tank. Their numbers kept shrinking, of course, because no matter what they did, or didn't do, the milk-making business couldn't keep all of them financially afloat.

Overseeing the era was King Richard, a governor who, in Frank Bryan's analysis, epitomized the system's axiom breed. The axiom, Bryan wrote, "holds that man is happiest in a rational arm's length relationship with others—lots of others—preferably of different varieties. Issues should be judged long range from a statewide or national perspective." Bryan's system axiom was cosmopolitan, goal oriented, and guided by a single overriding principle: efficiency. An interesting twist with Snelling was that he brought a very human temper into the system, upsetting its inhumanity with his outbursts and egotism, yet, at the same time, making himself less a governor than he otherwise could have been.

A middle-aged professional, a publisher from an old Boston firm, and I almost bumped into each other in a Montgomery barnyard one wintry night in the late seventies. He gazed around in the blowing snow like a dazed soul and declared, "We're living a Kafkaesque novel!"

His wife sat in the car, a blurry orange U-Haul to its rear. They had moved up finally, he said.

My older friend was one of a small, select, and often extremely influential group of newcomers of the mid- and late-seventies: the prematurely burnt-out professional eager to start over. With track records and decades of experience in whatever they had done, many of these skilled, middle-aged high achievers shoved quickly to the head of the economic ranks in their adopted towns. Some got involved in community service, others in politics. A rare few, like Blair and Ketchum, started enterprises that became synonymous with Vermont. But collectively, as their successes spread, they prompted the muffled outcry, "Flatlander!"

The so-called leap "from Brooks Brothers to L.L. Bean," as author Peter Jennison, a member of this loosely-allied fraternity called it, either meant picking up the pieces of a prior career or forging something new. Two who stayed with their careers were Russell Morse, an attorney from New Jersey who practiced law in Woodstock and went on to become a Superior Court judge; and Fred Pope, from Connecticut, who moved to Tom Salmon's office in Bellows Falls. One who changed was Wall Street broker-turned-innkeeper Max Commins of South Woodstock. There were a number of older journalists who found how little money you made following events from the back beyond. One was Pulitzer Prize winner Edgar May. May would, as a state senator in the eighties, watch his sister, Madeleine Kunin, wrestle her way through the gates of power and become Vermont's first women governor. A fellow from this older group who closely approximated the technocrat of Frank Bryan's imagination was Carroll Bowen.

Bowen had become a resident of Rochester in 1974 at the age of forty-four. He had grown up on a farm in Indiana where, he recollected, "The day electricity came was a miracle." As a young man he sold books for Oxford University Press and was the director of the MIT press for a while in the sixties. Then Bowen made the leap from text and paper to images and screens and became a telecommunications consultant. When Bowen first moved to Rochester, he kept forty or so beef cattle and calves, mostly for tax breaks, and drove back and forth weekly on I-89 to Boston. There he developed electronic-based continuing education programs for engineers. "Some weeks I wouldn't go at all," he said. "Particularly during haying."

Rochester had been badly depressed in the fifties when Bowen arrived. He had paid an average of thirty dollars an acre and slowly amassed thirteen hundred acres. During the eighties Bowen shifted his telecommunications consulting business to Vermont and expanded his farming considerably. By the end of the decade his North Hollow Farm leased twenty-six parcels of land from nine other owners to supply a large herd of Herefords, Hereford-Angus, and Hereford-Angus-Charolais breeds with corn, silage, hay, and pasture. "We do a three-breed cross for a slaughter animal," Bowen told me. "Lean, tender, and flavorful [beef] free from hormonal or pharmacologic contamination" was what North Hollow Farm sold, according to its sales flyer. The farm also sold pork from a Yorkshire-Landrace-Duroc breeding stock raised on organic feed, the bacon free of cancer-linked nitrites. Bowen marketed chickens, again naturally grown. These were white "Cornish Hallcross meat birds." Yard strollers, that is, rather than robotic chickens fed by conveyor belts in football field-size poultry factories.

Bowen no longer used his farms as a tax shelter, he said, and had relinquished much of the day-to-day control to his son Mike, a graduate of Rochester High School, and his high-energy daughter-in-law Valerie who raised the produce and watched over the yard stroller end of the sizable operation. Bowen himself continued to put in a quarter of his work week doing telecommunications consultation. "I'm a young sixty-five," he said, "a very young sixty-five. And ready to take great gambles."

One gamble was his purchase in 1990 of the Martin farm on the flats of the North Branch between Rochester and Granville. Carl Martin, a workaholic, had run the impressive farm, with its tall silos and low silhouette barn alongside Route 100, until his wife had died in 1987. Then he'd come apart and shot himself. It had been another lean time for farmers. The "whole herd buy-out," a federally subsidized program that cost $1.8 billion, was eliminating fourteen thousand dairy farmers nationwide. One hundred and ninety-two of them were in Vermont. The cows went to the butchers, and the farmers into early retirement. The Martin farm, though not part of the buy-out, seemed about to go out of business once Carl Martin was dead. The Vermont Land Trust, an organization committed to keeping farms in production rather than seeing them subdivided and sold as real estate, bought it. Operationally, the committed Martin family was replaced, Bowen said, with "casual, informal dairying that didn't work." Most of the farm soon came on the market again and Bowen picked it up.

In remarks to the press about the purchase, Bowen alluded to "those farm families that worked these lower mountain slopes and the river bottom farms, the Burroughs and the Taylors and Howes in Hancock, and the Warners and Beans of Rochester." He reminded everyone that "the families practiced diversified farming as we call it today, small-scale dairying, with pigs and chickens and other livestock and poultry. With very hard work, non-mechanical planting and harvesting, and family labor, they built and preserved the farms of the upper White River Valley." The Martins had started out with eight cows and rented pastures, Bowen said, and had grown to dominate farming in the valley. "We are another farm family," he added, an entrepreneurial farm family committed to "low-input, sustainable agricultural practices." Their farm married select farm values—in this case, the perpetuation of sustainable soils and healthy foods—with inspection and marketing technologies that allowed for point-of-growing and butchering sales, and had a sound scientific ethic of environmental concern. "We cultivate our corn rather than use weed-killer," Bowen said. "We spread our manure as our major soil nutrient. We strive for healthy animals and soils."

Down in Vernon, a town bordered by both New Hampshire and Massachusett, Paul Miller, fifty-four, was less of a New Age farmer than Bowen. A technocrat, nevertheless, he relied on technology to keep his 160-Holstein operation prosperous. The afternoon I stopped in, sunlight glistened on three blue Harvestore silos and corn snow blanketed the meadows. Across Route 5 sat a symbol of what many Vermonters had come to associate with technology gone awry: the Vermont Yankee nuclear power plant, a composite of huge blocks, a tall smokestack, and wires of considerable gauge swooping gracefully toward the horizon.

Paul Miller, a solid man with a deeply lined face, led me into his parlor past stacks of black and white photographs on a table and framed covers of the *American Agriculturist,* the *Ford New Holland News,* and other agricultural magazines on the wall. His hobby was photography, Miller said as I took a seat.

"Farming has lost its fun," he said when I asked how he felt about his occupation. "Who likes to run computers? A farmer likes to drive a tractor." He had an eight-thousand-dollar corn planter, he said. "I use it for four days." He had a fifty-thousand-dollar tractor. "I haven't started it in five months." He was more of a businessman than a farmer, Miller said. He had automated steadily ever since taking over the farm from his father in the early sixties. In 1990 Miller used free-stall-housing and milked ten cows at a time, which reduced labor substantially from the stanchion system where a farmer moved from cow to cow. He had small Bobcat loaders for all the shoveling jobs: bedding stalls, cleaning manure, feeding the cows. "We used to shovel almost all day, it seemed. Either shovel or pitch hay. Even throwing hay bales—that's pretty much eliminated now. We have elevators.

We have bale-kickers, to kick it in the wagons." However, Miller added, "To afford these things, you had to increase your income; that means more cows."

The last few days, Miller said, he had been pondering the latest thing in dairy farming: bovine somatotropin, or BST, the growth hormone. "Yesterday, the fellow from Monsanto was here trying to sell me on it." As a former biology professor (Miller had taught at Walla Walla College in Washington for a year in the sixties) he was intrigued. BST was "naturally occurring," he said. "People produce it. It starts out as a pituitary extract; that's where it's found, in slaughtered beef cows. They get this bovine growth hormone, isolate it, and then culture it with bacteria; then grow it as a bio-tech product. Then it's refined, purified, and I would buy it and have to inject it every two weeks." As a farmer, however, he was afraid of the hormone because consumers were leery of it. "We know we could ruin the market in a day or two."

Miller showed me the materials the Monsanto salesman had left to promote BST. The sheet that graphed potential profits made the hormone seem awfully inviting.

"With all the technology," Miller said, "we're really at the mercy of everything working right."

I asked him why he went into farming, and stayed in, despite changes he has not particularly liked.

"I just wanted to raise my kids on a farm. It's a way of life."

The way of life in a technocracy: lots of sophisticated machinery, a believe in science and old-fashioned rural family values—all within a shout of Vermont Yankee, the shadow of which might make some folks nervous—but not Paul Miller, who was a religious man, a Seventh-Day Adventist, the church descended from the Millerites of the 1840s, the sect that had sold all its worldly goods and hiked to the Jamaica hilltops to await the Second Coming. Paul Miller talked briefly about his church, but didn't proselytize. A train passed by and the parlor floor vibrated like a wooden tuning fork. Photographs danced on the table. Miller smiled. He used to catch the train from here to Brattleboro as a boy, right out in front of the house, he said. These days there was no passenger service and the propane cars worried him a little. "They could wipe me off the map, and I'd never know it. Take the farm with them."

Outside, leaving, I noticed the license place on Miller's Volkswagen read: *DAIRY.*

LEARNING ARTS

The arts are the privilege of the rich. Only wealthy individuals and wealthy societies afford them. Their functions are to fill out leisure time and to decorate dull spaces. That's the reality. But in spirit the arts are gods: they heal, revolutionize, fulfill, perfect. They can do all these things that we never dare to dream as possible, and they are dead-serious about it.

—*Peter Schumann, Introduction to* Bread and Puppet

*T*he rivers were high and brown, the sky low and grey, and the rolling terrain still blanketed in snow, though it was early April, as I came down the eastern flank of the Green Mountains and into the "kingdom," the tundra-like region of Vermont where many artists, writers, and poets settled in the seventies and gradually carved out reputations. In those days the Northeast Kingdom had been poorer, more isolated, and probably even a little more desolate than it seemed to me now. But for several reasons—land remained cheap, it wasn't *that* long a drive to Burlington or Montreal, and you were still in Vermont, albeit in a region where folks still possessed a distinct rural character—creative types had come here and stayed. They included Peter Schumann with his low-cost, high-drama Bread and Puppet Theater in Glover; Jay Craven with his Catamount Arts and Films, which brought world-class entertainers to scattered auditoriums in backwater towns; Don Sunseri, the founder and guardian angel of Grass Roots Art and Community Efforts ("Our message at GRACE," Sunseri often said, "is you should not know what you're doing"), which ran painting workshops for the elderly and the handicapped; Howard Frank Mosher, the Irasburg novelist who made "Kingdom County," as he called it, his fictional terrain; Claire Van Vliet of Newark, the recipient of a MacArthur Fellowship, or "genius grant," for handmade books; Don Bredes, an author who had struck first-novel pay dirt with his best selling *Hard Feelings*; Vermont's state poet Galway Kinnell, another MacArthur genius grantee who spent much of his time in Sutton; and many others less acclaimed.

Throughout the seventies, as a kind of counterpoint to the energy blues and zigzagging economy, art in Vermont created a much-needed cultural anchor. In a state seeking a new, post-agrarian identity, artists who had typically fled crowded cities and commercial art scenes sank roots into communities, and with words, paints, musical notes, and dancing feet helped ground this drifting place. Not that Vermont had been without art or culturally starved before then. The Marlboro Music Festival, the Vermont Symphony, Southern Vermont Artists, Bread Loaf Writers' Conference, and the Shakespeare Festival in Burlington, for example, had been active for years. But the audiences had been select, heavy with summer people, typically short on workboots and flannel shirts. Art and the common man, art and the local school—these were concepts not exactly integral to the state.

I remember the first time I ever met an artist. It was at Sugarbush in the mid-sixties. Even though I had seen a few museums and could even name a couple of painters, I marveled at the very idea that such an exotic creature was living there. My sentiments—I saw artists as rarefied, often aloof creators of stuff for the walls of the well-off before it got hung for the next few centuries on the walls of museums—were not unusual, even if they were totally stereotyped. Like many Vermonters I lacked any art education, knew little to nothing of the value of art, its magic and beauty and seditiousness. Attempting to jostle mindsets like mine, "to educate the audience," became a major goal of the Vermont Council of the Arts, which was founded in the mid-sixties as an offshoot of the National Arts and Cultural Development Act passed by Congress. The VCA awarded fellowships to artists and sponsored plays, art openings, dance programs, concerts, and readings in scattered halls, churches, Granges, libraries, and school auditoriums.

Drawing a broad audience to the events was a challenge, as was fund raising to make up for losses that were often a consequence of poor attendance. If art pushed into realms of expression some people associated with wasted time and wild ideas, there could be trouble. An exhibition of photography with a few non-bovine breasts exposed might please some transplants, for sure, but it was also likely to rile a few members of the broader audience being courted, prompting a critical letter to the local paper, as well as a few phone calls to state representatives, the callers asking why taxpayers' money was being spent on filth.

For artists grappling with the truth about a transforming Vermont, with the conflict between tradition and change, and between the images of tourism and the realities of many lives that were bleak, compromised, and often abused, the in-state marketplace for their work was limited. Nevertheless, as a good place to escape the cities and to squirrel up in a pastoral paradise, the circumstances here approached the ideal. In addition to relatively low costs compared to cities, you had a stimulating environment in which an older, traditional population was absorbing and being changed by a bright, ambitious, and typically liberal influx. Up in the three counties of Essex, Orleans, and Caledonia, of course, you were not only in Vermont, but you were in a separate kingdom where the moose outnumbered the lawyers and the rusty trailers outnumbered the Saabs.

I found Don Sunseri, a gnomish, self-effacing fellow in his mid-fifties, overseeing a GRACE workshop in Greensboro. Eight or ten elderly ladies, and a couple of younger mothers and brush-swirling children, sat at tables, painting. Sunseri had been a sculptor in New York City, but in the early seventies began disliking the commercial art scene. Determined to reaffirm the spiritual in art he moved to St. Johnsbury and took a job as the dishwasher at a nursing home.

"It was my first connection with old people," he told me. And the seedbed of GRACE.

Sunseri swapped his dishwashing apron for a box of paints after convincing the home administrator to give him a chance to set up a workshop as an alternative to the typical Bingo and card-playing sessions. Sunseri soon had workshops in several area nursing homes, but kept his art philosophy simple: "Anyone who has the urge can let it out, and do it. Training is nice, but not necessary."

Sixteen years later GRACE had uncovered dozens of talents. They included Roland Rochette, a jack-of-all-trades who had died at ninety-nine. Rochette made assemblages—farms, sugaring scenes, the interior of a logging camp, the statehouse in Montpelier—from little stones, wood chips, tiles and paint. Richie Delisle, a veteran who had been in a battalion that liberated the Dachau death camp at the end of World War II, painted disturbing pictures of crematory ovens and prisoners. GRACE's best-known artist was Gayleen Aiken from Barre. Suffering from a severe personality disorder since birth, she painted what her childhood might have been like if she could have stayed up late at night and played a grand piano beneath a full moon, gone sledding on snowy hills above the Barre granite quarries, and been in plenty of musical parades, usually accompanied by the Raimbillis, a family of twenty-four that she made up. In the late eighties, Aiken had a show at Lincoln Center in New York, had a documentary made about her life and work by Jay Craven (it was titled "Gayleen"), and found her oils in demand by folk art collectors.

At the Greensboro workshop Sunseri introduced me to Dot Kibbee, an effervescent seventy-three-year-old former nurse from Hardwick. Kibbee had GRACE painted across the shoulders of her jacket. She had recently completed an ambitious autobiographical work titled "All That Glitters." The painstakingly rendered painting consisted of dozens of two-inch squares, each with a scene from Kibbee's past, including a cornucopia, a registered nurse insignia, a black dog howling at the moon, and her mother and father.

"I emptied my head out," Kibbee said, then added in classic understatement, "Not much in it."

*T*he following day I found Jay Craven at Catamount Arts and Films in St. Johnsbury. Craven had started Catamount in 1977 and except for rare periods when there was an infusion of always desperately needed cash (in 1985 Catamount received an eighty-five thousand dollar Advancement Grant from the National Endowment of the Arts) had kept it aloft with the economic juggling skills of a bonds trader, the booking talents of a New York City impresario, and the day-to-day pragmatism of a master-sergeant. Nevertheless, after thirteen years as director, "It's the same old story," Craven conceded: too little staff, too many bills, not enough time.

Thin, thirty-nine, intense, today Jay Craven looked like a middle-aged rocker who had spent too many nights on the road. In his office, located in the rear of the former St. Johnsbury Post Office, now rehabilitated into a small theater, a gallery, and working spaces, there were stacks of post cards advertising the upcoming concert of country singer Reba McEntire. Mummenschanz, the avant-garde dance troop, had bombed last night, Craven said. But Catamount had lost only three thousand dollars, rather than eight thousand because he had renegotiated the contract at the last minute. Putting on shows fifteen of the last sixteen weekends had kept him running. He was trying to find enough time to finish the study guide for "High Water," a dramatic film based on a Howard Frank Mosher short story that Catamount had filmed in seven days. Craven directed, Don Bredes wrote the script. The study guide would complete an educational package—the film, a documentary of the making of the film, the short story, the script of the story, and the study guide—and Catamount would distribute it to schools. The film had just won the Golden Gate Award for Best Short Dramatic Film at the San Francisco International Film Festival.

Like Bread and Puppet's Peter Schumann and GRACE's Don Sunseri, Craven was a runaway from New York City. In the mid-seventies he quit the liberal anti-war movement ("I was ready to burn out and spend the rest of my life chasing Richard Nixon") and moved to the Northeast Kingdom with his girlfriend, Patty, the former wife of sculptor Claes Oldenburg. They discovered that folks there were not like them. The Vermonters were poorer and less intellectual for one thing. They were also living in a rural culture so indigenous that few of them seemed aware of just how far from the mainstream the region really was. That appealed to Craven, yet didn't help him find a job.

In 1976 he started teaching at Peacham School, an alternative school for grades seven through twelve in the town of Peacham, about a ten-mile drive southwest of St. Johnsbury. At the time alternative schools numbered about one thousand around the country. But they were particularly popular in Vermont, where the flower children of the sixties now had children of their own. Craven taught social studies, journalism, media, and film. Peacham School had a visionary director who fostered a sense of critical consciousness in students. There were no grades. Each student took a year of theater, a year of film-making and media. Craven's film program screened works by Truffaut, Godard, Bunuel, Antonioni and American films organized around single themes like "growing up." At Peacham School, Craven said, he came to grips with the fact that Vermont kids needed to find their own voices, comprehend their own history. Traditional schools tend to reinforce a sense of powerlessness, he said, which kids then take with them out into the real world. He found that particularly true in 1990. The family farm as the glue of community had lost its adhesion, leaving kids prey to external realities that were commercial, thought up by people hundreds of miles away, and often slick and soul-sapping. Pummeled by television images and cultural heroes whose relationship to Vermont were tenuous at best and non-existent most of the time, kids got lost. He said that three students at Lake Region Union High School in Orleans had committed suicide in the last eighteen months. They seemed to have been swept along by the vicarious bravado of violence and heavy metal, he went on, but lacked any authentic seeds of rebellion. The dead kids had, sadly enough, become cult heroes.

Although Craven was best known for having brought entertainers like Memphis blues legend B. B. King, folksingers Pete Seeger and Joan Baez, dancer Mose Allison, and the king of soul, Ray Charles, to halls and gyms in Vermont where their presence must have seemed as unlikely at times as an eighty degree day in January, the impresario's true forte was education. He strove to educate adults and children through art, to regenerate community and the human spirit with images, song, dance, and mystery. Over lunch Craven mentioned that he was considering basing Catamount's next film on a book by Garret Keizer, author of *No Place But Here*. Keizer taught English at Lake Region Union High School.

In his book Keizer touches on the need to honor the sacredness of kids, whether they're the misfits, the college-bound, or the Future Farmers of America in their conspicuous blue jackets. "We sigh our thanks for living in a better place and time, and we send the kids off to the video arcade," he wrote. "But the energy remains. That its use has often been tragic does not make its waste any less tragic. That we do waste it, that we have allowed it to be perverted into a subculture of obnoxious mannerisms and indiscriminate consumerism does not make it any less marvelous to consider."

Craven's unorthodox thinking and efforts on behalf of education in Vermont (Catamount's programs constantly integrated local artists and their work into the schools) brought to mind another renegade educator, Carl Borgmann, who had been president of the University of Vermont in the mid-fifties. Borgmann, a midwesterner, had pulled and pushed the state university out of its Ivy League coziness and exclusivity, had admitted that "the task that education faces is almost discouraging in its magnitude," and had, like proponents of alternative schools, believed "classrooms are just one part of the [education] process." Borgmann had the view that a good education made a "free man," one who recognized that ends achieved were no better than their means, that self-reliance did not exempt one from the necessity of cooperation, and that the pursuit of pleasure was not the same as the pursuit of happiness.

Both Borgmann and Craven, at heart, were educational philosophers. Borgmann had said education went forward in four key ways. First, it trained you to communicate by words, both spoken and written, and to listen well. Secondly, it gathered a broad storehouse of knowledge to deal with various demands, situations, and people. Thirdly, it refined skills of critical reasoning, to improve on your ability to separate right from wrong and to understand logical conclusions. And fourthly, education developed "good" qualities—honesty, sincerity, trustworthiness, and respect and love for others. Borgmann, in a speech in Strafford in 1954, where he was unveiling a historic marker honoring Justin Morrill, the Vermont senator who fathered the land-grant college and university system of the United States in the mid-nineteenth century, had added that his philosophy of education was "wrapped tightly to his faith that man . . . is capable of becoming and has an inner drive to become more Godlike."

An odd thing for an educator to say, or so it would seem from a perspective thirty-odd years down the road, when the mention of God in the schools, along with prayer and other rituals, including the saluting of the flag and the reading of the "Pledge of Allegiance," had become a no-no.

In 1984 Jay Craven was recognized in a special issue of *Esquire* as one of fifty Americans under the age of forty who had significantly affected American culture. About his accomplishments noted fiction writer Anne Beattie, who came to St. Johnsbury to interview Craven, said: "Imagine if you will the Metropolitan Museum of Art with its mummies stored in a library, its Old Masters in the auditorium of P.S. 11, and its sculptures in a bowling alley, all of which can be brought out if there's somebody strong enough to carry it. Having an edifice is crucial, as Jay Gatsby knew when he set out to become the Great Gatsby." But, as Beattie informed readers, there was no edifice in St. Johnsbury. Catamount was "a floating entity," anchored by a room with empty wine jug lights, a couple of desks, a sofa, and with maps of Vermont on the walls, pushpins shoved into towns where cultural growth was in progress. Also on the walls were a poster of Charlie Chaplin, one of Craven's heroes, and memorabilia from Craven's political past. "Like Fonda and Lennon," Beattie wrote, "Craven has a vision of what would be, at least, a more ideal society."

Don Bredes, a friend and collaborator of Craven's, lived a half hour north of St. Johnsbury, up in the hills near the Stannard/Wheelock town line. On my way there, I got a flat tire. Luckily, I was on the outskirts of Lyndonville. I thumped fifty yards to a garage where the sign said:

Open 7 Days a Week 7 A.M. to 7 P.M.

Inside I found a scrawny, rough-handed fellow who probably had not gone to Catamount's presentation of the Washington Ballet, nor to hear jazzman Wynton Marsalis blow his trumpet. For one thing, he didn't have the time. From nearby Sheffield he worked seven days a week here by himself, he said. He looked about thirty. "Don't even have time for a cold beer anymore." He laughed and poured hot water over instant coffee in a styrofoam cup.

"Word of mouth," that was what was going to build his business up, he said a few minutes later, having deftly removed my tire and replaced it with the spare, his hands oily and quick and graceful. Radio hadn't done it; he'd tried that. Cost $170, "but didn't do me no good."

Thirty minutes later I found Bredes' house overlooking a muddy back road in Wheelock. A somber man, he was graying around the temples. I asked him why he lived back in the country and he said he found "an enduring wildness."

Bredes had moved to the Northeast Kingdom in 1969 after graduating from Syracuse University. He taught English at Lake Region Union for three years, earning fifty-eight hundred dollars his first year, made friends with poet Galway Kinnell ("we played tennis together"), landed a writing fellowship to the University of California at Irvine with Kinnell's help, and out on the West Coast discovered the voice that made *Hard Feelings*, a quasi-autobiographical novel about coming of age in the sixties, a hit. The book's success put Bredes, who had returned to Vermont and was waiting tables at Carbur's Restaurant in Burlington, into the literary fast lane. *Hard Feelings* was the kind of first novel people who dreamily consider trying their hand at fiction fantasize about. In 1977 it was named one of the American Library Association's Best Books of the Year. Paperback rights sold for $185,000. The film rights got gobbled up. Bredes built his house from the proceeds.

Since then, however, a follow-up success had eluded him. His latest novel, one with a Northeast Kingdom setting, was making the rounds with publishers. It was about what became of counterculture people and their ideals, he said. "The whole notion of sixties' living is not as bankrupt as people today think it is."

Of the yet-to-be-filmed *Where the Rivers Flow North*, a fast-paced, evocative tale that takes place during the 1927 flood that left much of Vermont in ruins, Bredes said he had a good time writing the screenplay. As for *High Water*, he found the lead actor, a farm boy determined to get his jalopy to the track in Quebec despite a kind of Faulknerian hurdle— torrential rains that sweep away bridges—too overtly angry and fierce. Craven also penned in some changes Bredes didn't particularly like.

Before I left, Bredes said he didn't see himself moving from this house deep in the hills, where he lives with his wife and a child. But, he added as a literary afterthought, if you subscribe to the dictum, you must write out of your experience, this environment "does limit you."

*S*ince the cultural explosion of the sixties and seventies, when the Vermont Council on the Arts was spawned and the craft ethic elevated the handmade above the manufactured, both the cultural bureaucrats and the audience-at-large had been awaiting the coming of *the* Vermont artist. The vision of the artist had to contain Vermont in great distillation, like a super kind of maple syrup, grade A-plus-extra, so to speak. The vision needed beauty, edge, substance, historical resonance, and had to make the commercial crossover into the national art market. Declarations by the VCA, calls for new works by various art sponsors, statements by individuals, all emphasized the ideal that some Green Mountain Elvis, some Morrisville Marilyn, some backwoods Picasso or Joyce would spring forth, creating a big splash outside regional boundaries with work that said "Vermont" to a world audience.

There had been no lack of pretenders to the throne. Bredes was one. Galway Kinnell with his poems, Mosher with his novels and short stories were up there. So was playwright David Budbill of Wolcott, who wrote *The Chainsaw Dance* and *Judevine*. There was photographer Marion Ettlinger, and painter Lance Richbourg in his "Mad Dog" days in Burlington, when the artist lit gunpowder tracings on fire so they cut dog silhouettes out of plywood. And of course, Peter Schumann's puppet extravaganzas were always high on the list of Vermont-made art. As were, to more commercial minds, Sabra Field's woodcuts and Mary Azarian's prints of older Vermont scenes, like those in *A Farmer's Alphabet*.

Yet none of these quite made the great leap, quite bounded, like Frost's poetry had, or even Walter Hard's prose/poems had in a lesser way, across the abyss of greatness. No contemporary artist's work had yet pierced America's heart with the undeniable assertion: "Hey, here it is! This is Vermont, super-plus-ultra grade!"

PART FOUR

QUEEN CITY

Watch it—it's a wicked city.
—*Stuart "Red" Martin, 1991, founder and owner of WCAX-TV*

*J*ust how far Burlington had pulled away from most of Vermont by the early eighties was brought home in a story Lorraine St. Onge, the Montgomery village postmistress, told me. In either 1981 or 1982, Lorraine said, her boy and the neighbor's boy, Frankie, both of them teenagers, had gone to Burlington one Saturday to see a movie. For Frankie, it was his first trip ever to the Queen City, sixty miles from Montgomery. Before and after the film, Frankie walked around the streets in a kind of a daze, Lorraine recalled. Frankie wore a big smile on his face. Frankie kept saying to people they passed, "We're from Vermont!"

But Frankie was right. Burlington *did* seem like some other place: it didn't seem like Vermont, or it didn't seem like what Vermont was supposed to be—whatever that was.

In ten years the state's population had jumped by fifteen percent to 541,000, with 115,534 people—nearly twenty-one percent—concentrated in Burlington and suburban Chittenden County. Visually, economically, and socially, the Queen City, its bedroom communities in tow, had been leaving most of the state behind. As the population grew, farmers in the Chittenden County area became an endangered species, and lawn care services proliferated. Housing costs soared, poorer folks moved elsewhere, and the cultural scene grew richer.

With its downtown marketplace, enclosed mall, socialist mayor, art scene, jobs, historic architecture, colleges, medical center, beautiful views, political and financial clout, Burlington became Vermont's little big-hearted city. More than any other place in Vermont it pulsed to national currents, dreams, expectations, and neuroses. It was also home to the state's heavyweight media: the *Burlington Free Press* and WCAX-TV. And to the *Vermont Vanguard*, a liberal art/news weekly that merged with a monthly *Vermont Woman*, to become the *Vermont Times* at the decade's end. It had a Boston-like cluster of colleges. It even had its own Loch Ness-like monster, except this creature was a good monster with the nice name of Champ. On the streets you saw orange-haired punks, three-piece suits, blue-haired matrons, college kids, cops, brown-bag carrying drunks, even an occasional black, as well as a smattering of Vermont's homeless—all within a three- or four-square block area of Main Street. Yet, within a twenty minute drive was country: thousands of large lots for sale, shaded driveways, views.

Winooski tried to compete with Burlington for a while. The working-class town next door wanted to grow, too, hungered for some of the tourist state's retail dollars. The pigeons were evicted from the abandoned textile mills and the Champlain Mill mall opened. A wild-haired scheme to build a dome over Winooski got a lot of press. But people simply weren't fired up enough by Winooski. It was too blue-collar, too retro. There was something more ethereal and dreamy about Burlington across the river. Maybe it was the altitude, or the sunsets over the lake, or the High Peaks of the Adirondacks rising to the west. Burlington had the allure, particularly to urban types. City blocks, cafes, and festivals reminded them a little of back home. They slid into apartments and condos with ease. Not that the Queen City wasn't provincial in many ways, somewhat immune to self-criticism, and occasionally overwhelmed by so many college kids that it seemed like Fort Lauderdale North. Yet for many of the ambitious, if they were going to stay in Vermont, it was the only place to be.

The three main forces transforming Vermont throughout the eighties—land use (including gentrification of the old North End, a traditionally blue-collar community in Burlington), feminism, and independent politics—converged in the Queen City. But of the three, politics proved the most potent once socialist Bernie Sanders stunned the city's moribund political establishment in 1981 by defeating incumbent Democrat Gordon Paquette. Paquette, having served five terms, got lazy; he mistakenly assumed he was mayor for life and didn't even bother to campaign.

A year or so before his ten-vote loss to the upstart Sanders, I saw Paquette hanging out at Nectars, a Main Street restaurant and nightclub. A large, flaccid man, Mayor Paquette sat with several city aldermen and a few of their cronies around a table and in a couple of booths along the wall. They talked and joked behind a veil of smoke. A couple of them ogled the occasional coed who walked by. Music drifted in from the barroom where college students and older hipsters drank and danced. Paquette, oozing overconfidence, suggested a Vermont rendition of Chicago's long-time Mayor Richard Daley, complete with the retinue. Yet he knew something about Vermont outside the boundaries of Burlington. When I introduced myself and told him I was from Montgomery, the mayor thought a moment and then asked if I was from the village or the center.

When he challenged Paquette in 1981, Bernie Sanders was a thirty-nine-year-old perennial loser. He had moved to Vermont in 1968 with a degree in political science from the University of Chicago, done some freelance writing, including a short stint for Bun O'Shea in Enosburg where the Democratic loyalist had consolidated several Franklin County newspapers into the *County Courier,* and even banged nails. In 1972 Sanders first ran for the House of Representatives. He was the Liberty Union Party candidate and got fewer than two thousand votes. In 1974 he ran for the U.S. Senate and got almost six thousand votes. In 1976, still carrying the banner of the fringe Liberty Union Party, Sanders pulled in over eleven thousand votes when he ran for governor against Richard Snelling and Stella Hackel. But regardless of which seat he ran for or which year it was, Sanders was powered by an almost messianic glow and kept repeating three main convictions: the rich had too much of everything; the government was in collusion with them to make sure a redistribution never happened; and thirdly, the two-party system failed the poor, the elderly, and the working class, many of whom had given up voting.

Before 1981, though, Sanders' social idealism never meshed with Vermont's political realities. He was interesting, provocative, but not electable. Yet his dogged perseverence impressed even those who didn't like his message, which basically distilled into a warning: democracy is only working for a minority of Americans. His supporters, often young, bright, and energetic, sensed that with Sanders they had hitched onto a rising star. Each campaign he got more votes. But until 1981 he remained a loser—an interesting one, but a loser nevertheless. He needed a win. Even a die-hard socialist can suffer from a loss of self-esteem.

In Burlington, where a moribund administration was blind to the transformation going on around it, Sanders broke his losing streak. Subsequently, the city proved a great soapbox, a crucible for testing his mettle, and a flexible springboard for his leap into national politics.

To leap into the whirlwind of immense change, writes Eric Hoffer in *The True Believer,* a brilliant analysis of mass movements and of the leaders who inspire them, men must "be intensely discontented yet not destitute. . . . They must also have an extravagant conception of the prospects and potentialities of the future. Finally, they must be wholly ignorant of the difficulties involved in their vast undertaking. Experience is a handicap."

When Sanders beat a stunned Gordon Paquette, he wasn't burdened by an experience handicap. Of course, in Vermont he had predecessors. In 1946, for instance, war-hero Governor Ernest Gibson, Jr., had lacked any experience as an elected official, and sixteen years later Phil Hoff had had only one-term as a legislator behind him when he became governor and walked into his new office to find all the files missing. Sanders, Gibson, and Hoff, (as well as Eugene Spriggs of the Northeast Kingdom Community Church, for that matter) shared a common denominator, however. They were filled with the high-octane psychic fuel needed for any major political, religious, or social ascent: an unquenchable frustration with the status quo.

What distanced Sanders from Gibson and Hoff, if not from Spriggs, was the fact he was a complete outsider. Bernie Sanders was a Jewish flatlander, and a poor one at that. In Brooklyn, where Bernie was born, his father Eli had been a salesman always worried about making ends meet. The financial stress of Sanders' family life related in some ways to Arthur Miller's *Death of a Salesman*, with its vast hopes, ruinous family denials, and undercurrent of inevitable tragedy. The experience of growing up poor and Jewish seemed to have left an indelible stamp on young Bernie's psyche. In the years between Flatbush and Burlington, he transformed his anxieties and concerns into a kind of steam-roller activism, delivered with all the hand waving and fired-up righteousness of a tent evangelist.

Sanders' route to public office in Vermont had as many bumps as the roads John Finn had traveled in 1954, when he hauled the trailer around back roads for Frank Branon, the Fairfield dairy farmer with the Abe Lincoln profile. Sanders wore out a lot of shoe leather. In fact, a friend of mine, back in the seventies, picked Bernie up once when he was the hitchhiking candidate for governor. Later, Bernie's organization would get better. And his message would seem more prophetic. Sanders elucidated that message in his 1972 campaign for the House of Representatives, and refined it during his subsequent unsuccessful campaigns before he got to Paquette, the vulnerable mayor who drove nails into his own political coffin by refusing to even campaign.

In 1981, when Sanders took to the streets in Burlington, to describe democracy in the Queen City as hidebound was to be kind. Two years before, in 1979, eighty-three percent of the voters hadn't even bothered to vote for mayor.

Sanders, going door to door, hammered away at the administration's indifference to the majority of the city's people. He criticized the proposed property tax increase, which would fall more heavily on the working class. He accused Paquette of serving the city's ruling class. He defused negative feelings about his avowed socialism by explaining that he had never joined any socialist party (meaning "communist") and that his vision of socialism was of a system in which people ran the government and controlled their lives. One touchy issue Paquette had not dealt with, and that Sanders raised, was student sprawl. Since the mid-sixties, almost like lava, the University of Vermont had spread downhill from the campus into older, often blue-collar, neighborhoods, disrupting them and eliminating low-cost housing. The students never figured out that their hero Bernie was also their nemesis in this issue and voted for him just the same. But the pivotal factor in Sanders' upset was the candidacy of Independent Dick Bove. On election day Bove pulled in twelve percent of the vote. Thus, like Phil Hoff's unlikely victory nineteen years earlier, Sanders' win was made possible by an independent organization siphoning votes away from an indifferent incumbent.

Sanders' ten-vote win landed him in the fishbowl of Burlington city politics. He was initially treated like a barracuda. Few of those in power had any idea how to parry his relentless and direct aggressiveness.

They should have picked up a copy of *The True Believer*. Hoffer knew what they were dealing with. Fueled with frustration, energized by the momentum of a decade of accumulated support, Sanders was suffused with the fanaticism, enthusiasm, great hope, and intolerance of all true believers. With his newly hatched Progressive Party behind him, Sanders released what Hoffer identified as the common chord of elected, against-the-current idealists, "a powerful flow of activity in certain departments of life; all of them demand[ing] blind faith and single-hearted allegiance."

In a series of articles published in the *Burlington Free Press* at the end of Sanders' four terms, reporter Mary Ann Lickteig gave readers an idea of what Sanders—"Burlington's ranting and raving socialist mayor," she called him—had gotten himself into. During his first months in office, angry aldermen fired the mayor's secretary and refused to approve some of his other appointments. Forced to whisper confidentialities in his office because the City Clerk—one of "them"—might hear, Sanders met with his kitchen cabinet at night in safe houses reminiscent of Democratic meeting places in rural villages during the fifties. Sanders once found his rusty Volkswagen ticketed for being parked in the mayor's space on Main Street. Aldermanic meetings, previously dull and uninspired, came to life with confrontational democracy. Sanders accused his opponents of serving institutions that kept the poor in grinding poverty and the rich in cognac and tax shelters.

Years of low-budget campaigning, with its incessant demands on creativity and on gaining the ear of sympathetic reporters (or, at least, intrigued ones), had made Sanders a master of media manipulation. He both entertained and startled the public with his forthrightness and knack for drama. In his Brooklynese he berated the ruling elite, which included the University of Vermont (not responsive to the needs of the community), and developers ("Hey, you can't just move to the city and build anything you want anywhere you want"). He told the legislature to get out of Burlington's business, and on the national level criticized the Reagan administration's war in Nicaragua and its escalating arms sales in a world plagued with hunger. "Being mayor, at least the way I do it," Sanders said, "is a very hard job. Because I feel a responsibility to make certain that the streets get paved, that we stop the war against Nicaragua, and that we have a national health-care system. Plus a few hundred other things." He also said inspiring words Vermonters longed to hear, such as, "I want to see a rebirth of the human spirit in the largest city in the most beautiful state."

Sanders followed up on his promises to make city government responsive to people who had been excluded from its largesse. He introduced city-subsidized day-care, a community boathouse, a city arts office, and a city youth council. He even fell in love with his Youth Coordinator, Jane Driscoll. Divorced and a mother of three, after first hearing her future husband speak, Driscoll said to herself, "God, this man embodies everything I believe in."

If Bernie Sanders embodied a Che Guevara type in Yankee Vermont, Jane Driscoll suggested a grassroots Jane Fonda. An active political organizer, Driscoll had grown up in a household where she and her brothers had to work to make ends meet. Bernie understood poverty, Driscoll realized, whereas "most people don't."

But what was Sanders really like? What made him tick? He played basketball pretty well, liked softball. I even sat behind the mayor once at a Bob Dylan concert. But to really grasp the core of Sanders' drive, turn to Hoffer's analysis of the true believer.

Sanders, before gaining political notoriety, had tried to make it as a writer. And, there is, as Hoffer notes, "a deep-seated craving common to almost all men of words. . . . a craving for recognition; a craving for a clearly marked status above the common run of humanity." In addition, intellectuals, of which Sanders was a bona fide example, complete with the rumpled jacket and the glasses, possess "an irremediable insecurity at the core," Hoffer adds. "Even the most gifted and prolific seem to live a life of eternal self-doubting and have to prove their worth anew each day."

In the corridors of power in the Queen City, Bernie Sanders, craving recognition and getting more of it every year, proved his worth enough so that voters reelected him for three more terms, by larger margins each time. He had a tenacity few Vermonters could match. He demanded accountability. He also was lucky. His eight years as mayor coincided with Vermont's decade of prosperity. Even so, he didn't accomplish everything he had in mind. He couldn't get his Progressive Coalition candidates into a majority of the seats on the aldermanic board. He didn't manage to open the Burlington waterfront to the public. Nor did he get the Medical Center Hospital of Vermont to pay a $2,.8 million tax bill he sent them when city lawyers found a 1954 law that said (or so the lawyers interpreted—the Chittenden Superior Court eventually sided with the Medical Center) that hospitals could be taxed.

But Sanders did revolutionize the administration of city government and made Burlington proud of its reinvigorated political atmosphere. Even the business community, which he often berated, softened towards him. One member of "the establishment," Ernest Pomerleau, president of Pomerleau Real Estate Company, had been amazed by Sanders' victory. Here was "this tireless, ruffle-haired person . . . who had just taken over Burlington," Pomerleau told Licktieg. At the time, Pomerleau figured that in two years the hippy would be history. However, his father Antonio ("You see, Dad was the epitome of capitalism") proved more pragmatic about the new mayor. Antonio promptly visited Bernie, then shocked the business community by announcing that he and Bernie had discussed ways of working together.

By 1988 when Sanders first ran against Republican incumbent Peter Smith for Congress and lost, he had become a bigger-than-life folk hero, a Vermont celebrity who had been caricatured in "Doonesbury," the nationally syndicated comic strip, as the mayor of the People's Republic of Burlington. Burlington may not have been "right in the heart of Vermont," as Sanders had joked once over the radio, but he had managed, like the stray dog that wouldn't go away, barking ceaselessly at threats and predators, both real and imagined, to win his way into the hearts of tens of thousands of Vermonters. Said University of Vermont political science professor Garrison Nelson: "The city will never be the same. And every subsequent mayor is going to be compared to Bernie."

On November 6, 1990, election night, I decided to take my eight-year-old son to Bernie Sanders' campaign headquarters in Burlington to hear the returns come in, and, in all likelihood, to share in the excitement of a victory over Republican incumbent Peter Smith. We almost missed the excitement though. Expecting a late evening decision, Andrew and I went to a movie and then stopped at Al's French Fries on Shelburne Road. Casually, I asked a woman behind the counter how Sanders was doing. She passed the question along to a guy flipping fries.

"Sanders won," he said.

By the time we rushed into Sanders' headquarters in the bowels of Memorial Auditorium, a motley crowd was cheering and hooting. Like magic, Sanders appeared, grinning a toothy grin. As he passed us, I lifted Andrew and Sanders, somewhat repugnantly, I thought, and in kind of a daze, hugged him. A second later, three photographers took Sanders' picture, bulbs flashing. The victor embraced a woman, saying something into her hair. A band played loud music. We were swept first one way by the crowd, then the other. "Watch it!" someone shouted. "The boat is going to tip!" No, but it was tacking. Propelled along by the throng's momentum, we rounded the bandstand and involuntarily found ourselves in the far corner of the gymnasium-sized space, facing a huge video screen filled with Peter Smith's solemn face. Andrew leaped up, trying to see over the taller heads. Smith was conceding.

"Bernie! Bernie! Bernie!" a phalanx of supporters—mostly young and exuberant, but spotted with middle-aged people with salt-and-pepper hair as well—chanted as they lofted their hero to the stage. Disheveled as usual, Sanders faced the crowd.

"I know the pain he feels," he said.

It was a gracious nod. The final week of the campaign had turned dirty. Polls had told the forty-four-year-old Smith he was behind. Desperate, he had turned to commie-baiting, and to nasty—and many observers seemed to think, counter-effective—personal attacks on Sanders' character. But now, as Sanders squinted before the harsh media lights, all that lay behind.

The last time I had laid eyes on the candidate had been two months before, at Johnson State College where he had told gathered students and a few faculty members, "Politics is everything!"—including Air Jordan sneakers, moronic television ads, and high college tuitions. Restless, standing behind a podium on the foul lines of a gymnasium, both hands gripping the edges of the angled wooden lectern on which he had placed no notes, Sanders said that the quality of democracy was deteriorating, that a majority of Americans "have lost faith in the democratic process." Describing a system in which ninety-five percent of the incumbents were regularly getting reelected, and in which two-thirds of the voters would not even participate on November 6, Sanders used the words "rigged" and "undemocratic." He said, "The system doesn't want you to participate. It wants you to say, 'It's all bullshit, anyway!'" Sanders wrapped up his assault on the status quo with a call for the "revitalization of democracy." That meant, among other things, he said, cuts in military spending, a new relationship with the Third World, and the involvement of all the people in the democratic process, not just one-third of them who felt the process still had validity in their lives.

Between that speech at Johnson State College and election night, Sanders became the dark horse darling of some nationally syndicated columnists looking for barometers of change. For instance, Studs Terkel wrote, "A Sanders victory would mean a fresh wind blowing in Washington. It would mean that someone independent of the hacks can actually get elected to Congress."

Old Bernardo, as *Vermont Vanguard* columnist Peter Freyne labeled his most popular subject, also received an indirect pump from the video rock queen Madonna. On MTV Madonna, attired in a red bra, bikini panties, and an American flag, incited the indifferent young to get out there and do their duty. To vote, that was. Pouting and coaxing and strutting in combat boots with her flag cape, she sang: "Abe Lincoln and Jefferson Tom/They didn't drop the atom bomb/Dr. King, Malcolm X/Freedom of speech is as good as sex."

The young constituency Madonna hounded was the latest crop of the age group that had first lifted Sanders to prominence almost twenty years before. In the early seventies, unknown, idealistic, and clobbered at the polls, the indefatigable campaigner had cobbled together a battalion of what inexorably became Bernie's division and finally Bernie's army as he had run for one office after the other. By 1990, with Peter Smith bruised and beaten, Sanders had a broad cross section of Vermonters—young, old, blue collar, yuppie—X-ing his name on the ballot. Luck hadn't failed him either. In the 1990 campaign the Democratic candidate, University of Vermont professor Dolores Sandoval, took all the liberal stands, including legalization of marijuana. By placing herself in most voters' eyes to the left of Sanders, she gave the independent a big boost.

"We can show that the State of Vermont is prepared to lead the nation!" Sanders declared to the hooting, clapping crowd the night of his victory. Vermont had shown America how to step outside of the two-party system, he said, how to "stand up to the president and the vice president, and every multi-national corporation in America!"

That evoked a sustained chorus of screaming, foot stomping, and clapping from the crowd, above which the television lights glowed, bathing heads in a harsh glare.

"Congress is out of touch with the needs of the elderly, of working people, and of the poor! We, as a state, are prepared to radically change the priorities of this nation!

"As I stand before you," he concluded, "I think that our small state might go down in history as being the leading state in the fight for a political revolution—" Interrupting him the crowd went wild again, clapping and cheering. "A revolution that will take away power from from the multi-nationals and the wealthy and give it back to the people where it belongs." That raised the decibel level even higher.

Zydeco music erupted from the bandstand. Sanders eased into the arms of the jubilant throng.

A short while later, as the celebration wound down, Andrew and I walked out into the crisp autumn air. I felt enervated, a little giddy. Yet, for some odd reason, I recalled Norman Runnion's assessment of Bernie Sanders. When I had interviewed Runnion some months before, the long-time editor of the *Brattleboro Reformer* had seemed philosophically in tune with Sanders when he said, "We still live in a crummy, mean, materialistic world, and Vermont is part of that." Both national and state politics had become "morally corrupt," Runnion insisted. "Everybody has a special agenda." Runnion held little hope for the Vermont press to address grievances because most state reporters lacked experience and worked for publishers focused on the bottom line rather than on in-depth news coverage. The day we had talked in Brattleboro, Runnion seemed fired by the same dissatisfaction that drove Sanders. His own life was undergoing a sea change. At sixty, he'd quit his editing post and was bound for theological school to become a preacher. "There has to be an absolute moral revolution," he insisted. "Modern life is a complete failure." Talking about Sanders, the grey-bearded Runnion, who seemed to be a branch off the same tree, said he had always been fascinated by leadership. As a United Press International reporter, "I covered JFK from the day he went into the White House," he said, "until he went out in a hearse." Sanders just didn't do it for Runnion. "I think Bernie Sanders is one of the biggest political fakes I've ever covered in forty years of journalism."

By the front stairs to Memorial Auditorium, Andrew jolted me back to the present. "Dad, the firecrackers."

Oh yeah, we had brought some, just in case.

I sat the pack on the cement steps. To complete our political cheap thrill of sharing in Bernie Sanders' victory elation, Andrew cautiously lit a match, then touched the wick.

*S*hadowing the ascent of Burlington throughout the eighties (and, in fact, provoking a rather lethargic retail community in downtown to shift into gear and do something appealing, namely build a pedestrian marketplace) was a commercial bogeyman, a proposed regional shopping center called Pyramid Mall, a.k.a. Maple Tree Place. Begun as an option on a meadow in a still rural-looking Williston in late 1977, the saga of Pyramid Mall swept back and forth in the local headlines for years. Like a long-running soap opera, complete with a changing cast and eventually even a new name, the drama continued into the nineties.

As shopping malls go, Pyramid was only going to be medium-sized: eighty stores, a parking lot for two thousand cars, twenty acres of roadways. But it wasn't the size that bothered people so. It was the idea. A mall meant the big-hearted city had been sold out, that the region had passed through some modern rite of passage. To the more offended opponents a mall distilled disconnectedness, mind-numbing commercialism, and conformity; it was the American Way of Life Grade X, an unrelieved focus on shopping and consumption in a bland environment manned by underpaid personnel who knew little about the products they sold, and who changed jobs as rapidly as Vermont changed seasons. At the same time, as an archaeologist friend of mine had told me one night as we drove past a vast, brilliantly lighted mall in Ohio, "That's modern man's ceremonial center." Recently returned from eighteen months in Ecuador on a Fulbright fellowship, he had been digging in the sub-tropical rain forest. Lifting a hand from the wheel and pointing towards the mammoth parking lot bathed in an orange glare, the big squarish buildings in the background, their marquees aglow, he had continued, "That's where the young do their tribal dance. That's where they meet."

In a car culture obsessed with convenience, not only was the mall a teenager's nirvana, but it was where just about everything a person could desire in the material sense was available. All you had to do was hop in your car. And by the eighties that car was more important to the average Vermonter than a house, which was beyond his or her means. Like their contemporaries across America, Vermonters sought joy and meaning not in the old standbys of home and hearth, but in more readily accessible material goods. Shopping, epitomized by the mall, where everything seen on television could be reached with a car and bought with plastic, was at least within their grasp.

In the statistics game of new jobs created per year, which the state and regional development organizations played relentlessly and with great seriousness, much ink was spent on retail's new, low-quality opportunities which attracted teenagers like fake bait snagged hatchery-raised fish. Wriggling and thrashing they got caught by something they knew nothing about before they even got to live. Mall jobs, with their part-time hours, low wages, and non-existent benefits, had a special allure for sixteen, seventeen, and eighteen-year-olds, yet typically sapped these students of the very energy and time they needed to put into school in order to lift themselves above such jobs. At the same time, mall retailers eliminated the traditional family-owned stores, in which you knew a clerk, or your mother had known the owner, or that reflected any of those other old-fashioned human connections integral to country life. Mall stores were usually units of some far-away, centralized financial entity. District managers visited occasionally to verify proper execution of the corporate manual.

In Williston, Pyramid Mall was going to be enclosed, too, thus eliminating the final Vermont variable, the one that still cut across class, status, and attitude: the weather.

For kids, however, just as my archaeologist friend had said, a mall was the promised land. There, they could find the latest funky gear and avoid their parents. A mall brought television merchandising to life right before eyes groomed on an average weekly dose of seventeen hours of tube-think. It was the straight umbilical plug-in for the commercial-driven generation. And frankly, at the mall there was action, stuff going on, communication among peers, playfulness, intimations of sex. If TV was the medium and the medium was the message, then being at the mall was living the message.

Kids didn't have much power, though. In 1983 Pyramid went down to its first defeat at trying to give the Burlington area, and its bedroom communities, their own ceremonial center, one compatible with the region's growing population and economic verve. The loss followed forty-three days of hearings over fifteen months in late 1982 and early 1983. The District Four Environmental Commission denied Pyramid's land-use permit, ruling that the mall would bring too much traffic, overload local services, and radically alter Taft Corners, which still had some farms and hay fields nearby.

The Pyramid Mall imbroglio resumed in 1987. Robert Congel, whose headquarters were in Syracuse, New York, and who controlled Pyramid Companies through a closely-held private partnership, recognized that Chittenden County was a more lucrative market than ever. Besides, there was his credo—"the most important thing in life is persistence"—to uphold.

Various local opposition groups, again spearheaded by the Williston Citizens for Responsible Growth, resumed their defensive positions. "They're BAAAAAAAAAAAK!" screamed CRG eye-catching ads. "They Came From Outer State." One ad showed bug-eyed pyramids floating around like UFOs and referred to "an unoriginal score featuring the hit song

'Mall Me,' available on Maple Tree Records & Tapes."

Not only had the imperturbable Congel not given up on his dictum about perseverance, he had repackaged Pyramid in a slightly smaller shape and given it a less inflammatory name: Maple Tree Place.

"Well, I think they're coming back a little bit smarter," CRG long-timer Hal Painter of Williston warned. "They've hired local people—the architect, lawyer, and their traffic, water and sewage people are local, so there's more of a local flavor."

The opposition manned the same defenses: traffic, air pollution, quality of life. In 1988, however, the question of saving the rural quality of Williston seemed moot. Its town plan, rather than curtailing commercial sprawl, had fostered it. A motley assortment of new commercial buildings in two business parks and several small clusters of stores had sprung up near Taft Corners. Ironically, Pyramid's seventy-two-acre site, much of which was meadow, began to look out of place with nothing on it. Maple Tree Place's front man, a flannel shirt-wearing lawyer from Stowe named Ben Frank, argued that everything had changed since the Act 250 rejection. Downtown Burlington had traffic congestion the mall would eliminate, Frank insisted. The rural character of Taft Corners was gone, he said.

The battle continued. It had been going on too long for either side to gracefully withdraw. Like many conflicts, its origins and real meaning were lost somewhere back in piles of transcripts, human intransigence, and the dance of protracted antagonism. That Congel and his mall would not go away simply validated how lucrative a market Chittenden County and northwestern Vermont, which included Franklin, Grand Isle, and Addison counties as well, had become. By the late eighties the region had about one-third of Vermont's population, forty percent of the jobs, and forty percent of the productive farmland.

Pyramid came on strong. Frank played an upbeat, positive role. The Act 250 defeat of five years before had been a costly setback for Congel, the former pipe fitter who had a reputation for remaining unemotional during protracted controversies. For in the wake of the recession of 1982 Vermont had taken off on an economic joyride, with Chittenden County in the front seat. Between 1982 and 1987 statewide retail sales jumped sixty percent while the nationwide increase was forty-four percent. Vermonters bought more wine and beer, new clothes, new cars, and building materials than their contemporaries elsewhere. For once the supposedly frugal showed the rest of America how to shop. And did it pretty much without big shopping malls.

Writing about Congel and his Pyramid companies in the *New York Times Sunday Magazine* at the decade's end, Roberta Brandes Gratz said that Pyramid had staked out New England as its shopping mall galaxy, and that with the exception of Burlington neither organized downtowns nor concerned environmental groups had stopped the juggernaut for long. An investigation by the New York State Commission on Government Integrity (its spokesperson described Pyramid as "a company that defines the American dream as a mall in every wetland") had brought to light the fact that Pyramid had pumped $750,000 into crooked city elections to buy a zoning change for a huge mall project in Poughkeepsie. New England now caught Congel's eye, despite being over-regulated and environmentally pesky, because the six states had a concentration of bodies and unexploited potential.

Facing the revived project adjacent to his city, Sanders' successor as mayor of Burlington, Peter Clavelle, snapped, "This is not new retail dollars. This is displaced growth. If we haven't learned the lesson from national experience that regional malls suck life blood out of downtowns, then we haven't paid attention."

In November 1989, when I visited Tim Murphy, who had just been made a temporary replacement on the District Four Environmental Commission that ruled on Pyramid's Act 250 permits, he was sitting alone by a table covered with folders.

"UPS came today," Murphy said. The files contained his Maple Tree Place documentation: two piles of transcripts, each pile six inches high, from previous environmental hearings; a pile of assessments; a half-dozen large maps; and a small stack of District Four memos about Pyramid Mall prior to its reincarnation as Maple Tree Place. In three weeks Act 250 hearings were scheduled to resume. Murphy, a Montgomery contractor with a Harvard degree and a pugnacious nature, waved a hand over the table. "There are reams and reams and reams of testimony," he said. "That tells you something right there. The case is being overrun by legalities."

Murphy couldn't comment on the merits of the case, or he'd be off the commission. But basically, as he explained it, the board of laymen he was joining would rule on the testimony of eighteen lawyers. For his role as an environmental judge, Murphy received fifty dollars a day, plus mileage and a per diem. Pyramid's cost for filing for permits was sixty-eight thousand dollars, with the projected construction cost just over twenty-seven million dollars. Murphy did not get paid for the time he had to spend studying the piles in the light cast by his television set.

The controversy over Pyramid had entered a new phase, prompted by changes in the Williston Town Plan. Pyramid had finally gotten tentative approval but Williston had altered the rules. Congel, who never appeared in Burlington in person, ordered his subalterns to take the Williston town fathers to court.

One reason Williston had revised its town plan was a workshop conducted by Burlington architect Rolf Kielman and several planners in May 1988. After examining the in-place town plan, Kielman and the others had pushed development to the theoretical legal limit. "It was scary," Kielman recalled. There were buildings everywhere, Taft Corners looked like suburban New Jersey. "This kind of development was staring us everywhere in the face," Kielman said.

"How did Williston react?"

"It was like we'd thrown bricks through their windows."

The crux of the problem was that Williston's planners had not done their homework. Not that they were alone, or had intended to wake up one morning, rub their eyes, and say sleepily, "Where to hell am I?" But they had adopted a poor town plan. Like many Vermont towns, Williston had invested lots of energy in selling the idea of a plan and in getting it passed. But they had spent far less energy actually conceiving the plan itself. Most plans tended to be taped-together regulations taken from plans conceived elsewhere, typically from towns in Connecticut, Massachusetts, and New Jersey. Once such a plan was in place people thought everything was okay if the plan was enforced. Everything was not okay. The plans tended to be car-culture inspirations that would eventually efface the historic settlement patterns of Vermont rather than reinforcing them. "Then when it's all built and looks like New Jersey," Kielman said, "they're horrified."

The lesson of Williston was that the suburban nebulas, road networks, and gauntlet-like development of countrysides of more populous states were doomed to be repeated in the Green Mountain State unless plans sympathetic to Vermont's small town patterns—commons, pedestrian walkways, and an architecture of human scale—were integrated into revised and flexible plans. That such a simple reality—the pedestrian ought to be fundamental—*was* fundamental to enduring community because pedestrians stopped, talked, interrelated in ways vehicles did not, had been lost to the car culture.

Despite the challenges they faced, during the mid- and late-eighties dozens of development projects sprang off drawing boards across the state and headed into labyrinths of regulations and meetings with opposition groups and compliance agencies. Some projects were big, like Sherman Hollow in Huntington and Waterland in Montgomery. Others were small, a three-store cluster anchored with a Quik Stop, or five modest homes on lots at the edge of town. Others were illegal, including subdivisions in the Northeast Kingdom that used dummy corporations to avoid Act 250's review process.

Many Vermonters were worried about disappearing open land and about the homogenization of the Vermont scene. They worried about growth increasing school enrollments, which in turn raised property taxes. They worried about traffic, sewage, garbage, and the elusive "quality of life." Development was promoted as a way to broaden the local tax base and to lower tax pressures on property owners. Yet except where single large projects dominated the economy, this accepted truth was seldom validated. With growth, taxes went up regardless. While citizens griped and complained about loss of control over the future, developers gnashed their teeth over state bureaucratic red tape and over infringements on their property rights. On the sidelines environmentalists decried the loss of countryside silence, clean water, and wilderness.

Planning, the great white hope, tried with various degrees of success to balance the forces at work into harmonious coexistence. Some developers were cooperative with town officials and planners. Others fought them. A few towns simply ignored planning, expecting the regional environmental commission and Act 250 to handle any major headaches for them.

De facto growth quotas, like those passed in Iowa during the seventies to protect farm land, didn't gain favor in Vermont's legislature as a means of keeping rich soil in agriculture. Nor did the lawmakers identify, as Oregon had with its state land-use plan of 1973, so-called Exclusive Farm Use zones based on soils. Instead, tax abatement programs were passed to subsidize dairy farmers and a current use reimbursement program paid landowners to keep their properties undeveloped. These measures, however, relied on high revenues, which Vermont enjoyed between 1983 and 1989.

Before the boom went bust, Act 200, the Vermont Growth Bill, passed in 1988. Proponents, led by an embattled Governor Kunin, tiptoed through a minefield of opposition, claiming Act 200 made the state more responsive to local decisions, revitalized local control of town plans, and attempted to balance economic and environmental needs. Opponents countered that the vague and badly-written law was a Draconian measure lawyers loved and people, if they could understand it, hated. By 1990, led by a statewide group called Citizens for Property Rights, thousands had signed petitions demanding the law be repealed. A landmark attempt to confront the tremendous complexities of land-use, Act 200's test would come in the nineties. Meanwhile, it became a political punching bag.

In counterpoint to Pyramid Mall, the success story of Ben & Jerry's Homemade captured the support, enthusiasm, and limited investment dollars of many Vermonters.

The company went public in May 1984. It was a xenophobic affair: for Vermonters only. The prospectus was heavy with warnings: the offering was in excess of book value; there was no market for the stock; if you decided to sell your shares within nine months another bona fide Vermonter had to take them off your hands. Proceeds from the offering, around $700,000, were to be used to buy equipment and land for a new plant. Ben & Jerry's planned to expand to meet the demands of scoop shop franchises and supermarkets in the Northeast that wanted to sell superpremium ice cream with the pictures of two hippies on the top and with down-home copy ("This carton contains some of the finest ice cream available anywhere. We know because we're the guys who make it") on the side. The whole scheme sounded just crazy enough to work. I bought fifty shares at $10.50 a share.

What the prospectus had failed to tell me about was the biggest threat of all to Ben & Jerry's: the Doughboy. The Pillsbury Corporation's Doughboy, that is. Pillsbury, owner of Häagen-Dazs, the Danish-named superpremium ice cream, wanted to eliminate "the best ice cream in the world," as an article in *Time* had called Ben & Jerry's Homemade in 1982, from supermarket shelves.

Ben Cohen, thirty-three, and Jerry Greenfield, also thirty-three but semi-retired ("Mr. Greenfield does not participate in daily management," the prospectus said), were the company founders. They had started the business in a rented gas station on the corner of Pine and College streets in downtown Burlington in 1978 and expanded slowly and not without a certain amount of sixties' ambivalence about being in commerce. For instance, a friend of mine went to the ice cream shop one day only to find the door locked and a note posted. Business was harder than the owners had anticipated, the note said, and they had taken the day off "to get their shit together." My friend said he particularly remembered the last phrase. By 1980 operations had smoothed out enough so that Ben & Jerry's opened their first franchise in Shelburne. In 1984, the year of Orwell's Big Brother and the Island Pond Raid, they decided to go big-time. Recent requests from ice cream distributors in New York and Washington, D.C., the prospectus said, had been turned down for lack of product.

An article in the *New Yorker* in 1985 by Calvin Trillin described Ben & Jerry's ice-cream-making facility as "a tiny galvanized-tin building that a Ford dealer had formerly used to repair trucks—a production setup that a succinct visitor might have described as five dropouts in a garage." But the heart of the piece contrasted the unconventional Cohen and Greenfield and their rise to respectability, albeit with no cashiering of their hippy souls, with the story of Reuben Mattus, the corporate hero of another business era and the fellow behind Häagen-Dazs. Because Mattus, a Jewish streetfighter who had survived ice cream wars in New York for decades, had sold his company to Pillsbury, staying on as manager, he became the heavy in the article. Cohen and Greenfield looked like New Age folk heroes.

Trillin's account was a classic David and Goliath tale. Little guys lobbing ice cream bombs at a giant named the Doughboy. Counterattacks at Pillsbury's illegal tactics in pages of *Rolling Stone.* Bumper stickers asking "What's the Doughboy afraid of?" An 800 number to call if you wanted the true scoop, from the little guy's side, and packets of information mailed free to explain what was happening. In effect, taking one scoop counter-culture idealism, two scoops Jewish chutzpah, and a lot of high-butterfat milk from Vermont dairy cows, the hippies had fought back.

The media loved the story of two guys who looked like munchy-crazed remnants of the cannabis culture on their pint lids taking on big business without losing their cool. Here were two graduates of liberal arts schools, Cohen from Skidmore and Greenfield from Oberlin, who gave MBAs pause. The twosome had no business training, Trillin wrote, and had "capped off their preparations by sending away to Pennsylvania State University for a five-dollar correspondence course in ice-cream making—two-fifty apiece." Like a lot of people who were in college during the late sixties and early seventies, they had been educated to "think small."

And dream big.

One unorthodox corporate ritual the ice cream makers had initiated was something called the annual Fall Down. At the Fall Down Jerry Greenfield, who flew in from Arizona, swung a sledge hammer and smashed a cinder block on Ben Cohen's sizable stomach (too much product testing, Trillin thought), and then partying commenced.

Reuben Mattus liked the boys' sense of humor and even their product. Nevertheless, they should have borrowed some money and gone into bagels, he concluded, rather than compete against Häagen-Dazs. When the two hippies from Vermont wanted to place their crazy brands of rich, expensive ice cream, with names like Dastardly Mash and Heath Bar Crunch, along the more sedate chocolate, vanilla, and coffee containers of Häagen-Dazs, Mattus transformed into the streetfighter—or in this case, supermarket shelf-fighter—of old. Except now, as a member of the Doughboy's family, he had more muscle.

"We were really scared," Chico Lager, president of Ben and Jerry's in 1985, told Trillin. Though the company's corporate style seemed predicated on fun and laughter, and on crazy stunts and weirdness, Lager said, "This was not a joke to us. How we responded was a lot of fun, but the matter itself was very serious."

The matter was unfair competition, a violation of the Clayton Act. Ben

& Jerry's lawyer, Howard Fuguet of Boston's prestigious Ropes and Gray, who handled the case against Pillsbury's formidable legal department, which had been acting as if it was brushing the gnat off its sizable back, got the defendant to see that an out-of-court settlement was to his advantage. Pillsbury had already gotten a taste of the unorthodox countermeasures dreamed up by the hippies in their fairy-tale hangout up north. And how the measures had generated thousands of column inches of press patter, very little of which made Pillsbury look like anything but a greedy giant and Ben & Jerry like the boys next door. Boys who used to make you wince with their antics but who now were intent on playing hard ball.

Said Fuguet to Pillsbury: "It would be wishful thinking on the part of your subsidiary's offices to imagine that it can bully Ben & Jerry's, stifle its growth, and cause it to roll over." He listed precedents. The Doughboy backed off.

Ben & Jerry's adroit publicity campaign not only increased sales, but captured the admiration of dozens of other eager nouveau-capitalists. Cohen soon achieved a national stature similar to that of Paul Hawken, the driving force behind Smith and Hawken, a Mill Valley, California, gardening tools company that had made quality, the environment, and customer service its themes. The philosophy that united Ben & Jerry's Homemade with Smith and Hawken, and that linked them to hundreds of lesser though like-minded ventures begun in the eighties, was that you could disdain the more oppressive corporate conventions while still adopting good operating methods; you could make a healthy profit without selling your soul; and you could employ people and remain sensitive to their humanity. These were lessons big business, like the ice cream giants squeezing milk out and puffing air in their products, still were fighting. Lessons the Japanese had taken to heart.

Ben & Jerry's also emerged in Vermont as leaders of the "Made in Vermont" phenomenon of the eighties. From chocolates and running bras to recycled fertilizer and computer software, the eighties witnessed a boom in small entrepreneurships. Many new businesses united handcrafted quality with innovations in sales and marketing. Their products often bore the state-approved "Seal of Quality." Social activism and corporate responsibility integrated with more traditional company goals, like making a profit, drew non-business types into the corporate fold.

THE TESTOSTERONE PARADIGM

"Tie *You* Up"
—*Pamela Polston, songwriter and vocalist, The Decentz, 1982*

*T*here has been a conspicuous absence in this book so far: women. Sure, I have talked about my sister, and I mentioned that women in hill farm Vermont were the soul of the Grange and the pillars of the church. But in the corridors of power and in the written histories, women were mostly behind the scenes. In 1977 Faith L. Pepe, a museum exhibition curator teaching at the Community College of Vermont, published a bibliography of writings by and about Vermont women in the spring issue of *Vermont History*. In an accompanying essay she echoed the common complaint that "man," as found in most writing, implied that man was the representative for all humanity. Pepe pointed out that Walter Crockett's five-volume *History of Vermont* listed only eight women in its index. Of course, there had been the famous editor Abby Hemenway and her five-volume *Gazetteer*, a compendium of town histories published in the second half of the nineteenth century. In the twentieth century Dorothy Canfield Fisher established herself as a nationally known writer from Vermont, and in 1954 Consuelo Northrup Bailey became the first woman in Vermont—and the nation—to be lieutenant governor.

But then came the eighties. Joining ranks with the national woman's movement, which had gained momentum in the late seventies, Vermont women surged forward, not to be denied. Across the spectrum, from artists to housewives, women took themselves more seriously. They competed for jobs traditionally reserved for men. In 1984 they helped elect the first woman governor in Vermont history, Madeleine Kunin.

My sister Barbara, though unknown to most of these women, was the kind of old-fashioned, spirited fountainhead from which their movement drew energy and inspiration, whether they realized it or not. To me, she was simply the most indomitable and big-hearted person I ever knew.

Barb was dying when the decade opened. She was riven through with cancer: rot spreading in a still standing, vaguely majestic, but doomed tree. As she tottered she once said to me, "It takes a hell of a lot more to pull down a person of strength than it does one who's weak to begin with."

Like the grandfather in Rainer Maria Rilke's *The Notebooks of Malte Laurids Brigge*, Barbara's death grew and swelled and overflowed our family in the very same way her life had, bringing us together. She wouldn't let go. She wavered in the wind of illness but with her roots absolutely refusing to give up. As Rilke wrote, "Who is there today who still cares about a well-finished death? No one. Even the rich, who could after all afford this luxury, are beginning to grow lazy and indifferent; the desire to have a death of one's own is becoming more and more rare. In a short time it will be as rare as a life of one's own. Because, my God!, it is all there. You come, you find a life, ready-made, you just have to slip it on. You leave when you want to, or when you're forced to: anyway no effort: *Voila, votre mort, monsieur.* You die as best you can; you die the death that belongs to the sickness you have. . . ."

The sickness Barb had was the sickness permeating America's health: cancer. But she had never slipped into a ready-made life, she had tilled the land and been a mainstay of the last Vermont textile mills. That June we hovered around her death bed in the Gifford Memorial Hospital in Randolph, her husband Raymond way past sympathy, the nurse wonderfully consoling, the grandchildren scared and often crying, the room a steadily changing scene of friends and relatives and neighbors coming and sitting for a while, and then leaving.

How long does it take for a strong Vermont woman to die? She was bloated with fluids. Her eyes were glazed. Frances held her mother's hand. We heard her struggling breathing. Her hair was a white nimbus from the chemotherapy. "All through this she never cried once," Raymond said. "Except on the phone when she was worried about Dad." She had swollen up so the hospital had to cut her clothes off. They couldn't drain her legs, which bulged beneath the bedspreads. The nurse kept repeating that grief was nothing to be ashamed of, that crying and getting it out was better than withholding. We joined hands and said prayers. Raymond, stoic, leaned by her ear: "I'm right here, Barb. I'm right here."

Barb was fifty-seven. She was buried in Tunbridge on a sunny day, cows grazing alongside the headstones, the World's Fair grounds in the distance. On her gravestone, a slab of Rock of Ages granite from Barre, there is an engraving of a little village, a steeple jutting up, and of a horse on a treadmill. "Pull together," the inscription says.

My sister's death pulled the woman's movement with its invisible strength. I know it did. The lives and deaths of so many Vermont women fed the movement, directly and indirectly. If the woman's movement needed its goddesses, women of the near and distant past to venerate—not sex goddesses like those of the silver screen and the magazine cover—but of fertility and of the earth, and of love, they needn't look back as far as Isis in Egypt, or Hera in Greece, or Cybele in Rome, although those were powerful and resonant, but to those thousands of farm women who carried on well into this century in the hills and valleys of Vermont.

One young woman who rode the current of feminism into the early eighties was Pamela Polston. From Nebraska, Polston had moved to Burlington in 1975, when she was twenty-six, to get her doctorate in experimental psychology at the University of Vermont. By the end of the decade, however, while studying the psychology of women and sexual behavior, "I realized it wasn't the correct course for me to take," she said, "as in 'path of life.' But it took a long time to accept that and to leave that safe little world of school. I left UVM in December of 1980 and six months later I was in the first New Wave rock band in Vermont, the Decentz, with a z. It was a big change."

New Wave music, raucous electrified sound overlaid with often searing lyrics, found a waiting audience in Burlington. The music's popularity had begun with the Sex Pistols in England. The anarchy and nihilism that lead singer Johnny Rotten, along with infamous guitarist Sid Vicious, had screamed about in their songs, together with a blatant disregard for the commercial conventions of the music business, had shaken the foundations of the music establishment. Polston and the Decentz, a kind of second-generation punk band, though way out on the edge for Vermont, came along when New Wave no longer caused riots nor handwringing in the offices of music industry executives.

"We got together and started writing songs," Polston recalled about the band's classic punk beginnings. Two guys who could actually play, including guitarist Jimmy Ryan, whom Polston married, grounded the group. She and Brett Hughes, who had never performed either and who strapped on a rhythm guitar, gave the Decentz both the right "look," and the serendipitous spirit of blatant amateurism that punk personified.

"I was already thirty-two years old," Polston recalled in 1991. "I hate to use the word liberated."

Now forty, with thick red hair and Valentine-shaped lips, Polston was a journalist who wrote about the arts and women's issues. As the frenetic lead singer of the Decentz, she had also written most of their songs, including "Seems So Strange," "Compared to You," "Hold Me Tight," and "Tie *You* Up." The last was "a controversial song," she said. "Some people were offended by it."

"Like who?"

"Feminists. Women. It was a spoof."

The Decentz played in local clubs: The Mill in Winooski, Hunt's in Burlington. The other popular punk band was Pinhead. "The music scene was very vibrant and inspired," Polston said.

"How did it make you feel, being a lead singer in a punk band?"

"It was a wonderful alternative to grad school," she said with a poker face. "It was a lot more creative." Performing dropped her reserve, brought out another Pamela Polston, one "sort of opposite of my reserve and decorum." A little laugh came from the full lips whose previous musical experience had been at the small end of a trombone in her high school band in Nebraska. "It was kind of wild. I was jumping around the stage a lot. I was very energetic. It was one of the reasons people liked us, because the energy was very infectious".

Jolting towards success, the Decentz played all over New England and in New York. "We were making our living completely from the band. Because of the early success, we figured we could take it a step higher. We did get some national airplay from our record. It was called, 'Get In Trouble.' A song that I wrote."

Most of Polston's songs were about relationships. "They expressed my feminism sensibility: sometimes an angry one, sometimes funny. It had to do with being a female in this country in this century." Though she never sought a sexy look, Polston acknowledged, "Some men perceived me that way. I think my look was pretty goofy, actually. I was not a 'boy toy,' à la Madonna. I got into the punkette thing." Punkette in 1981 meant leopard-print fabric, ripped T-shirts, dyed hair. "I dyed my hair every color there was. I also cut it off."

One factor that helped the band draw crowds was the eighteen-year-old drinking age, which the legislature would soon raise to twenty-one. Though Polston hadn't enjoyed teaching undergraduates as a doctoral candidate, they made a good audience, one that liked to dance drunk. An occasional member of the punk throng that savored the Decentz music and coopted its attitude was UVM student Stuart McGowan, who became a Burlington videographer later in the eighties. An army brat who had lived in Japan, Korea, Europe, and Argentina, as well as a few states, McGowan remembered the drinking scene at the Redstone Campus in those days as "unbelievable. There was this alcohol culture. There were eighteen-year-old alcoholics." *Playboy* had labeled UVM one of the best party schools in America. "It was a fuck-a-thon," McGowan said, laughing. "You had to be dead and not have a dick not to go home with somebody."

While the high times lasted, doctoral dropout Pamela Polston pranced and leaped across various stages, playing dress up and letting go for the audience. "I've always been a rule breaker," she said.

And across Vermont thousands of other women were doing the same, albeit usually in moderation. Many of them had had it with the testosterone paradigm ("Tie *You* Up"), with the "God is a man" theme of the Old Testament. Others simply wanted equal pay for equal work or a husband who washed the dishes. As for really standing out in the crowd, Polston said, "It was easier to be different then. How far can you push the envelope?"

The Decentz never got the envelope open quite wide enough to fill it with national success. The image of a rainbow-haired songstress with Valentine lips pouring out commentary on the dire straits of American relationships is an enticing one. But Polston and the band's leap for stardom fell short. The roots of New Wave may have needed more serious urban trampling than a small city on a pristine lake could provide. Being on the road a lot made things tough, too. When the Decentz came home, Polston recalled, they didn't want to see each other, never mind practice. It was an old artistic conundrum: being out there doing what you did well exhausted you so that you didn't have any energy left over to keep on growing.

At any rate, Brett Hughes quit the band in October 1983. Polston left soon afterwards. With the captivating synergy gone, the Decentz, with a z, lasted another six months. Vermont's first queen of punk went to work temporarily at Bookstacks in Burlington, then moved to France for nine months.

*T*he woman looked tired. But she smiled, pulled a chair out in the middle of the room, and sat. Her eyes glowed a light blue. She wore a maroon jacket, a maroon skirt. She had bracelets on one wrist. She glanced out a big window at white puffs of cloud coasting across a pale blue sky. Just out of the frame was the golden dome.

"It's hard to think of yourself as history," Madeleine Kunin said.

But she was. It was August 2, 1990. Four months before, with some of her staff crying, Governor Kunin had announced she was bowing out. No possible fourth term for her. She was going to relax, enjoy private life, teach and possibly write.

During her six years as governor Kunin had pulled more women into Vermont politics than had ever been there before. She had been a hands-off leader, a stalwart environmentalist, and a big spender on education. Openly pro-choice, Kunin had also gotten behind formation of the Vermont Family Court, which put divorce, family abuse, and domestic problems together under a single legal umbrella. Her fall from popularity began slowly, in 1988, when she aggressively championed Act 200, the long-awaited but now vigorously opposed second leg, the land-use planning one, of Act 250. The presidential election of 1988 also revealed fissures in the state's Democratic party, which had been Kunin's other power base. While she supported Governor Michael Dukakis, the Vermont delegation to the Democratic convention favored Jesse Jackson and his Rainbow Coalition. Attacks on her managerial skills intensified. She wasn't assertive enough, critics said. "I don't govern like a man" was what they meant, she countered.

Madeleine Kunin's ascent to power had a lot of the American dream about it. She had come to America in 1940 at the age of six, sailing past the Statue of Liberty aboard a ship of refugees, which included her ten-year-old brother, Edgar, and her mother, who was forty-one. Swiss Jews, the Mays were fleeing the threat of concentration camps, fearful that Hitler's armies would invade Switzerland. The mother spoke some English, but the vocabulary of the children, according to Edgar May, added up to three words: "yes," "no," and "bathroom." The family settled in Pittsfield, Massachusetts. Madeleine went to the University of Massachusetts, then to Columbia, where she got a masters degree in journalism. A possible job at the *Washington Post* as a reporter terminated on a sexist note (her predecessor had been raped in a parking lot, Kunin was told, so the job was going to a man). Kunin moved to Vermont, where her Pulitzer prize-winning brother Edgar had settled. In the late fifties she worked at the *Burlington Free Press* as an education reporter, met and married doctor Arthur Kunin, and slipped into domesticity. She took care of the house and had four children.

Then, in 1971, the year Swiss women finally won the right to vote in their federal elections, Kunin visited Switzerland. There when her fellow Swiss finally won complete suffrage, it dawned on Kunin how slight a dent American women had made in her adopted land's political institutions, despite having the right to vote since 1920. The Holocaust weighed on her mind, too. Remaining passive, as millions of Jewish victims had, and being acted upon by outside forces, was not the way to head into the future, she decided. Back in Burlington in 1972 Kunin ran for a seat on Burlington's male-dominated aldermanic board. She lost by sixteen votes. Undaunted, that fall she emerged the Democratic winner of her district for the Vermont House. In 1978 she defeated Governor Richard Snelling's favorite, Peter Smith, for the lieutenant governor's slot. As lieutenant governor she got into some scuffles with King Richard. Their lack of love for each other was obvious before Kunin, then chairperson of the House Appropriations Committee, even defeated the Ivy Leaguer Smith. "I don't agree with her philosophy on lots of things," Snelling told the press. "And she doesn't agree with mine."

Four years later Kunin ran for governor. She announced her candidacy after Snelling had said he wouldn't run for a fourth term. But he then did an about-face and beat Kunin in November. Two years later she tried again. She took on Attorney General John Easton, who still had egg on his tie from the ill-conceived Island Pond raid that June. She snuck past Easton by sixty-two votes. Kunin inherited a twenty million dollar deficit and the gender gap. As the Vermont economy turned rosier, high revenues wiped out the deficit, creating surpluses that fed government growth with Kunin's encouragement. But the gender thing had several thousand years behind it. Kunin, traveling with her husband, Arthur, frequently found him, or one of her male advisors, being mistaken for the governor. She, of course, was perceived as the governor's wife.

Like Sanders, who was building a reputation in Burlington, Kunin benefited from the strong economy. Her critics tabbed the governor as a Swiss "Jewish mother" type with a bleeding heart and a love of centralization. She wanted to control "growth," they said, but never clearly defined what growth was. Her supporters praised her genuine sense of caring for people, her vulnerability, and her willingness to give her subordinates great latitude to make their own decisions, a trait that not infrequently got Kunin into political trouble. No doubt, she did spend money, but the legislature went right along with her. Spending on human services and state aid to education both about doubled during her tenure. Property tax relief almost tripled, and the current use reimbursement program (it paid property owners to keep their land undeveloped) went up like a rocket. Big surpluses in 1988 and 1989 helped pay for the expanding programs. The surpluses ended, but not the need for more revenues. During Kunin's six years in power, total state spending increased seventy-two percent, from $589 million to almost $1.3 billion in 1990. The bureaucracy grew to seventy-eight hundred employees; it had numbered around seven thousand when Kunin had first taken office. By 1990, though, the average per capita income for a Vermonter was $16,400, slightly below the national average of $17,500, and well below the New England average of $21,500. And when the economy went sour in 1989, so did Vermonters' attitudes towards a lot of taxes and spending. Glancing next door, they could see that neighboring New Hampshire, with neither an income nor a sales tax, ranked fiftieth, or dead last in taxes paid per resident. At home they saw a large bureaucracy. They saw waste and favoritism. For instance, Special Funds, an umbrella spending category known for favoring pet projects close to powerful legislators' hearts, had jumped 192 percent in six years.

If fiscal restraint and a lean bureaucracy were not Kunin's strengths, environmental activism and the empowerment of women were. Leading an activist administration drained Kunin, however. "As uncomfortable with authority as a man in a badly fitting suit," a *Burlington Free Press* editorial described her.

Kunin lived the paradox of the power-based feminist. It was a constant struggle to be a woman in what was still a man's arena. She talked to fellow female politicians about this in early 1990. Getting the technical edge of politics down hadn't been her problem, she said. It was the challenge of acquiring "a comfort level with power itself. We are still learning the culture of public life," she said. "Dealing with conflict, going into battle, and emerging from battle with the strength to continue the fight. . . . Each day we go through not only outer skirmishes but inner ones as well."

Sitting in the waiting room adjoining her office in the Pavilion Building, weary-looking yet also at ease, Kunin sounded rather philosophical. "Even as we change," she said to one of my questions, "we can keep the qualities that drew us here." Shifting to her favorite topic, women, she said she liked to recall the stories of single mothers going into the labor force through the "Reach Up" program. "Reach Up" gave single parents day-care, transportation, and education funding so they could acquire the skills to get off welfare. The success tales there "have been marvelous," Kunin said.

While governor, Kunin refused to consider any list of nominees that did not include women's names. She insisted her advisors find qualified women. By 1990 forty percent of the state commissions, agencies, and boards were female. In the 1988 elections more women ran for office and more won. One-third of the House was women. The Senate remained a male stronghold, however, with only six women members. The total of 56 out of 180 representatives, or thirty-one percent, far surpassed the male/female makeup of the U.S. Congress. There only 27 women held seats of power amidst 508 men, a mere five percent.

If Kunin had gone out of power more propitiously, she might have elected to run for national office. She did become influential at the National Governors' Association where she urged other governors to get involved in global environmental issues. Because of her experience in Vermont, with its reputation as an environmentally progressive state, Kunin was listened to. Recycling, energy conservation, affordable housing, ways to protect farmland—all the issues Vermont was struggling with she encouraged her fellow governors to take sides on.

Governor Madeleine Kunin's picture appeared on the first cover of *Vermont Woman* in 1985, together with nine other women, and on the last cover five years later, solo. The giveaway monthly, which was published in Burlington by Suzanne Gillis, had a feminist slant and celebrated diversity. It ran features on politics, fashion, and the arts, as well as on controversial subjects such as incest and abortion. With the controversial reportage, though, there was a big problem: advertisers.

"Whenever we tackled a hard-hitting issue," said Ricky Gard Diamond, the monthly's first editor, "the next issue our advertising revenue fell off. It was maddening. Commerce loves pablum."

Even the readership blasted the paper. Liberals and lesbians said, "Not radical enough." The right urged, "Be more conservative, please."

"Some families were afraid to even put it on the coffee table," Diamond said.

While editing *Vermont Woman,* which she did for two years, Diamond learned that rural women wheeled substantial informal power, yet lacked much power up front. Diamond knew a little about power. From Michigan, divorced, with three kids, ages six to eleven, she had moved to Vermont in 1980 and enrolled at Goddard College. In Michigan, she had started to write, but had come face-to-face with a harsh economic reality.

"I found I couldn't make it."

Eventually she got a B.A. from Vermont College and went to work for the Central Vermont Community Action Council, an anti-poverty agency. Diamond was director of communications for the council and edited *People's Voice,* which circulated to fifteen thousand readers, many of them poor and on welfare. She took the helm of *Vermont Woman* in 1985 and subsequently returned to Community Action as development director. There she realized that the same people who were poor and on welfare ten years ago, when she came to Vermont, were still poor and on welfare. They were mostly women and children. Only today there were more poor families, greater pressures to economize, and a social system with bigger holes. If there was one constant, Diamond said, it was the tradition in American politics—as ingrained as the longing to be modern was ingrained in the culture—that people programs got the knife first when money was tight.

"Poverty is so multi-faceted," Diamond lamented. It has the kind of relentless and all-sided aggressiveness of below zero weather encountering a tarpaper shack. Bad housing consumes paychecks for heat. Lumps in breasts and wracking coughs get ignored until the poor are wheeled into the doors of emergency rooms. Emotional impoverishment in families starves kids of love and can make them cold, heartless, and violent. One indicator of heartlessness in modern Vermont was the rash of man/woman homicides. Right before I interviewed Diamond in the summer of 1990 there were several of them: Shirley LeClerc, thirty, had been raped and strangled in Enosburg; Cynthia Thow, twenty-three, had been killed when her insanely jealous boyfriend drove her, and himself, headlong into a tree on U.S. 7 in Pittsford; Charles Ducharme, twenty-three, was shot and killed in Burlington by Darren Couture as Ducharme was watching TV with Couture's supposed girlfriend; and Lynne Corey of Milton, thirty-nine, shot her old boyfriend William Dandrow, who wouldn't leave her alone—"I don't know what hell's like," Corey said, "but I feel like I've lived it"—after numerous complaints to the police had accomplished little.

Poverty also gripped, often hardest of all, Diamond said, proud Vermonters who "didn't know they were poor until we told them." She was alluding to the not-so-well-off who couldn't find work or help and who were just hanging on, hoping, in the words of my sister, "that things would get better."

But during the eighties, for most of them, things got worse.

What Diamond called "life-changing" programs, including job training and education, had taken a beating under President Reagan. In 1990 Diamond said she saw more people in Vermont hopelessly entrenched in poverty than in 1980.

There were plenty of bright spots, Diamond added. In particular, though she didn't say it, was her own story. A down-on-her-luck housewife, she had forged a reputation and centered herself in the maelstrom of change. She found that in Vermont you really could make a difference; that wasn't a cliché. Yet, she mused towards the end of our talk, she saw fewer people these days putting out the effort to make that difference.

"I almost feel a sense of resignation, of inevitability that this place won't be able to continue to be so different. A requirement of Vermont citizenship ought to be an annual trip somewhere else."

No shortage of people saw poverty differently than Diamond. Some of them wanted the government out of it altogether. Others insisted, "Let business take care of it." Currently gaining supporters was the radically old-fashioned idea of putting welfare back into the hands of communities where recipients live. In *The Vermont Papers* by Frank Bryan and John

McClaughry, a 1989 book that decried the state of democracy across America and championed a return to human-scale politics and power bases, the authors acknowledged, "Every society must face squarely the problem of the chronic poor." Bryan and McClaughry exhorted Vermonters to make their state into a series of "shires," or clusters of towns, each self-governing, with broad, discretionary powers. With each responsible for the health and welfare of its citizens, including the poor, the addicted, the abused, and the elderly. Local knowledge of specific circumstances would be the basis for dealing with each case differently, rather than lumping, say, the poor, into categories that were all treated the same way, as most state programs did.

Many social scientists, politicians, and therapists agreed with the two Vermont authors that large-scale human service systems were a failure, an economic albatross born in the thirties and fattened in the sixties. Community-based approaches to human problems promised to empower towns and villages, or shires, to displace the human service hierarchies that were manned by officials who often distained community, sought out only other experts' testimony, and competed for money and power by making the poor into consumers just as surely as did IBM and Coke. A community-based system seemed a possibility for returning a little heart and soul to the never-ending tragedy of increasing numbers of poor people, both in Vermont and nationwide.

THE LATE GREAT
FAIRY-TALE STATE

It's a pretty heavy burden being mythologized.
—*Scott Hastings, Jr.,* Always in Season

*T*he eighties were, in a word, complex.

From the fertile seeds of the sixties, washed over by the waves of the seventies, grew a tough tangle of characters, issues, and causes, all intertwining and determining the state's future. From having been a remote world of small mill towns and hill farms only thirty years before, Vermont now found itself within a day's drive of sixty-five million people. Tax subsidies were needed to prop up agriculture as a livelihood and as a visual backdrop for tourism. The state was laced with a plethora of environmental and social programs that required steadily increasing revenues, along with a large bureaucracy to implement them. And looming over the state and the times was yet another painful paradox: growth threatened Vermont's special sense of place, yet maintaining that sense of place, with its pastoral look, open spaces, and small towns, threatened to make Vermont elitist, an upscale getaway for the rich.

Politically the state remained highly centralized. A leadership vacuum existed in many towns. Elected officials often lacked experience or, worse yet, common sense. Along with wizards of oratory, who were indifferent to the quiet groans as they stood up, again and again at public forums, to pontificate on whatever issue was being debated, they drove the public away from faith in a return to real local control. The concept put forth in *The Vermont Papers* by Bryan and McClaughry of making Vermont "a demonstration project of the future" appealed, in theory, to many sensibilities. Eliminating system solutions to human problems, as the authors urged, and fostering human-scale resolutions to problems seemed not impossible here. Yet all too often the collective will to change seemed wanting. There were too many special agendas, too many people convinced they knew what was good for everyone else, too much apathy and contentedness with the status quo, and not enough vision and direction.

Ironically, the independence so integral to the Vermont myth seemed partially to blame for the lack of a common mission. Political labels became practically meaningless during the eighties. No single dominant issue subdued the decade's fractiousness for very long. Across Vermont, advocates of all stripes—for and against abortion, for and against gun control, for and against animal rights, gay rights, children's rights, the rights of single mothers, for and against regional planning, preservation, better-paid teachers—jockeyed for power year in and year out. It often seemed that the Green Mountain State had transformed from a land of the tolerant and the laconic into an upscale kingdom of the garrulous and the feisty. Practically everyone seemed to have something to say, far less time to listen. Commissions to take their testimonies were duly appointed and traveled the length of the state, holding meetings, scribbling notes, publishing their findings at just about the same time a new issue had captured the public's concern.

Moving along just beneath the surface however, out-of-sight but immensely influential, was an undercurrent of morality, of fairness. This sense of morality, it seemed to me, nourished much of the public debate, from education spending to affordable housing to condom giveaways to what to do about the garbage. The burning question was, "Are we doing it right?" Without this sense of morality how could socialist Bernie Sanders have gotten elected to Congress as an Independent? Incredibly, a rabble-rouser had transformed himself into a political seismograph. His zigzagging political ascent plotted the way many Vermonters, both native and newcomer, felt towards the traditional system. Sanders said all these things about poverty, class, and power that no native had had the guts to make his or her protracted crusade. His rise to power could only have occurred in a transforming and rudderless Vermont. Sanders came to symbolize the long cry for fairness, for a better distribution of the spoils, for a new morality that so many newcomers had dreamed about, had moved to Vermont to find or shape, but had witnessed gradually, inexorably, irrefutably, slipping from their grasp.

By 1990 Vermont had reached Robert Frost's metaphysical fork in the road. The question was, which road would it take? Would those in power, primarily newcomers who had arrived since the sixties and who, with rare exception, dominated banking, politics, and education, continue to make life possible for not only the well-to-do but for the not-so-well-off, many of whom were second- and third-generation native sons and daughters cut off from the opportunity to buy land or own a home? Would the new Vermont make room for the old, not just on bookshelves or along isolated stretches of back roads, but in its collective upscale heart, in its twenty-first-century technocratic soul?

Often, traveling around, much of the state struck me as a kind of theme park. The theme was "funky rural": wildflowers along the highways, gourmet meals in historic houses, general stores selling brie, characters out of storybooks: the bearded logger, the gnarly farmer, the spinsterish schoolmarm, the thievish town clerk, the equestrian bitch, the remorseless teenage delinquent—an assortment, a sampler of them, mingling on Church Street Marketplace in Burlington, at the Montpelier Fools Fest in July, at the Tunbridge World's Fair as the songbirds flew south. I'm not talking Walt Disney here. I'm talking modern fairy tale: Robert Frost out chasing his wife on a four wheeler; dark and light; the open meadow and the dank swamp; good and evil. All of the characters lived and their interrelationships unfolded in a theme park whose population in 1990, 572,000, was about the same number of people who passed through Grand Central Station in New York City during a day.

As a park Vermont satisfied the classic criterion laid down by landscape architect Frederick Law Olmsted over a century ago. That is, much of it remained pristine. Here, a weary urban soul could find much-needed psychological balm. At the same time Vermont was a shrinking pristine place, a pricey balm. In the open spaces between villages, and on the sprawling outskirts of the small cities, grew an ultimate suburbia of four- and ten-acre lots, each with a view and a road cut. The growth created gauntlets of wood and glass through which commuters rushed daily, but above which tourists could still gaze, imagining deer and bear and owls in the woods. Out of this woods wandered a moose named Bullwinkle who fell in love with a cow.

The oddball romance, which really did happen on Larry Carrara's farm in Shrewsbury in the fall of 1986, got the kind of media attention America usually reserves for small children stuck in mine shafts. And, of course, reinforced the image of the Green Mountain State as a place that could be both "on the cutting edge of political weirdness," as *Roll Call* staffer Glenn Simpson, who wrote for an audience in Washington, described Vermont during Sanders' campaign for Congress in 1990, and be the home turf of Ben & Jerry's Homemade, a company that boasted about its sense of social responsibility and vigorously challenged such American shibboleths as defense spending.

Economically, the eighties started out okay, stumbled a little during the national recession of 1982, but then took off on an economic joyride the likes of which the state had never known. Buoyed by increasing revenues, lower taxes, and optimism, and stoked on the national level by tax breaks, defense spending, and a huge increase in the federal deficit, Vermonters savored their prosperity while state government went on a binge. But the decade went out with a WHOOSH: the sound of a balloon losing air. Richard Snelling came out of political retirement in 1990, won his crown back, and inherited a record-setting deficit in the vicinity of one hundred million dollars only to die of a heart attack in August of 1991.

Reality had caught up with the fairy-tale kingdom.

The forties and the fifties seemed a long time ago. They had been decades of protracted loss and private tragedy, brightened here and there with optimism sparked by skiing and tourism. The sixties had become a time of official recognition of Vermont's long-suppressed needs for dramatic change. Those years witnessed the arrival of thousands of young people whose liberating, if untenable, idealism cherished the dying-out Vermont Way of Life. They were joined by a growing number of professionals, both young and middle-aged. The seventies had brought new technologies and successive waves of resettlers, as well as the energy crises that impacted everything and slammed "the beckoning country" doors closed. But it was a little late for that. Before the seventies ended, the American Way of Life prevailed over the Vermont Way of Life practically everywhere in the state. Sure, there were hold-outs: retrograde hippies still loading ash into their Home Comforts, loggers skidding hemlock with horses, even a dozen or so surviving one-room schools. But they were mostly quaint anachronisms, compliments to a fairy-tale kingdom, photo opportunities for camera carriers.

The eighties, by default, inherited all the momentum of the transforming past. All the newcomers who had gotten into positions of power, all the crafties who had become capitalists, all the poor who had become homeless, all the developers who had been waiting their chance, all of these and so many more, in the Reagan eighties, in the decade of "touching base" and "product" and "networking," wanted their piece of the Vermont pie. And the pie had become expensive. No longer could the average Vermonter afford even a sliver of that pie, if a sliver happened to be for sale anywhere but in out-of-the-way places, such as at the junctions of roads halfway between towns. There, in newly sprouted neighborhoods of motley dwellings inhabited often by the not-so-well off, by an occasional direct descendant of the Green Mountain Boys, folks hung onto scraps of land and threads of independence. Driving by, you'd see a log cabin, maybe a few trailers, a ranch house, a couple of lean-tos, some junk cars, snowmobiles, woodsmoke if it was cold, and kids. Along with maybe an older farmhouse in which the heirs of the last farmer on the land had been born, raised, and died. "No turning" signs greeted you in the driveways. "Beware of the dog" signs hung by doors. More than the welfare rolls, more than the growing number of trailers, more than the special education loads in the schools of have-not towns, these neighborhoods, symbolized the rift in Vermont's soul, probably because they were still isolated, still rooted in the Vermont of the recent past, the Vermont of the tinkerer Egbert Buckley who kept everything out back because it might have some use in the near future. But also because they personified the land-use problem. How long could a family subdivide sixty acres?

Nevertheless, despite the displacement of the poor, the moral over-reaching, and the seemingly endless meetings of earnest citizens trying to decide what to do about everything, Vermont retained a degree of fascination. Smallness helped. Along with Wyoming and Alaska, relatively vast spaces, Vermont remained one of the three most rural states in America. A third of the inhabitants lived in the towns and cities, so the density in the countryside remained low. Of course, that could change on holiday weekends in second-home regions. During the Christmas holidays in 1989, for instance, it took me almost thirty minutes to drive through Waitsfield, now a cluster of inns, restaurants, and commercial ventures hugging (some might say "strangling") Route 100.

There was also a greater diversity of people here than ever before, although ninety-eight percent of them were white. One black man, Larry McCrory, dean of Allied Health Services at the University of Vermont, told me that when he had first moved to Burlington in 1966 he had gone to a meeting of the NAACP only to open a door on a room full of white people. "I started to close the door," McCrory recalled in amazement, "thinking I was in the wrong place. But I wasn't." In Vermont the NAACP was merely another white-skinned branch of the ongoing morality play that wanted to make things right.

Smallness and diversity made Vermont a microcosm of white middle-class America, a place whose problems, as opposed to those of big states, seemed resolvable. Here you could simply see the issues more clearly, identify the key players, and still enjoy the view.

Vermont also had some challenges uniquely its own. For instance, could tourism, farming, and environmentalism be rural bedfellows? Or was three a crowd? Self-esteem questions inherent in a culture that more and more sold itself, or a fictitious vision of itself, to strangers waited for answers. What myths and traditions wove themselves around tourism and recreation? One long-time observer of Vermont's evolution into a state of tourists and second homes was Professor August St. John, who taught marketing at Long Island University and owned a second home in Manchester. Dubbed "Professor Doom and Gloom," St. John identified a cycle a tourist town went through as it evolved from an open-armed showplace eager to please into a hodgepodge of architecture, heavy traffic, and chamber of commerce boasts about the uniqueness of a homogenized place. Tourism itself was not the villain, however, St. John said. It was development. And development, of course, with its planners, lawyers, builders, engineers, and suppliers all making a living off growth, stimulated the economy and provided jobs.

During the eighties, more than in the agrarian past, Vermonters got involved with the whirl of the larger world, yet still raised gardens. Culturally, the arts flourished. The summer months in particular brought musicians, artists, writers, and actors to numerous festivals, workshops, institutes, and summer theaters. Vermonters were also becoming more political. As the two-party system collapsed, anybody could run with a chance of winning. All you needed was fifty signatures on a petition. In 1988 I challenged my district's Republican incumbent Merrill Perley, the affable "Road Warrior," as he was called by editor Chris O'Shea in the *Country Courier* because of his fixation on potholes and dangerous corners. I financed my campaign, for which I coined the slogan "Nickels for Change," with thousands of returnable cans and bottles that my supporters left at gas stations. I knocked on every door in my district, which covered Montgomery, Enosburg Falls, and Bakersfield, and which has over a hundred miles of dirt roads. Some of my prospective constituents lived in the fast lane on a dirt road. Others were dirt poor. More than I care to remember told me they were related to Merrill Perley. Though I didn't beat Perley, I came away from the campaign with a renewed appreciation for the diversity of humanity in my neck of the woods and remain convinced that I was the only political aspirant in America that year who got chased back to his car by a pig. That alone, however, did not justify all the effort; after campaigning hard, I learned, you do want to win.

ACROSS THE FENCE
AND INTO THE FUTURE

It pays to know this. It pays to know there is just as
much future out there as there is past.
—*Loren Eiseley,* The Immense Journey

*A*mericans' images of Vermont are often startling
and strange, or given a bucolic, romantic spin. Larry, Darryl and Darryl, the
rubes on TV's "The Newhart Show," a popular 1980s situation comedy
about a flatlander who buys a country inn, synced into the national
consciousness, at least from the feedback I received from people in the
South and Midwest where mention of where I was from often evoked the
names of the threesome. Tourists leave with odd impressions of Vermont
as well. For instance, I overheard a fellow once in the Pittsburgh airport
talking about Woodstock and Quechee, where his family had just spent a
few days. "Don't go to Woodstock!" he advised a fellow flyer. "Kee-chee,"
as he pronounced it, was the place to be seen because it was where the
classy, rich people lived. Woodstock—actually one of the wealthier, historic
towns in the state—still had little old gas pumps where a car could barely
squeeze between them and the steps of the store, the man said, laughing,
and was only noteworthy as a place to drive through on route to the Norman
Rockwell Museum in Rutland, a stop he highly recommended and that I had
not, until that moment, known existed.

Instate, the most pervasive imagemaker was television. It had been
practically since 1954 when Stuart "Red" Martin had built WCAX, Channel
3, in Burlington, and had put a static test pattern—an Indian head with lines
radiating from it—on the air for ten days before regular programming. "At
a conservative estimate, I received over two hundred letters describing that
test pattern," Martin recalled many years later with a sly chuckle. "That
shows you the hunger for the new medium."

Vermont was the last of forty-eight states (Alaska and Hawaii were still territories) to have its own television station. Two years later, in 1956, Channel 3 received nearly one hundred thousand letters and cards, more than the total estimated number of television sets in the state. During the era of television's tremendous growth and transformation from furniture with a picture in it to image-shaper, Red Martin (he not only founded WCAX but had been its sole president) had overseen Vermont's diet of visuals. Not until the eighties, when cable networks, satellite transmissions, and Vermont Educational TV came on strong, was there serious competition for viewers.

A conservative, witty character, Martin talked about his station's history and impact to a small audience in the Fletcher Free Library in Burlington one spring evening in 1991. A slight, white-haired septuagenarian with a dry delivery and a fondness for cigars, Martin was a guest speaker for Part 6, "Frontier to Global Village," part of a two-year series called *We Vermonters: Perspectives on the Past.* An oral and visual exploration of Vermont history, the series was sponsored jointly by the Center for Research on Vermont, the Fletcher Free Library in Burlington, and the Vermont Historical Society, received a generous grant from the National Endowment for the Humanities, and was indicative of the blossoming of regard for regional studies.

Martin talked about TV reception in Vermont in the pre-Channel 3 days as "some kind of snow." One heard voices in the background, usually cowboy voices as westerns were extremely popular. He had come to Burlington, he said, intending only to help his stepfather, C.P. Hasbrook, who owned WCAX radio, convert it to the newer medium. But Hasbrook had taken sick. Martin, then in his early forties, found himself swiftly pulled into the new medium's vortex. He located the transmitting antennae atop Mount Mansfield after hiking around up there with ski-trail design master Charlie Lord to find the ideal spot, and built a studio with a direct line-of-sight connection with the tower, which was necessary in those days, in an old warehouse off Pearl Street. The studio overlooked the American Woolen Mill Company in Winooski, which was closing.

"We had a monopoly on home entertainment," Martin said. And incredible power to give birth to local personalities. "Any personality who appeared was instantly widely liked unless he had a revolting personal habit." He mentioned one fellow, "a thoroughly likeable idiot" by the name of Dusty Boyd who introduced westerns, then took a shot at a selectman's spot in South Burlington and won. "But the ultimate in TV influence," Martin went on, was Ed Keenan. Ed Keenan was famous for giving reports on ice fishing. Keenan advised viewers to store fish eyes in their mouths, just like he did. Keenan, Martin said, after an appropriate pause, got elected mayor of Burlington. People knew him from television.

The medium had changed a lot since those days, Martin conceded late in his lecture. "In the nineties, TV is undergoing a sea-change because we've lost our monopoly." Cable networks and VCRs had decimated Saturday night network viewing, down to six percent of the Vermont audience from ninety percent in the sixties. Another big change was news coverage. Channel 3's news budget for 1990 was $1.5 million. It paid for twelve reporters, three news bureaus, and engineering support, including a $350,000 satellite truck with a dish on the roof. "It can go anywhere," Martin told us. "Even Hardwick."

TV had also devastated literacy in students, Martin acknowledged, and been less than a boon to good drama. On the other hand, he said, it gave Vermonters "a homogeneous experience to talk about, which makes the bonds of community."

Of the shows on Channel 3, the most popular and enduring was "Across the Fence." Started in 1956 by the University of Vermont Extension Service, "Across the Fence" was a down home kind of program that dealt with farming and Vermont issues. It beamed into living rooms with little errors intact. Thirty-five years later, it retained a refreshing lack of slickness and had become, Martin said, "the longest running program of its kind in the country."

In 1983 a fateful twist had put twenty-year-old Stu McGowan, the punked-out army brat who liked the Decentz, behind a video camera shooting segments of "Across the Fence." As McGowan remembered it, he had a dismal work-study job cutting open rats in a biology laboratory and a friend, who had an opportunity to study abroad, asked him if he wanted a better job shooting video. Though McGowan had never used a camera before, he switched. Training amounted to a couple hours learning how to shoot and a couple hours editing. Unlike his pre-vet studies, which he stayed with because he didn't know what else he wanted to do, McGowan was enthralled by video. "I was doing real life stuff," he said, "and getting college credit for it. But I had to perform."

A year later, driving home from a shoot of the Vermont farmer of the year, McGowan and his executive producer, a TV veteran named Lyn Jarvis, got to talking about dream jobs. Jarvis said he had been thinking about a series focused on people in Vermont. McGowan suggested going into towns, filming everybody they could find, then editing a show from the footage.

By the end of the drive, Jarvis told him, "If you want to do it, I'll give you a two-week slot. I'll give you ten days, in January and February. You produce them. You do it."

McGowan targeted twelve towns, called the Town Clerks, arranged interviews. Jarvis assigned him an assistant, another twenty-one-year-old named Luke. The first shoot was in Danville during its annual dowsers convention. But there was a glitch. McGowan arranged for a taciturn Vermonter to interview people and the fellow didn't have a knack for it. "So our next show was Tunbridge. We get there and all of a sudden we don't have anybody to interview. I said, I got to do it! My hair is bleached white, for some reason or other—I don't know why. Bleached half white and half brown. I had a black, sleeveless, cut-off T-shirt on. I was like this kid from hell coming into Tunbridge.

"But the fair worked, because it was kind of nutty anyway. So I just did the interviews. And it was the first time that Luke had ever filmed."

They played up the contrast between the old and the new Vermont. They shot bikers, yuppies in their Saabs, and Joe Tuttle, the quintessential old Vermont farmer. The Tunbridge town show "won a national award for student productions," McGowan said. "Grand prize. Best of show. It just cleaned up. Joe Tuttle was the reason I won the show, incidentally. We put him on and I had the guts to leave him on for five minutes straight. Nothing but Joe. He just blew the judges away."

Four years later a headless Joe Tuttle, then ninety-three, appeared on the rear jacket of Peter Miller's *Vermont People*. Miller cropped Tuttle's head and showed his gnarled hands holding an old framed photograph against his stomach. In the caption Tuttle says he can't understand some of the new people around Tunbridge. "They buy a place in good condition," he says, "and tear out every partition and pretty near wreck it, and then start over and build it again. God, but I guess they need to spend money."

*T*he Tuttle farm sits high above the North Branch on the South Strafford Road, the barn leaning and guarded by two old red Farmalls, the house brick and attached to a woodshed and fronted by a rough circular drive. On the wet November afternoon I pull into the drive, a huge cabbage fills a chair on the porch. I knock and the glass pane in the door rattles. "Come in!" a friendly voice says from out of sight.

I find Joe Tuttle, Mrs. Tuttle, and a fellow named Tom Kellogg eating ice cream around an oval table in the parlor. Mrs. Tuttle, a round, short lady wearing a hat with a green plastic visor, rocks back and forth like a buoy when she walks to the kitchen. She returns with a bowl of ice cream for me. It isn't Ben & Jerry's.

Once he finishes his ice cream, Joe Tuttle lights a pipe. "Born right there in that room," he says, pointing past a wooden clothesrack draped with pants and shirts. He was an only child, a rarity in turn-of-the-century Vermont.

"On a rainy November day forty years ago," I ask, "what would you have been doing?"

"Cutting wood," Kellogg volunteers while bussing ice cream dishes.

"Would have been cleaning out the stable," Tuttle says. "Cleaning off cows and horses. Oiling harnesses. God, there was a lot to do in them days."

"You were still working with horses?"

"Well, I guess we had one tractor, a crawler tractor. It was an Oliver. But we done most of the work with the horses."

His son Fred returned from the European theater after the end of World War Two, Tuttle says. They milked between twenty and twenty-five Jerseys. They took their milk down to the Tunbridge Creamery, just like Raymond Young had.

"Did you do a lot of canning?"

"Oh God, always."

"Did you miss working with your horses once you had tractors?"

"You're damn right. I'd have horses today, but I can't go down to the barn. My God, I don't know. I never was a lover of baled hay. I know it's easier to put in, it's quicker. You can handle more. But, my God, ain't good for your health, I don't believe." Tuttle looks at Kellogg. "Hard to get it and not get it dusty, isn't it, Tom?"

Tom Kellogg shakes his head yes. He's gotten curious about my questioning and asks about the book. I tell him it's about change in Vermont.

"I'll tell you what's changed the most," Tuttle says, poking at his pipe. "Taxes."

A cuckoo clock chimes on the wall. It's beside a U.S. Springfield muzzle loader, pre-Civil War vintage. A log smolders in the fireplace and Tom Kellogg flops down into a stuffed chair draped with a blanket. To his right are a large ceramic cat and a big plastic chicken perched on the mantel. Kellogg tells me he sold his large Holstein farm in Bethel two months ago. "Just got sick of it," he says.

"So, what do you think's going to happen?" I ask. "The farms that are still going, are they going to stay in business, or are they going to keep gradually going out until there are hardly any farms in Vermont?"

"We'll lose half as many as we got now," Kellogg says.

"Milk's going up," Tuttle says. He puffs on his pipe. Sallow cheeked, with a few days of stubby white whiskers, he speaks slowly and thoughtfully. "It may help the farmer."

Going into the room where he was born, Joe Tuttle soon returns with a map, Vermont circa 1865. He unrolls it on the table. Kellogg and I stand on either side of him. The population of Tunbridge is less today than it was then. Montgomery's population was double what it is 125 years later.

A few minutes later Joe Tuttle's son Fred comes into the parlor. A bandy-legged man with the strong odor of the barn, Fred eases down into an armchair, his cane against one knee. Around sixty, he has a squinty-eyed face that reminds me of the cartoon character, Mr. McGoo. The others tell him why I'm here. "By gosh, you got a lot of writing to do," Fred says to me.

Mrs. Tuttle laughs.

"Take more writing than you can do in one lifetime, won't it?" Fred says. He glances towards Tom Kellogg in the next chair. "It's all gone, Tom, isn't it?" Before Kellogg can answer, Fred continues, "I never seen a town go like Tunbridge. It's completely gone."

Then the three men all start talking at once, Fred Tuttle about the present, Joe Tuttle about the past, Tom Kellogg about the future. Their conversation echoes about the parlor and off the worn wooden floor like thousands of previous conversations have. The television is shoved back in the corner, there's no music, only rain on the roof.

"Shit, thirty years ago, you got sick," Kellogg says, "somebody'd come up to see how you are. Today, they wait for you to die so they can put your place on the market."

"Four pounds for a dollar," Joe Tuttle says, talking about how much butter once cost.

"I guess Tunbridge has changed a lot," Fred says, staying focused. "All gone. Strafford's all gone. Quechee's all gone."

Fred pulls out his Red Man chewing tobacco and stuffs a wad into his mouth. He and Kellogg start talking about real estate. Joe Tuttle puffs his pipe.

"They've made Vermont so accessible," Kellogg says, "they priced the natives right out of business."

Suddenly, Kellogg jumps up. Fred has said something that seems to have riled him. A rugged, medium-height fellow in his early fifties who looks ten years younger, Kellogg fishes a wad of money from the pocket of his jeans. "Money doesn't mean nothing," he declares, flipping the wad. He's got on black rubber barn boots, just like the Tuttles', and a black Harley-Davidson T-shirt. Stepping towards me, Kellogg fans the wad of bills, all hundreds, thirty or forty of them. Fred has lifted off his chair slightly, both hands on his cane. Maybe Kellogg hasn't shown his stash to Fred before. Sounding slightly alarmed, Fred says, "Tom, you carry that much money with you?"

"It doesn't mean nothing," Kellogg tells him. "Money doesn't mean nothing anymore."

"When we going to have a Depression?" Fred asks a moment later, after mulling things over.

"You asked me that fifteen years ago. They ain't going to let it happen."

Fred squints at me. He chews. He doesn't seem convinced. Mrs. Tuttle slides a guest book in front of me, then a pen. Kellogg starts talking about flying. He has his own plane. He mentions a friend who won't ride across the road in a pick-up with him but who will fly with him anywhere.

"Tom, I'm kind of afraid of airplanes," Fred says. "Ever since they bombed London during the nighttime."

"I love to fly at night."

I sign my name in the guest book beneath Tom Kellogg's. Mrs. Tuttle seems pleased. Sunlight suddenly streams through the parlor windows, laying a sharp shadow across the plastic chicken. The rain has stopped and a manure spreader, red and heaped with cowshit, sits spotlighted on a luminous green meadow across the road. How beautiful it can be here all of a sudden, I think, listening to Fred Tuttle and Kellogg talking. Joe Tuttle leans close and tells me Mrs. Tuttle wants to show me her salt and pepper shaker collection.

ACKNOWLEDGMENTS

*I*f I have managed to loosely tell the story of modern Vermont during the last half century, it's because dozens of people shared their anecdotes, observations, and insights with me. And, on several occasions, lent me their spare bedrooms. For their cooperation I am thankful, and if I have misinterpreted any of their perspectives to reinforce my own prejudices, I apologize. Writing contemporary history is risky business.

In particular I want to thank Joseph Bortugno, Joe Tuttle, Carroll Bowen, Tom Kellogg, Ryle Dow, Paul Miller, Fred Tuttle, and Esther Swift for their input on farming. Don Albano, Tim Murphy, Rolf Kielman, and Bill Schmidt talked to me about development and land-use issues. Bill Blair, Chris O'Shea, Norman Runnion, Stuart McGowan, Stuart "Red" Martin, Dan Neary, and Tom Slayton all contributed stories, memories, and information relating to the media and its characters and influence in Vermont. Don Bredes, Don Sunseri, Dot Kibbee, and Jay Craven shared with me their experiences in the arts and literature. State politics were clarified and expanded by Robert V. Daniels, the late Deane C. Davis, John Finn, Ernest Gibson, III, Robert Gibson, Stephen C. Terry, Philip Hoff, Madeleine Kunin, and Stephen Morse. Insights into Vermont's architecture were given me by Paul Bruhn and Martin Tierney. In addition, Bruhn shared his views of how Burlington has changed. The chapter on violent crime came out of interviews with Nelson Lay, Elton Hislop, and James Ryan.

Lengthy interviews I conducted with my sister Barbara in the early eighties play a significant role in the text, as do those with her husband

Raymond and their daughter Frances Clark and her husband Freeman Clark. My own memories of skiing were fleshed out and broadened by those of Hap Gaylord, Charlie Brown, Lloyd Boston, Betsy Pratt, and Jim Boyce. The transformation of Quechee came into clearer focus with the help of Josephine Dupuis, Ed Hughes, Melvin Young, Walter Spencer, Walter Henson, and Carol Dewey Davidson. And the chapters on the counterculture were given their heart and color by Richard Wizansky and Fritz Hewitt, and spiced by the recollections of Kingman Brewster, Jr.

D. Gregory Sanford and Perry Merrill provided insights into numerous dimensions of evolving Vermont. Larry McGrory and Lorraine St. Onge added personal anecdotes.

Ricky Gard Diamond, Pamela Polston, Joan Watson, Megan Camp, and Christine Lynch generously discussed with me the changing roles of women in Vermont and details of their careers.

Everyone I interviewed had stories whose loose strings linked together with the stories of other folks I talked with. Those intertwining strings provided much of the backdrop and continuity of this tale. I mention this as an extra note of thanks to all of them.

I researched and wrote this book in eighteen months. A generous grant from the Franklin-Lamoille Bank in St. Albans helped me tremendously. I want to thank bank president Bob Gillis for making that grant possible. I wrote most of it in the front parlor of Laura Crane's big old farmhouse in Montgomery and am grateful for Laura's generous hospitality.

For one of the themes in this book, the trading of the Vermont Way of Life and its regionalisms for the American Way of Life, I am much indebted to historian C. Vann Woodward's *The Burden of Southern Identity*. Woodward's analysis of the South as a place unique and apart has many parallels with Vermont's history, at least until recently, and I drew on some of those parallels liberally to advance my own arguments.

Lastly, I want to praise my editor, Peter Jennison. His light-handed yet sure guidance is the kind writers hope for but all too rarely receive. Also, to copy editor Susan Bartlett Weber, hats off for smoothing my somewhat shaky syntax and for an overall fine-tuning of the narrative.

BIBLIOGRAPHY

Beck, Jane C., ed. *Always in Season: Folk Art and Traditional Culture in Vermont.* Montpelier, Vt.: Vermont Council on the Arts, 1982.

Besser, Gretchen R. *The National Ski Patrol, Samaritans of the Snow.* Woodstock, Vt.: The Countryman Press, 1983.

Borgmann, Carl W. "The Education of Free Men." In *Vermont History,* Vol. 25, no. 1, January 1957.

Bryan, Frank M. *Yankee Politics in Rural Vermont.* Hanover, N.H.: The University Press of New England, 1974.

Bryan, Frank, and McCLaughry, John. *The Vermont Papers: Recreating the Past.* Chelsea, Vt.: Chelsea Green Publishing Co., 1989.

Broehl, Wayne G., Jr. *Precision Valley, The Machine Tool Companies of Springfield, Vermont.* Englewood Cliffs: Prentice-Hall, Inc., 1959.

D'Agostino, Lorenzo. *The History of Public Welfare in Vermont.* Winooski, Vt.: St. Michael's College Press, 1948.

Daly, Yvonne. "Home Comfort, The Reunion of Total Loss Farm." In the *Sunday Rutland Herald and Times Argus,* November 20, 1988.

Donnelly, John. "The Northeast Kingdom Community Church." In the *Burlington Free Press,* October 23-27, 1983.

Gratz, Roberta Brandes. "Malling the Northeast." In *The New York Times Sunday Magazine,* April 1, 1991, pp. 35-59.

Green, Susan. *Bread and Puppet: Stories of Struggle and Faith from Central America.* Burlington, Vt.: Green Valley Film and Art, Inc., 1985.

Hambourg, Stephen, photographs, and Perrin, Noel, and Breisch, Kenneth, essays. *Mills and Factories of New England.* New York: Harry N. Abrams, Inc., Publisher, 1988.

Hand, Samuel B. "Friends, Neighbors, and Political Allies: Reflections on the Gibson-Aiken Connection." In "Occasional Paper No. 11." Burlington, Vt.: University of Vermont, Center for Research on Vermont, 1986.

Hard, Walter. *A Mountain Township.* New York: Stephen Daye Press, 1933.

_____. Hard, Walter, Jr., and Graffagnino, J. Kevin, eds. *Vermont People.* Middlebury, Vt.: Vermont Books, 1981.

Hastings, Scott, Jr., and Ames, Geraldine S. *The Vermont Farm Year in 1890.* Woodstock, Vt.: The Billings Farm and Museum, 1983.

Hoffer, Eric. *The True Believer.* New York: Harper & Row, Publishers, 1951.

Huffman, Benjamin L. *Getting Around Vermont.* Burlington, Vt.: The University of Vermont Environmental Program, 1974.

Jennison, Peter S. *The Roadside History of Vermont.* Missoula, Mt.: Mountain Press Publishing Company, 1989.

Keizer, Garret. *No Place But Here.* New York: Penguin Books, 1988.

Lickteig, Mary Ann. "Bernie Sanders." In the *Burlington Free Press,* January 8, 1989.

McKnight, John L. "Regenerating Community." In *Social Policy,* Winter, 1987, pp. 54-58.

Meeks, Harold A. *Time and Change in Vermont: A Human Geography.* Chester, Ct.: The Globe-Pequot Press, 1986.

Merrill, Perry H. *Vermont Under Four Flags.* Montpelier, Vt.: published by the author, 1975.

_____. *The Making of a Forester.* Montpelier, Vt.: published by the author, 1984.

_____. *Vermont Skiing.* Montpelier, Vt.: published by the author, 1987.

Meyer, Peter. *Death of Innocence.* New York: G.P. Putnam's Sons, 1985.

Moffett, Hugh. "The Ruckus in Irasburg." In *Life*, April 4, 1969, pp. 62-71.

Morrissey, Charles T. *Vermont: A History*. New York: W.W. Norton & Company, 1984.

Muller, H. Nicholas, III, and Hand, Samuel B., eds. *In A State of Nature: Readings in Vermont History*. Montpelier, Vt.: Vermont Historical Society, 1982.

Mungo, Raymond. *Famous Long Ago: My Life and Hard Times with Liberation News Service*. Boston: Beacon Press, 1970.

_____. *Total Loss Farm: A Year in the Life*. Seattle: Madrona Publishers, Inc., 1977.

Otto, H.A. "Communes: The Alternative Lifestyle." In *Saturday Review*, April 24, 1971, pp. 16-21.

Pepe, Faith L. "Toward a History of Women in Vermont, and Bibliography." In *Vermont History*, Spring 1977, pp. 69-101.

Pollack, Richard. "Taking Over Vermont." In *Playboy*, April 1972, p. 147.

Stephens, Ross. "State Centralization and the Erosion of Central Autonomy." In *Journal of Politics*, no. 44, 1974.

Terry, Stephen C. "The Hoff Era." In the *Rutland Herald*, seven-part series, December 23, 1968, to January 1, 1969.

Wines, James. *De-Architecture*. New York: Rizzoli International Publications, Inc., 1987.

Vermont Commission on Country Life, The. *Rural Vermont: A Program for the Future*. Burlington, Vt.: 1931.

INDEX